SHINGON BUDDHISM:
THEORY AND PRACTICE

SHINGON BUDDHISM: THEORY AND PRACTICE

BY

MINORU KIYOTA

BUDDHIST BOOKS INTERNATIONAL
Los Angeles-Tokyo

Library of Congress Cataloging in Publication Data

Kiyota, Minoru, 1923–
Shingon Buddhism.

Bibliography: p. 186
1. Shingon (Sect) I. Title.
BQ8965.4.K59 294.3'92 77–27894
ISBN 0–914910–09–4
ISBN 0–914910–10–8 pap.

Printed by Kenkyusha Printing Company
Tokyo, Japan

TO

NOREEN AND EILEEN

CONTENTS

PREFACE

Shingon is the Japanese version of Tantric Buddhism systematized by Kūkai in the ninth century. This book explores Shingon and is divided into five parts: the first establishes the Indian foundation of Tantric Buddhism; the second discusses the major tenets of Buddhist systems of thought as conceived by Kūkai; the third is an exposition of basic Shingon doctrinal concepts; the fourth describes those concepts iconographically in terms of *maṇḍalas;* the fifth is an interpretive account of practice. The rationale underlying this division—and hence the rationale underlying this work—is to investigate the Indian foundation of Tantric Buddhism upon which Shingon doctrine and practice are based, to survey the Shingon system of doctrinal classification, based upon a Chinese model, as a means to establish the necessary doctrinal perspective to examine and to contextualize the Shingon development of doctrine and practice, and to study Shingon in terms of its doctrine, *maṇḍala* and practice. A treatment of Shingon in terms of its doctrine, *maṇḍala* and practice is imperative to provide a structured approach: the doctrine provides the theoretical basis of Shingon; the *maṇḍala*, an iconographical representation of Shingon doctrine, personifies states of mind, religious qualities and virtues; and practice is the instrument through which what has been described doctrinally and iconographically is actualized. The Epilogue identifies and describes Shingon as an entity of Mahāyāna; it is a summation of Shingon theory and practice from a Buddhological point of view; it articulates the fact that Shingon is an experiential philosophy, not a form of mysticism.

This work takes a Buddhological approach; that is, it presents Shingon in terms of its doctrine, *maṇḍala* and practice based upon philological and textual studies. Hence primary sources (Buddhist *sūtras* and *śāstras* contained in the *Taishō Tripiṭaka* and classical Shingon works contained in the Shingon canons) and works by modern Japanese Shingon scholars and practitioners are extensively employed in interpreting Shingon theory and practice. I have done so to avoid the danger of treating Shingon simply as a system of speculative thought.

This work is primarily designed for students and specialists in Buddhist studies who are interested in examining the Japanese development of Tantric Buddhism. It presupposes some knowledge of Buddhist doctrine and practice; it is not a phenomenological study nor is it a historical treatment of Shingon and its founder. Because this work is not a historical treatment of Shingon, I have not attempted to describe the historical circumstances surrounding the development of what I have referred to as orthodox and neo-Shingon, nor the personalities associated with these two traditions. These traditions and personalities associated with them are mentioned (in Part III-5) merely to indicate a problematic issue inherent in Shingon doctrine.

The theme underlying this work is the integration of man with the cosmic Buddha (*Dharmakāya* Mahāvairocana). The purpose of this work is to present a system of Buddhist doctrine and practice which deals with a spiritual realm beyond verbal description (a realm in which the self is completely liberated in and integrated with the infinite world of *Dharmakāya* Mahāvairocana), to circumscribe such a realm within the limits of verbal description, and to examine Shingon as a cross-cultural product.

Since Sanskrit is the *lingua-franca* of *Mahāyāna*, I have attempted to reconstruct technical terms into Sanskrit and standardize them in Sanskrit, whenever possible, though technical terms of Japanese origin and/or those most popularly employed in Japanese have been retained in that language. Whenever a technical term is introduced, an attempt is made to define it as comprehensibly as possible. But here we must note that sometimes a clear distinction between terms or an interpretation of a term consistent with a given definition become difficult in Shingon. For example, *Dharmakāya*, by definition, is Dharma-body, a term employed in contradistinction to *Dharmadhātu,* the Dharma-world. But it becomes difficult to distinguish the 'body' from the 'world' simply because Shingon conceives the *Dharmadhātu*-world as *Dharmakāya* Mahāvairocana, the 'body' of the personified Dharma which constitutes the *Dharmadhātu*-world. *Tathatā* is another example. This term literally means 'thusness', in contrast to the concepts of the 'this' and the 'that'. But in this work *tathatā* is often translated as 'ultimate reality' or even 'cosmic harmony', the last being more to the point in Shingon. And the term *Dharma* is translated as 'truth', 'principle', 'emptiness', or 'middle path principle'; *pratītya-samutpāda* is translated as 'co-arising', 'dependent origination', 'conditional causation', 'interdependence', or 'relative'; *prajñā* as 'wisdom', 'knowledge', 'right cognition' or 'perfect understanding of Buddha-nature'. Buddhist terms must be understood within the given doctrinal context in which they are being discussed. A term taken out of that context and interpreted on the basis of a traditionally established definition contributes to confusion, if not an error, in interpreting a given doctrine. This is particularly so in the case of Shingon.

A selected and annotated bibliography on Shingon is attached to this work. It consists largely of Japanese sources, because Western sources on Shingon are limited. Chinese and Japanese primary sources (works included in the *Taishō Tripiṭaka* and in the Shingon canons) are not cited in the bibliography because they are already available in Yoshito S. Hakeda, *Kūkai, Major Works: Translated with an Account of His Life and a Study of His Thought,* (New York and London: Columbia University Press, 1972, pp. 281–83). Nor are Indian Tantric sources cited in the bibliography for they are available in Agehananda Bharati, *The Tantric Tradition* (New York: Doubleday and Co., Inc., Anchor Books Edition, 1970, pp. 303–36). A comprehensive glossary of Sanskrit technical terms with Chinese characters is also attached to this work.

Names of Japanese personalities are indicated by last name first and first name last, following Japanese custom, though names of Japanese-American personalities are rendered in the usual Western tradition. The Hepburn system is observed in the romanization of Japanese terms and personality names, unless the personality in question employs another system of romanization to indicate his name.

In the preparation of this work, I am grateful to Dr. Nagao Gadjin, Professor Emeritus of Kyoto University, for his critical examination of the first draft of the chapter on the Indian Foundation; to Professor Nakagawa Zenkyō, rector of Kōya-san University, whom I have consulted over the course of many years during my visits to Japan, for his keen insight into Shingon theory and practice; and to my former professors of Tokyo University who have provided me with the basic Buddhological discipline. And to Mr. Dennis Lishka, a student in the Buddhist Studies Program of the University of Wisconsin-Madison, for his time consuming efforts in preparing the glossary of technical terms and for his assistance in the preparation of the first draft of the manuscript; to Mrs. Mary Jo Smith for typing out the second draft; to Mr. Otis Smith and Mr. Nobuo Haneda, both students in the Buddhist Studies Program, for reading the manuscript and providing me with valuable suggestions.

I am also grateful to Dr. Sawa Takaaki who has kindly allowed me to use the pictures of *maṇḍalas* which I have extracted from his *Mikkyō no bijitsu* (Tokyo: Heibonsha, 1964); and to the editors of the *History of Religion* (University of Chicago), in whose journal my essay on the *maṇḍala* first appeared in 1968, for allowing me to use portions of that essay in this work. I wish also to acknowledge gratitude to Dr. Alicia Matsunaga, editor of the Buddhist Books International, Los Angeles, whose perceptive understanding of Buddhism and painstaking editorial efforts have enhanced the readability of this otherwise jargon-heavy work. Finally, but not the least, I am grateful to the Graduate School and to the Department of South Asian Studies, both of the University of Wisconsin-Madison, for providing me with research funds, including some funds for research assistants, over the course of many years, without which the completion of this work would not have been possible.

Minoru Kiyota
University of Wisconsin-Madison
Summer, 1977

Chapter One

THE INDIAN FOUNDATION OF TANTRIC BUDDHISM

1. Basic Suppositions

The term 'tantric' is derived from *tantra*, literally meaning a 'thread'. It is identical in its literal meaning to the term *sūtra*, that is, "a thread, yarn, string, line, cord, wire," which later came to mean that which "holds everything together, rule, direction, or manual of teaching in ritual, philosophy, grammar."[1] *Sūtra* is a religious literature which contains the alleged sayings of the Buddha, but *tantra*, in contradistinction to *sūtra*, specifically refers to a type of religious literature which deals with incantation (i.e. *mantra* and *dhāraṇi*), divination and magic, and on occasions, iconographic (i.e. *maṇḍala*), sexual and other devices to symbolically illustrate what the writers conceive as the truth. A system of thought which has incorporated these elements is referred to as Tantrism. Tantric elements can be found in ancient Indian literature, such as in the aboriginal Dravidian literature as well as in the Vedic literature of the Indo-Āryans. Interestingly, they developed most prominently in areas of ancient India where cultural intercourse with alien elements was most pronounced, such as in the west, where commercial seaports developed, and in the northwest, which bordered on the Silk Road. But the origin of *tantra* remains obscure and efforts to define the range of *tantras*, whether on a ritual, symbolic, or philosophical level, have been a frustrating experience. Bhattacharya therefore rightly points out "the writers of the *tantra* were most erratic and never followed any definite plans."[2] It can be assumed that various schools of tantrism and forms of tantric expression existed in ancient India, of which one was Buddhism.

Tantric Buddhism is a term used to characterize a school of Buddhism systematized in India by incorporating tantric elements. Matsunaga Yūkei defines Buddhist *tantras* as follows:

> ... religious texts developed within Indian Mahāyāna Buddhism after the eighth century, and which came to replace the literary genre of *sūtra* which has previously been the major literary form of Buddhist scripture.[3]

But here we must note that what Matsunaga refers to are 'pure' tantric texts, in contradistinction to 'miscellaneous' tantric texts. The former refers to tantric texts which have incorporated the philosophical tenets of Mādhyamika and Yogācāra, while the latter refers to a wide range of texts which have incorporated folk cult practices, such as incantation, divination and magic. Matsunaga therefore says,

> The transition from Miscellaneous Esoteric Buddhism to Pure Esoteric Buddhism was a gradual one, and indeed it is difficult to separate clearly the division between the two, but the following consideration may be relevant here. Scriptures of the Miscellaneous Esoteric tradition generally take the form of sermons preached by the Buddha Śākyamuni, and concern magic and ceremonies designed to avert evil and bring about blessings. There is no unitary religious practice involving [*mantra* and] *dhāraṇi*, *mudrā* [finger signs], or meditation, nor are the various Buddhas and *bodhisattvas* systematized into the scheme of a *maṇḍala* [iconographic representation of truth]. The scriptures of the Pure Esoteric tradition are preached by Vairocana *Tathāgata;* in the practice of the teachings set forth in these scriptures, meditation is combined with *mudrā* and *dhāraṇi* (*mantras*), and the interrelationship between these three—which now have as their goal the attainment of the full illumination which is Buddhahood—is strongly stressed. Also a variety of *maṇḍalas* are depicted in these Pure Esoteric Scriptures.[4] (Note: Brackets are mine.)

As it is apparent, tantrism *per se* did not develop in the eighth century, it developed before that period. What did develop during this period, in the tradition of the evolution of Buddhist literature, is pure Buddhist tantrism. Pure Buddhism tantrism is different from miscellaneous tantrism in that the former constitutes the basic literary material for the development of an independent school of Buddhism—Tantric Buddhism—with a distinct religious organization. In other words, pure Buddhist tantrism employs *tantras* as a means to interpret its Mahāyāna doctrinal contents. Granting that tantric elements are inherent in Mahāyāna literature *per se*, these elements are, however, of the miscellaneous type, constituting popular beliefs, which the writers of Mahāyāna literature have incorporated simply following a folk tradition. As such, the mere fact that this type of literature incorporated tantric elements does not necessarily warrant its classification as tantric. Mahāyāṇa literature incorporating miscellaneous tantras is Mahāyāna literature, not Buddhist tantric literature, because it does not conceive *tantra* as a means to interpret its doctrinal contents. For example, the *Prajñāpāramitā* and the *Saddharmapuṇḍarīka* literature incorporate forms of incantation, but these are miscellaneous *tantras*. In the Shingon tradition, the composition of the *Mahāvairocana* and the *Tattvasaṃgraha Sūtras* signals the beginning of pure Buddhist *tantra*. Thus the process of development from miscellaneous *tantra* to pure *tantra* took several centuries, that is, pure *tantras* developed after the development of major Mahāyāna *sūtra*, the *Mahāvairocana* and *Tattvasaṃgraha Sūtras* being later Mahāyāna compositions. But this is not saying that the two—the pure and the miscellaneous—are independent, that they are totally unrelated. The composition of miscellaneous *tantra*, extensively incorporating popular belief, constitutes the period of preparation for the development of pure Buddhist tantric texts. But, as Matsunaga has rightly pointed out, the division between the two is not a clear one, and though Shingon does not identify texts such as the *Guhyasamāja*, *Pañcakrama*, and others as pure Buddhist tantric texts, they are nevertheless Mahāyāna texts in which tantras are conceived as fundamental and employed to interpret Mahāyāna doctrines. With these suppositions in mind, we are now ready to examine the circumstances under which *tantras* penetrated Buddhism.

2. The Impact of Non-Buddhist Thought upon the Development of Mahāyāna

Śākyamuni, who is assumed to have lived in sixth century B.C., prohibited the practices of incantation, divination and other forms of religious practices of Brahmanic origin, and he is said to have accused the mantra practitioners as transgressors of *pātayantikā*, a moral offense related to speech.[5] Primitive Buddhism was, most likely, able to eliminate this deep rooted Brahmanic tradition primarily because it existed at a time of the declining prestige of the ancient clan system associated with Brahmanism and during the rise of a new socio-political order.

By the sixth century B.C., the Indo-Āryans—the carriers of the Brahmanic tradition and the conquerors of the natives of the Indian subcontinent—had firmly settled themselves in the Ganges Valley. They established village communities and exercised absolute spiritual authority over these natives. But intermarriage between the Āryans and the natives brought about a new breed, a generation indifferent to the Brahmanic tradition, aspiring to find new types of expression. Economically, the development of agriculture produced surplus goods which gave rise to commerce, industry, money economy, and cities. Socially, economic prosperity enticed the minds of people into seeking pleasure in material goods and in realizing immediate benefits. Politically, local kings, who once had governed a territory consisting of groups of cities, were gradually absorbed by more powerful kings, the latter developing a system of absolute monarchy and enforcing the traditional social caste system against which the people rebelled. Religiously, the sacrifices to gods to realize good fortune and the desire to ascend to heavenly paradise, which characterized the traditional religion of the Vedas, were observed with varying degrees of skepticism. For example, the Brahmans assumed fire to be sacred. Yet, the city dwellers felt that if fire were in fact sacred, it would be the blacksmith whose profession is the most sacred, not the Brahmans. The Brahmans also held that water was sacred and performed rites of purification along the Ganges River, but the urban populace felt that if water were actually sacred, it would be the fish of the Ganges

River who would be assured of liberation, not the Brahmans. The ancient religious rite and incantation associated with the conservative socio-political system were met with growing disbelief, so a new religion of a local clan of Magadha spread throughout India with astonishing speed. This was one of the free-thinking, anti-establishment systems of thought of the time—it was called Buddhism.

But Brahmanism was a force with which Buddhism had had to reconcile itself. It eventually proved to be the dominant force underlying ancient Indian civilization. It absorbed Buddhism, and, in spite of Buddhism's success in penetrating other areas of Asia, in due time, Buddhism was rendered imperceptible in the land of its birth. An historical investigation of Buddhism in India shows distinctly its reaction to Brahmanic tradition during its formative years and a gradual process of its absorption by Brahmanism thereafter, as we shall now see.

Though Śākyamuni established the four categories of disciples (*bhikṣu*, *bhikṣuṇi*, *upāsaka* and *upāsikā*) and is said to have invited men and women of all classes into the *Saṅgha*, there was a definite distinction between monks and laity and between monks and nuns in the makeup of the early *Saṅgha*. The role of monks was to exemplify enlightenment and that of the laity was to support monks; and legend has it that Śākyamuni accepted nuns only upon the urging of Ānanda though he personally thought women to be detrimental to the maintenance of discipline within the monk-oriented *Saṅgha*. Apparently, the early *Saṅgha*, notwithstanding Śākyamuni's popular appeal, was an astute organization which emphasized an elite monastic *Saṅgha*. Iwamoto Yutaka claims that over fifty percent of the Buddha's direct disciples were of Brahmanic origin (and over twenty-five percent of *kṣatriya* origin), based upon his investigation of the Pāli *Anguttara-nikāya*, the Chinese *Anguttara-āgama*, and the *Sumagadhavadāna*.[6]

Though Śākyamuni himself was not of Brahmanic origin, and though he proposed the middle path between the pleasure of the flesh and the humanly unbearable forms of ascetic practices in seeking enlightenment, the effect of a Brahmanic cultural orientation—which fostered an intellectual elite—is evident in the makeup of the early *Saṅgha* and in the composition of the Buddha's immediate disciples. It was this basic cultural orientation which provided a favorable Brahmanic beachhead within Buddhism and for Brahmanism to exercise a significant impact on Buddhism.

The Maurya Dynasty began from 317 B.C. and lasted until about 180 A.D. Chandragupta, its first king (reigned ca. 317–293 B.C.), established a central government. This dynasty also marked the time of the first major schism of the Buddhist *Saṅgha* into Theravāda and Mahāsanghika, the so-called 'conservative' and 'progressive' elements, respectively. However, no religion seems to have been persecuted under Chandragupta's administration. Buddhism, Jainism, and Brahmanism flourished without political discrimination. By the reign of King Aśoka (ca. 256–232 B.C.), Buddhist influence was felt even within the Mediterranean region. But the territory ruled by King Aśoka was extensive, and in spite of the great zeal with which this Buddhist king attempted to spread Buddhism, the new religious outlook, which transcended the limits of incantational practice and magic, failed to penetrate the outer fringes of the vast kingdom, where the traditional Brahmanic outlook remained solidly entrenched. Even the early splinter schools, such as the Vātsīputrīya and Dharmagupta, compiled texts called *paritta*, a collection of *mantras*, and claimed that *mantras* were the concoctions of Śākyamuni. Undoubtedly, *mantras* were practices which even the early Buddhists, particularly among those of Brahmanic origin, could not completely abandon.

Alexander's expedition to northwest India (327–325 B.C.) left a great impact upon the development of Indian Buddhist thought. A Greek colony referred to as Yavana was established in Bactria in the late third century B.C. It contributed to the development of Greco-Gandhāran art at about the beginning of the Christian century. This art depicted the Buddha anthropomorphically and gave rise to the cult of deification, and subsequently to the concept of the enlightened body as eternal, transcending the historical Buddha. This is not saying that the cult of deification was completely absent in the preceding period. It was not, as can be attested by the creation of many *stūpas* immediately after the death of the Buddha. Nevertheless the depiction of the Buddha anthropomorphically represents the concretization of the Buddha as an eternal enlightened body, transcending the historical Śākyamuni. Added to the influence of the Greco-Gandhāran art was the influence of the nomads of Central Asia, who, even prior to the beginning of the Christian era, invaded the agricultural communities of northwest India whenever their trade was frustrated. To these tribes, immediate secular profit and the concept of a supernatural being, rather than speculative philosophy—which characterized the conservative elements of the splinter schools—had a greater appeal, and this impact most likely also contributed to the development of Buddhist devotionalism and the cult of deification which transcended the historical Buddha.

Buddhism thus developed its ideas and practices beyond the scope envisaged by its founder, incorporating the Brahmanic practice of incantation and divination and encompassing within its pantheon a host of deities of Brahmanic and perhaps other origin, and was most likely inspired by the Greeks, central Asians and western Asians, as it approached the beginning of the Christian era and during the period immediately thereafter. Buddhism owes much to these external influences, particularly in the development of Mahāyāna. What then are the major doctrinal themes developed in Mahāyāna?

During the reign of King Kaniṣka (128–151 A.D.), the *Abhidharma-mahāvibhāṣa-śāstra*, an encyclopedic work of the splinter schools and a culmination of previous Abhidharma studies, was compiled. Abhidharma scholarship dealt with theories of existence and the individual's path to liberation. Possibly in reaction to a highly meta-physical (and analytic) approach—which obviously appealed only to the intellectual—Mahāyāna literature developed. Mahāyāna, or larger vehicle, is a term used in contradistinction to Hīnayāna, or lesser vehicle, though these terms are of Mahāyāna origin. The early portions of the *Prajñāpāramitā* literature, the first among the Mahāyāna works, were composed just before the beginning of the Christian era. This *sūtra* emphasizes *bodhisattva* practices to bring about universal salvation. The *Sukhāvatīvyūha*, composed in the second century, conceives a universal Buddha transcending the historical Buddha and directs its followers toward a devotional approach. The

Saddharmapuṇḍarīka, composed over a period between 50 and 150 A.D., also conceives a transcendental Buddha and enunciates the Ekayāna (catholic) doctrine of universal salvation. The *Vimalakīrtinirdeśa,* probably composed before the second century, demonstrates that the enlightenment of the laity is of a kind not unlike and possibly superior to that of monks. The *Śrīmālādevīsiṃhanāda,* composed perhaps sometime after the *Vimalakīrtinīrdeśa,* portrays the dignity of woman in pointing out the path to enlightenment. Some definitions might be in order at this point.

A *bodhisattva,* in the Mahāyāna context, is one who willingly renounces the possibility of realizing self-enlightenment, identifies himself with the problems of the world of sentient beings, and improvises skill-in-means to alleviate the sufferings of others. *Bodhisattva* practices designed to alleviate the sufferings of others articulate an experiential approach. *Ekayāna,* an entity within the Mahāyāna tradition, means a universal vehicle which makes no distinction between man and woman, monks and laity, insofar as realizing enlightenment is concerned. As such, Mahāyāna literature extensively employs such terms as *kulaputra* and *kuladuhitṛ,* good sons and daughters, making no distinction whatsoever between monks and laity as it does in pre-Mahāyāna literature. Hence we can now see that Mahāyāna literature emphasizes universal salvation, conceives a transcendental Buddha, and articulates *bodhisattva* practices. It is devotional, directing its faith to a transcendental Buddha, and experiential, emphasizing practices directed to deal with the problems of the empirical world and the beings of that world in its approach to salvation. This is particularly so of the schools of Mahāyāna based upon the *sūtras* mentioned above.

The rise of Mahāyāna was evidently a gradual one, and despite speculation that many Mahāyāna schools were targets of persecution by the established schools, Hīnayāna and Mahāyāna apparently co-existed for a considerable length of time in India, as Hsüan-tsang, for one, reports in his travel accounts. But most important to note here is the consistent impact of non-Buddhist thought in the course of the development of Buddhist thought and practice in India, particularly of Brahmanism and particularly in the course of the development of Mahāyāna, notwithstanding the fact that Buddhism originated as a reaction against Brahmanism. It is upon the historical background as we have just described that we will now examine the gradual development of Tantric Buddhism.

3. Events Surrounding the Development of Tantric Buddhism

Before we attempt to trace the history of the development of Tantric Buddhism in India, we might note here, as we have briefly noted before, that tantric elements can be found in early Mahāyāna literature. The *Aṣṭasāhasrikā-prajñapāramitā-sūtra*, which is believed to contain the earliest of the literary layers of the *prajñā* literature and to have been composed some sixty years before the beginning of the Christian century, employs *mantras;* and Nāgārjuna, who is believed to be the earliest of the Mahāyāna *śāstra* writers and to have lived in about 150–250 A.D., cites *mantras* in many of his works, apparently following the tradition established by the *prajñā* literature. Furthermore, Lokakṣema translated into Chinese the *Pratyutpanna-samādhi-sūtra*, an early and apparent tantric text which is no longer known to be extant in Sanskrit, in the second century. It is then obvious that, following a popular tradition, tantric elements, particularly the chanting of mantras and of visualizing deities, were accepted as supporting entities of meditational discipline, if not a form of meditation *per se*, by the early writers of Mahāyāna sūtras and *śāstras*, even prior to the systematization of Buddhist Tantrism. But we cannot overlook the apparent external influence in the development of Buddhist Tantrism.

In 168, during the Kṣāṇa period, an epidemic spread throughout India which brought terror to the masses and possibly produced a favorable condition for the popular resurgence of incantational practices and magic. The Kṣāṇas originally came from central Asia, a shaman territory, where incantational practices and magic have had a great appeal, and Mahāyāna, with its catholic outlook, obviously demonstrated less resistance to incorporating non-Buddhist ideas, practices and institutions than did the early schools of Buddhism. As a matter of fact, it can be established that the development of Mahāyāna during the Kṣāṇa period was greatly enhanced by incorporating tantric elements.

In the early third century, the power of the Kṣāṇas in northern India and of the Āndras in southern India declined, and for the next hundred years monarchs warred against one another. Written Chinese sources contain rich information for examining Indian Buddhism of this period. Dharmarakṣa (ca. 230–308) and an Indian monk whom the Chinese refers to as Chu Lü-yen (mid-third century) and other Buddhists from northern India and central Asia translated Buddhist tantric texts into Chinese. Dharmarakṣa (not to be confused with Dharmarakṣa of the fourth-fifth century), variably known as Bodhisattva Yeüh-shih and Bodhisattva Tun-huang, was a native of Yüeh-shih whose parents eventually settled in Tun-huang, though another account says that he was a native of Tun-huang and that his parents came from Yüeh-shih. At any rate, he traveled extensively throughout central Asia, introduced many Buddhist Sanskrit texts to China, lived in Ch'ang-an and Loyang, then the centers of Buddhist studies, and translated some 260 items of Buddhist Sanskrit texts into Chinese in those cities, among which were the *Prajñāpāramitā-*, *Saddharmapuṇḍarīka-*, *Vimalakīrtinīrdeśa-*, *Sukhāvativyūha-*, and other important Mahāyāna-*sūtras.* He also translated Buddhist tantric texts, as for example, the *Sūgara-nāgagarāja-sūtra.* Chih-ch'ien, a member of the nomadic Yüeh-shih tribe, who subsequently became a naturalized Chinese, translated some fifty-three Buddhist Sanskrit texts into Chinese, between 223 and 253, some of which were tantric texts, as for example, the *Puṣpakuta-dhāraṇi-sūtra*, *Amitāmukha-guhyadhara-sūtra*, etc. Fo T'u-ch'eng (232–348), another monk from central Asia, was favorably received by the emperors of north China. He incorporated incantation, divination and magic, through which he spread the Dharma. The Dharma was also spread by the introduction of many *dhāraṇi* texts designed to cure toothaches, eye diseases, etc., as was in the case of Dharmakṣma of late fourth century. Many monks who came to China between the late Han and early Six Dynastic periods spread the Dharma in these manners. Obviously, Tantric Buddhism exercised a significant influence in northern India and central Asia during the third and fourth centuries as can be clearly seen reflected in the type of literature—Buddhist tantric literature—that was carried into China by Buddhist monks during this period. But what is most important to note here is that regardless of the early period of the composition of Buddhist tantric texts in India—as judged from extant Chinese records—these were not 'pure' Buddhist tantric texts. Further examination of the socio-political situation of India is in order to see the gradual rise of Vajrayāna, one of the systematized forms of Buddhist tantrism which employs 'pure' Buddhist tantric texts.

Chandragupta I founded the Gupta Dynasty in 320 and his son Samdragupta (335–375) established a central government. The Gupta kings exercised power in northern India until about 470. The Gupta represented the period of Brahmanic renaissance. Brahmanism became the state religion, the traditional caste system was observed, and civil law based on Brahmanic texts was re-established. Trade and commerce developed, Indian merchants traded with the Romans, Greeks, and Iranians, and Roman currency flowed into India in substantial amount. Buddhism of this period, more than ever before, utilized various forms of *mantra* designed to cure the sick, to accumulate wealth, to prevent misfortunes, to insure longevity, to bring about rain, and to realize a bountiful harvest. Tantric texts—which were designed to foster secular satisfaction—were most likely composed in significant number during this period. (Many of these texts are no longer extant in Sanskrit but are preserved in the Chinese translation.) Gurus appeared and functioned as spiritual authorities. Buddhism, at least in its outward appearance, became increasingly difficult to distinguish from Brahamanism during the Gupta period.

The Roman Empire fell in 475 and the flow of Roman currency to India—which had begun in the Kṣāṇa period—came to an aburpt end. In addition, the Huns invaded northwest India in the late fifth century, destroying many Buddhist monasteries and *stūpas*. The Indian economy was seriously threatened because the Huns used a new kind of currency. The plight of this economy created social unrest and in all probability further stimulated the development of magic. In the sixth century, Bodhiruci (not to be confused with the monk of the same name of south

Indian origin) and Buddhaśānta, both of north Indian origin, escaping from the threatening Huns, came to China, carrying with them some Tantric Buddhist texts, though most of these texts had already been introduced by previous Buddhist missionaries from central Asia.

In the early seventh century, the Harṣa unified northern India. Hsüan-tsang (600– or 602–664) made his pilgrimage to India and returned in 645. Among the many Buddhist texts he brought back were about ten Tantric Buddhist texts, some of which had previously been known in China. Indications are that tantrism became the major school of Buddhism in India immediately after Hsüan-tsang returned to China. In southern India, the Pallavas, who had come to power in the fourth century, exercised a dominant influence from the early sixth through mid-seventh centuries, but were defeated by the Cholas in about 750. The Pallavan converts to Tantric Buddhism sought refuge in Orissa. This period marked the decline of Tantric Buddhism in southern India and its rise in Orissa, where Vajrayāna became popular.

King Indrabhūti (678–717)—who, incidentally, was the father of Padmasaṃbhava, the prominent monk who entered Tibet in about 747 and who is the founder of the Tibetan rNin-ma-pa school—is the author of *Jnānasiddhi*, *Kurukullāsādharma*, and other Buddhist texts. He is the alleged founder of the Vajrayāna school of Tantric Buddhism. The term '*vajra*' means 'diamond', though it also means 'thunderbolt', 'weapon', etc. Vajrayāna means the 'indestructible vehicle'. It prescribed methods for attaining the indestructible body (*vajra-kāya*) by realizing the nature of emptiness (*śūnyatā*), and it incorporated the tantras then popular among the masses of the Bengal region and contributed much to developing unique Buddhist literature written in local vernacular, like the *Apabhraṃśa*. This unique collection of literature is called *caryāgiti* or *dohā* and was developed by the Sahajayāna branch of Vajrayāna. The Sahajayāna attempted to realize the ultimate truth within one's own physical body (*sahaja*). (*Vajra-kāya* was conceived within *sahaja-kāya*.) Though this theory has a solid doctrinal basis, it nevertheless led to moral depravity in practice, as in the case of *mahāsukha*, the union of male and female energy—the former representing the seeker of truth and the latter truth *per se*. But it is an open question whether moral decadence was the result of tantrism or whether the type of tantrism which developed during this period reflected the moral decadence of its society. Even if the former is true, Vajrayāna did manage to produce prominent and respectable philosophers, like Atīśa (980–1052), who entered the kingdom of King 'Khan-Ide of Tibet, upon invitation, and contributed much toward reforming the Tibetan *Saṅgha*. It would be erroneous to simply associate Vajrayāna *per se* with moral decadence.

In the wake of anarchy which characterized northern India during the first half of the eight century, the Pālas (possibly of non-Brahman and non-Kṣatriyan origin) emerged and expanded their empire throughout this area. Gopāla (reigned ca. 765–770), the first Pāla king, built water reservoirs, developed irrigation systems, and promoted agriculture. Tantric Buddhism entered Bengal from Orissa at about this time. Gopāla became a Buddhist convert and he established a Buddhist academy, the Odantapuri. Dharmapāla, the second king, established the Vikramaśilā University in the late eighth century. This was the center of Vajrayāna studies to which monks from Tibet, Nepal, Śrivijaya, and China came to study. In the ninth century, Devapāla established the Somapurī University. It is a safe assumption that the Pālas supported Buddhism as a reaction against their predecessors in northern India, the Brahmanic Cholas and Guptas, but the type of Buddhism which they supported was that which already manifested a heavy trace of Brahmanic influence. At any rate, Tantric Buddhism in Bengal received the support of the Pāla kings until the early thirteenth century, a period which signaled the Moslem invasion of the Bengal region which essentially wiped out what remained of Buddhism. Fortunately, Mahāyāna was already introduced to East Asia, making possible its survival in that area and marking that area as a distinct Mahāyāna complex.

4. The Tantric Transmission to East Asia

Śubhākarasiṃha (637–735), Vajrabodhi (671–741), and Amoghavajra (705–774), a disciple of Vajrabodhi, carried with them a vast collection of Buddhist tantric texts when they entered China. Śubhākarasiṃha entered China by the northern land route, from central Asia. Vajrabodhi and Amoghavajra entered China by the southern sea route, from Southeast Asia. The routes they took are suggestive of the popularity of tantrism in those areas at that time. Because tantrism incorporated astronomy (and astrology), phenology, music, art, and folklore as methods of projecting its world view of a type which was apparently a product of synthesis of various world views representative of various cultural entities, the introduction of Tantric Buddhism contributed much to stimulating the growth of Chinese culture of a cosmopolitan dimension.

Buddhism was already popular in Southeast Asia in the fifth century, as attested by the vividly portrayed travel accounts of Fa-hsien (340?–420?). And it is very possible to assume that Buddhism had penetrated this area much eariler, as can be attested by the legendary accounts related to the transmission of the Dharma held to by the native of this area and through early Chinese historical records. The Chinese monk I-ching (635–713), who studied in Nālandā for some ten years, continued to study Sanskrit in Palembang on the eastern coast of Sumatra on his way back to China, suggesting that Buddhist scholarship had already established deep roots in this area by the seventh century. In the first half of the ninth century, the Pālas, under King Devapāla, engaged in diplomatic relations with King Bālaputradeva of the Śailendra Kingdom of Java. The Vajrayāna tradition of Vikramaśilā was introduced to Java at this time, culminating in the world renowned Boroboudour, its architectonic *maṇḍala.* Jayavarman II of Java entered Cambodia in the early ninth century and became the king of the Chen-las. Angkor Tom, completed in the twelfth century, and Angkor Vat, completed in the early thirteenth century, are modeled upon Boroboudour. The Vajrayāna impact on the development of culture in the Hindu-Buddhist countries of Southeast Asia is thus apparent.

The two sūtras—*Mahāvairocana* and *Tattvasaṃgraha*—form the basis of the Japanese Tantric Buddhist tradition and were transmitted from China. The *Mahāvairocana Sūtra* was introduced to China from India by Śubhākarasiṃha, a monk of royal origin, who studied at Nālandā and entered Ch'ang-an in 716. The *Tattvasaṃgraha Sūtra* was introduced to China by Vajrabodhi and Amoghavajra in 720, four years after Śubhākarasiṃha had arrived in China. The Japanese monk, Saichō (767–805), the founder of Japanese Tendai, studied under Shun-hsia, whose master, I-lin, studied the *Mahāvairocana Sūtra* under Śubhākarasiṃha. Kūkai (774–835), the founder of Japanese Shingon, studied under Hui-ko, who in turn studied the *Mahāvairocana* tradition under Hsuan-ch'ao, a disciple of Śubhākarasiṃa, and the *Tattvasaṃgraha* tradition directly under Amoghavajra. Thus the Buddhist tantric tradition in Japan is represented by two major schools, Tendai and Shingon. The Japanese tantric tradition incorporated within Tendai is called Taimitsu, while the Japanese tantric tradition represented by Shingon is called Tōmitsu. Kūkai's Shingon (Tōmitsu) represents a systematized doctrine based upon a synthesis of thoughts derived much from the *Mahāvairocana Sūtra* and the *Tattvasaṃgraha Sūtra*.

5. The *Māhavairocana* Sūtra: Its Origin and Transmission

This *sūtra* probably was known in full as the *Mahāvairocanābhisaṃbodhivikurvitādhiṣṭhāna-sūtra*. It is extant in the Chinese and Tibetan translations. It is not known to be extant in Sanskrit. The Tibetans refer to this sūtra as *rNam-par sNam mJad chen-po mÑon-par rGogs-par Byañ-chub-pa rNam-par sPrul-pa Byin-Gyis rLob-pa Sin-tu rGyas-pa mDo-sDei dBañ-poi rGyar-po ṣes-Bya-bai Chos-kyi rÑam-Grans*, according to the *sNar-than* edition, a probable translation from the Sanskrit *Mahāvairocanābhisaṃbodhivikurvitādhiṣṭhanāvaipulyasūtren-drarājanāmadharma paryāya*. The *Ta-ji ching su* (Commentary on the *Mahāvairocana Sūtra*), composed by Śubhākarasiṃha and the Chinese monk I-hsing, calls it the *Ta-kuang-po ching yin t'o-lo*, a probable translation from the Sanskrit *Mahāvaipulyasūtrandrarāja*. It is commonly known as the *Ta-ji ching* in Chinese and *Dainichikyō* in Japanese, that is, the *Mahāvairocana-sūtra*. It is most popularly studied in Japan. Kūkai called Mahāvairocana the '*Dainichi joan henmyō-jo shokakuja shinpen kaji-kyō taishaku ō*', meaning the "King [who interpreted] the *sūtra* on the miraculous transformation of the power of the

One who has realized the supreme enlightenment and whose great light is omnipresent and [capable of] illuminating [all darkness]." Mahāvairocana literally means 'the great light'.

The *Mahāvairocana Sūtra* is not mentioned in the following Chinese travel accounts: a) *Fu-kuo chi* (Record of the Buddha-land) written by Fa-hsien, who observed India and Southeast Asia for a ten year period, from the late fourth century through the early fifth century; b) *Shih hsi-yu chi* (Record of the Mission to the Western Region), written by Hui-shen, who was in India for three years in the early sixth century; and c) *Hsi-yu chi* (Record of the Western Region), written by Hsüan-tsang, who stayed in India for sixteen years in the first half of the seventh century. However, I-ching, who entered India in 671—some twenty-six years after Hsüan-tsang returned to China—and who remained there for the next twenty-five years, speaks of the *Mahāvairocana Sūtra* in his *Shi-yu ch'iu-fa kao-seng chüan*[7] (The Biography of Eminent Monks Who Sought the Dharma in the Western Region). Furthermore, Wu-hsing, who arrived in India about the same time as I-ching, sent a copy of this *sūtra* to China, and states in his letter that the teaching of the *mantra* is honored by many people.[8] I-ching, speaking of himself, writes that though he has gone to Nālandā, "he has found the teaching of the *mantra* very difficult."[9] Ch'ang-min also arrived in India at about the same time as I-ching, and he writes in his *Yu t'ien-chu chi* (Record of Travel to India) that Vairocana is worshipped by many people in Vaiśakha in central India.[10] Judging from these accounts, it may be surmised that the *Mahāvairocana Sūtra* was composed sometime in mid-seventh century, that is, between Hsüan-tsang's return to China in 645 and I-ching's arrival in India in 671, as it is speculated by Toganoo Shōun.[11]

Since the *sūtra* makes reference to things like an ocean, salt and merchants, and describes the garment worn by the Buddha as a *patta*, an extremely light garment, and also describes great cities and many deities, it can be assumed that the composer of this *sūtra* was knowledgeable of an ocean, lived in a tropical area, and was exposed to a variety of religions of a cosmopolitan setting. Interestingly, among the fifty-six monks to whom I-ching refers to in his *Shi-yu ch'iu-fa kao-seng chüan*, four are identified as converts to the Mahāvairocana cult. All four monks had made plans to go to the western coast of India, and two of them, Hsüan-chao and Tao-lin, went to Lāṭā in the Kathiawar peninsula on the western coast of India. Furthermore, Bharukaccha, that is Broach, once the capital of Lāṭā, was an important port city which ships from Greece, Egypt, Persia and other countries of the Mediterranean frequented. Here material goods and ideas were exchanged and various religions of the world —like Jainism, Brahmanism Hīnayāna, Mahāyāna, and Zoroastrianism—co-existed. It was one of the port cities destroyed by the Arabs in the ninth century. Both Hsüan-tsang and I-ching were familiar with this general area and identified Mālava and Valabhī, the neighboring cities of Bharukaccha, as prosperous commercial sites and great academic centers of Buddhism. It is very probable that the wealth of this area contributed much to the development and the maintenance of the cave temples of Ajantā, Ellora and Nāsik, sites found just southeast of this general area, and that Tantric Buddhism was very popular within this region as can be attested by the archeological remains found along the trade routes within this region.

Since I-ching says that the *Mahāvairocana Sūtra* was studied at Nālandā, it can be assumed that the *sūtra* was introduced to Nālandā by way of Uddiyana, following the established trade route of that time. It can also be assumed that Nālandā, at the time of I-ching, was one of the great centers of Tantric Buddhist studies, though the condition of tantric studies after his departure remains uncertain. Most likely, the Rājputs brought the once prosperous Tantric Buddhist center to an end. Subsequently, it is further assumed, the *sūtra* was introduced to southern India. Whether the *sūtra* was introduced to Ceylon or not is not, however, clear. But a Chinese record indicates that at the time of the reign of Emperor Hsien-tsüng (805–820) of T'ang, a Tantric Buddhist text called the *Hsin-ti kuan ching* (The *Sūtra* on the Meditation upon the Original State of Mind) was presented to the court by the king of Ceylon.[12] Tantric Buddhism, in fact, was popular in Ceylon even before the ninth century, but because Ceylon was a stronghold of the Vibhajyavādins, it is quite obvious that Tantric Buddhism did not exercise any significant influence there for any length of time.

With reference to its introduction to the northern region, a preface to the *Mahāvairocana Sūtra* (the *Zokuzō* version) says that this *sūtra* was transmitted to Bolora in Kashmir.[13] Toganoo cites a story from a commentary which mentions that Śubhākarasiṃha instructed the king of Gandhāra in worship of the Buddha based upon the *Mahāvairocana Sūtra.*[14] Though this story may be mere legend, it is possible that the sūtra was introduced to northwest India, Karakorum and Khotan, from Bolora, to give rise to such a legend.

According to I-ching's account, Wu-hsing, whom I-ching had met in India (and, incidentally, the only known Chinese who had studied under Dharmakīrti, the renowned Indian logician), attempted to carry the Sanskrit manuscript of the *Mahāvairocana Sūtra* to China on his way back. Wu-hsing unfortunately died in northern India in 674, but the manuscript was nevertheless carried to China by one of his disciples. The sūtra was then translated into Chinese by Śubhākarasiṃha and his disciple I-hsing (683–727) in 725. They used the Sanskrit manuscript which had been carried into China by Wu-hsing's disciple.

Many studies on the *Mahāvairocana Sūtra* are available in Chinese and Japanese, but very few in Tibetan and none yet discovered in Sanskrit. Yamada Ryūjō speculates that the system of direct transmission of the Mahāvairocana tradition, from master to disciple—a system extensively observed among the tantric traditions—might have been abruptly terminated because of political reasons in some countries, such as in Tibet, but since the Chinese and Japanese tantric tradition, based upon the *Mahāvairocana Sūtra*, allowed for textual study as well as direct transmission, the Mahāvairocana tradition survived in these two countries, regardless of whether the system of direct transmission was terminated or not.[15]

6. *The Tattvasamgraha Sūtra:* Its Origin and Transmission

The *Tattvasaṃgraha Sūtra*, known in full as the *Sarvatathāgata-tatıva-saṃgraha-mahāyānābhisamaya-mahākalpa-rāja-sūtra*, is retained in the Chinese Tripiṭaka in three versions: the first translated by Vajrabodhi into four *chüan*, the second by Amoghavajra into three, and the third by Dānapāla (late tenth century) into thirty. The *Tattvasaṃgraha Sūtra* is a part of a Tantric Buddhist text which Matsunaga refers to as the *Vajrosṇisa Sūtra*,[16] a collection of texts consisting of sermons delivered by the Buddha at eighteen assemblies and organized into 100,000 verses. The Chinese holds that Amoghavajra obtained the entire collection from King Silamega (733–772) of Ceylon and died after translating the *Shih-pa-hui chih-kuei* (The Outline of the Eighteen Assemblies). Sections of this outline, but not the contents of all eighteen assemblies, are retained in the Chinese *Tripiṭaka*. What is commonly referred to as the *Tattvasaṃgraha Sūtra* in the Shingon tradition, actually refers to the contents of the first assembly.

The *Tattvasaṃgraha Sūtra* describes a realm of enlightenment in terms of the fivefold Buddha assembly and the practices to realize that realm in terms of the five stages of meditation. But the fivefold Buddha assembly first appears in the *Pu-k'ung chüan-so ching*, probably known in Sanskrit as the *Amoghapaśa-sūtra*, which Bodhiruci (of South Indian origin) brought to Loyang in 693, or which found its way into China by some other means, even before that time. The fivefold Buddha assembly is also described in the previously mentioned *sūtra*, the *Hsin-ti kuan ching*.

Because the *Amoghapāśa* forms the model for the *Tattvasṃgraha*—as can be clearly seen upon examining the doctrinal contents of these two *sūtras*—we can assume that the *Tattvasaṃgraha* was composed after the composition of the *Amoghapāśa;* furthermore, the fact that the *Amoghapāśa* makes frequent reference to the *Mahāvairocana* (but not to the *Tattvasaṃgraha*) is suggestive that the *Mahāvairocana* was composed prior to the *Amoghapāśa*. In other words, among the three *sūtras* under consideration, the order of their composition may be as follows: *Mahāvairocana*, *Amoghapāśa*, and *Tattvasaṃgraha*. But this theory must be held as a tentative one, because another account holds that the *Amoghapāśa* was translated into Chinese by Jñānagupta (late 6th century to early 7th century) before 600, a date preceding the probable date of composition of the *Mahāvairocana*. What is relatively certain, however, is that the composition of the *Mahāvairocana* preceded the composition of the *Tattvasaṃgraha*.

Since Vajrabodhi studied in southern India and introduced the *Tattvasaṃgraha* to China in 720, it can be concluded with some degree of certainty that this *sūtra* was popular in southern India in the early eighth century, and that it was subsequently intoduced to Orissa, then to western India, and subsequently to China and Tibet. This speculation generally corresponds to a Chinese account recorded in the *Chin-kang-ting ching i-chüeh*, Vajrabodhi's commentary on the *Tattvasaṃgraha* and recorded by Amoghavajra, that the *Tattvasaṃgraha* is of southern Indian origin, and that it became popular throughout India in the eighth century. But it must be added here that the *Chin-kang-ting ching i-chüeh* is of dubious authorship. It is not recorded either in the K'ai-yüan or Chen-yüan catalogues.

7. Conclusion

Though details surrounding the origin and the Indian transmission of the two basic Shingon *sūtras*—*Mahāvairocana* and *Tattvasaṃgraha*—do not go beyond speculation, we may tentatively conclude that the *Mahāvairocana* was composed somewhere in the Kathiawar peninsula in mid-seventh century and was subsequently transmitted to various regions of India, and that the *Tattvasaṃgraha* was composed shortly after the composition of the *Mahāvairocana*, perhaps in early eighth century, somewhere in southern India. What is certain is that these two *sūtras* were transmitted to China in the eighth century and that, regardless of the degree of popularity they enjoyed in India and China, they became the two basic canonical sources of Japanese Shingon. We do not know for certain whether the doctrines of these two *sūtras* were integrated and contributed to the development of a distinct system of Buddhist tantric thought in India, as they did in Japan. They probably did not, notwithstanding the fact that they were known and were popularized in various regions of the Indian sub-continent at one time or another. And, notwithstanding the fact that these two "pure" Buddhist tantric texts—the *Mahāvairocana Sūtra* and the *Tattvasaṃgraha Sūtra*—were transmitted to China from India, and notwithstanding the fact that two great "pure" Buddhist tantric masters of India—Śubhākarasiṃha and Vajrabodhi—came to and resided in China for some time, Tantric Buddhism based upon the tradition of these *sūtras* and masters failed to establish deep roots in China and to sustain the interest of the Chinese, as it did in Japan. In other words, granting the fact that Shingon is largely based upon texts of Indian composition and that its tradition was transmitted to Japan from China, the formulation of Shingon doctrine, the systematization of Shingon as a distinct religious order, and the identification of Shingon as a distinct entity of Mahāyāna are attributed to the creative efforts of Kūkai.

Some basic historical issues, however, still remain unresolved. Matsunaga claims that "pure" Buddhist Tantric texts developed after the eighth century in India, while Toganoo speculates that the *Mahāvairocana Sūtra*, a "pure" Buddhist tantric text, was composed in mid-seventh century. On speculating the date of the composition of the *Mahāvairocana Sutra*, I have more-or-less followed Toganoo's line of reasoning. But both Matsunaga and Toganoo entertain the view that Vajrayāna, which has had considerable impact on the formulation of Shingon, developed in eighth century India, a view extensively entertained by most Indologists and Buddhologists today. But what remains puzzling is the evolution of the terms 'Vajrayāna' and 'Mantrayāna', terms obviously indicating schools or sub-schools of Indian Buddhist tantrism and which appear extensively in the *Mahāvairocana Sūtra* and the *Tattvasaṃgraha Sūtra*, as well as in other Buddhist tantric literature. We do not know for certain which came first. Furthermore, was there in fact a school called Buddhist Tantrayāna in the same vein that we refer to and distinguish the major schools of Buddhist thought, such as Hīnayāna and Mahāyāna, and *Triyāna* and *Ekayāna*? Clarification of these matters must wait for further investigation by the Buddhologists.

Chapter Two: THE SHINGON SYSTEM OF DOCTRINAL EVALUATION AND CLASSIFICATION

1. The System of Doctrinal Evaluation as a Spiritual Biographical Testimony

Shingon, or Shingon *Mikkyō* in full, is the abbreviation of *Shingon-darani*, the Japanese rendition of *mantra* and *dhāraṇi*. *Mantra* in the Shingon context means a formula into which the teachings of the Buddha are distilled. It does not refer to "words in praise of gods," as the term means in the Vedic literature. *Dhāraṇi* is another word for *mantra*. But whereas *mantra* represents the ultimate distillation of truth expressed in a simple syllable, *dhāraṇi* is a description of truth in a simple verse.

Shingon, in the Sino-Japanese characters, literally means 'true word'. It refers to Mantrayāna, the Mantra School. *Mikkyō* literally means the 'secret teaching'. It is a term used in contrast to *Kengyō*, the 'revealed teaching.' *Mikkyō* and *Kengyō* are important terms in the history of the development of Japanese Buddhist thought. *Mikkyō* specifically refers to the teaching of the secret (unrevealed) Buddha, who is *Dharmakāya* Mahāvairocana. (The meaning of the term *Dharmakāya* Mahāvairocana will be discussed in detail in Chapter III-2, Mahāvairocana). *Kengyō* refers to the teachings of Śākyamuni, the historical (revealed) Buddha, who was enlightened through his insights into *Dharamakāya*. Shingon *Mikkyō* therefore means the secret teaching of the *mantra* school systematized by Kūkai (774–835), who is posthumously known as Kōbō Daishi.

Shingon *Mikkyō* is a school of Buddhism systematized in Japan and is dedicated to support the principles which Kūkai conceived. It is the Japanese version of Tantric Buddhism based on the Mahāyāna philosophy of Mādhyamika and Yogācāra. It interprets these philosophical tenets through symbolic and iconographic representations and extensively employs the tantric practices of *mantras*, *mudrās*, and yogic meditation. Its purpose is to actualize the integration of man with Mahāvairocana. Though Kūkai makes reference to a variety of Buddhist literature representing a wide range of schools of thought, his ideas are fundamentally based upon two *sūtras* and two *śāstras*. These are the *Mahāvairocana* and *Tattvasaṃgraha Sūtras*, and the *Bodhicitta Śāstra* and the *Commentary on the Awakening of Mahāyāna Faith*. The last two are alleged to have been composed by the tantric master Nāgārjuna. Kūkai's major compositions are the *Ben kenmitsu nikyō-ron* (Discourse on *Mikkyō* and *Kengyō*), *Jūjū shin-ron* (Ten Stages of Mental Development), *Hizō-hōyaku* (Jewel Key to the Secret Store), and the *Sokushin jōbutsu-gi* (Buddhahood Realized in the Present Body).

Ben kenmitsu nikyō-ron distinguishes between *Mikkyō* and *Kengyō*, *Jūjū shin-ron* and its abridged version *Hizō-hōyaku* synthesize various schools of thought within the context of Shingon *Mikkyō*, and *Sokushin jōbutsu-gi* articulates the theory of 'instant Buddhahood'. *Ben kenmitsu nikyō-ron*, *Jūjū shin-ron* and *Hizō-hōyaku* represent Kūkai's system of doctrinal evaluation and classification. This system is ahistorical. It is based on a doctrinal value judgement. Kūkai's particular system of doctrinal classification is based upon a Chinese model. The historical circumstances which contributed to the development of the Chinese system of doctrinal classification now needs to be examined.

Buddhist thought in India evolved in a rational sequence, from the primitive to the analytic and speculative Abhidharma, to the synthetic and experiential Mahāyāna, to the symbolic Tantric Buddhism. Buddhist literature was introduced to China at a time when the Chinese had already realized a sophisticated form of civilization with distinct, native thought and institutions already developed; it came in several waves at various historical periods, and in a manner which did not correspond to the pattern of development of Indian Buddhist thought. Furthermore, the development of schools of Chinese Buddhism was affected by established political powers. That is, Confucianism, supported at time by Taoism, or vice-versa, represented native thought, molded socio-political thought and stimulated xenophobia among the tradition-oriented intellectuals, a great number of whom represented the state bureaucracy. The socio-political circumstances under which Buddhism was introduced to and domesticated in China, contributed to the development of the '*chiao-pan*' (Jap. *kyōsō hanjaku*, or *kyō-han*) system of doctrinal evaluation and classification. This system was designed to show that a doctrine which had developed in China was in no way inferior to that which had been developed in India. The criteria for evaluating the superiority of a school was rationality in synthesizing several schools of thought and practice demonstrating this rationale. The purpose of the Chinese system of doctrinal evaluation and classification was in developing *Ekayāna*, the universal vehicle, which synthesized various schools of thought based upon this rationale.

Though the system of doctrinal evaluation and classification is ahistorical, it represents a biographical testimony of one in pursuit of truth. It selects doctrines and ideas regardless of historical development, based upon a specific theme which its author conceives to be the ideal principle (Dharma) and from which other schools of thought are critically examined and incorporated as a method to realize the Dharma; it distinguishes the method—*upāya* (skillful means)—from the ultimate truth (Dharma); and it systematizes schools of thought based upon that Dharma. In other words, the system requires not only an arbitrary evaluation and classification of schools of thought but also a perceptive understanding of those schools, the selection and interpretation of Buddhist literature appropriate to solving the problems faced by its author, and a root text or texts to synthesize schools of thought.

The Shingon system of doctrinal evaluation and classification follows the Chinese *chiao-pan* tradition and claims that the teachings of the historical Buddha are designed to reveal the supreme truth through skillful means. The supreme truth of Shingon is represented by the secret Buddha, *Dharmakāya* Mahāvairocana, while all other teachings are conceived as methods to realize the realm of *Dharmakāya* Mahāvairocana. The *Ben kenmitsu nikyō-ron* identifies the teaching of *Dharmakāya* Mahāvairocana as *Mikkyō*, and all other teachings as *Kengyō*. The

Hizō-hōyaku describes ten schools of thought. It recognizes the 'seed' of Mahāvairocana in each school and emphasizes that the means (to realize Buddhahood) and the end (i.e., the realization of Buddhahood) are not distinct and apart, the premise being that the goal is inherent in the means. The theory of Buddhahood inherent in the present body, as articulated in the *Sokushin jōbutsu-gi*, is based upon this premise. Let us now trace the development of thought as Kūkai himself has experienced it, for Shingon, like many other schools of Buddhism, was founded as a way to solve the paradox of human existence as experienced by its founder. The *Hizō-hōyaku* begins in verse as follows:

Unknowable, unknowable
    It is completely unknowable,
About the Buddha and the non-Buddhists
    There are millions of scrolls;
Dark, dark, it is very dark,
    Of the way that is spoken there are many paths.
What is left
    When the copying and chanting of scriptures stop?
No one knows, no one knows
    And I too do not know,
Though they consider and speculate
    Even the wise do not know.[1]

It further says:

> Life is that which man did not desire and death is that which all men abhor. However, life continues to revolve around the six destinies and in death we sink into the path of delusion. Even our parents, who gave us birth, do not know the origins of birth. And we, who have received life, do not know where death leads to.[2]

Faced with the futility of knowledge and the uncertainty of life, Kūkai attempted to seek the existential nature of man. But he realized that what is sought is ultimately empty and that there is essentially nothing to be grasped, because life is not based upon a first cause nor a first principle. He therefore says:

> There is nothing that is not created by conditions. But that which is created by conditions must be based upon a definite cause—the creator of conditions. Upon contemplating on the creator of conditions, we realize that the creator is also created by conditions. What then is the source of the conditions which created the creator? We then come to realize that an 'original state' is devoid of a creator-essence. One who has realized this original state knows the true nature of self. Knowing the true nature of self is the wisdom of all wisdoms.[3]

Kūkai negated the Brahmanic concept of creation because, according to the principle of conditional causation (*pratītya-samutpāda*), a creator too is subject to the law of origination and extinction. Thus, if a creator is subject to extinction, he is no longer a creator. 'Wisdom of all wisdoms' denotes the 'original state of mind' (pure mind), unpolluted by acquired knowledge. It is acquired knowledge which fragments the world into fixed conceptual categories, establishes the dichotomy (such as the creator and the created), and conceives conceptual categories as entities of true reality. Kūkai called the moment of this realization the state of awakening (*citta-utpanna*) or the state of revival (*āśvāsa*).

Kūkai considered insight into the emptiness of all things to be the key to ultimate liberation from ignorance. Emptiness is the doctrinal basis of the Mādhyamika school (see Sanron, this chapter). The moment one realizes insight into emptiness is referred to as awakening. It corresponds to the Yogācāra notion of *parāvṛtti*, literally a revolution or transformation. In that revolution the mind turns round completely and sees the world from an entirely different perspective (see Hossō, this chapter). The new world unfolded is termed *Dharmadhātu*, the world of emptiness.

Insight into *Dharmadhātu* requires an understanding of Mādhyamika. The *Mādhyamaka-kārikā* says,

> What is dependent co-arising we call emptiness;

This serves as a designation
And is the same as the middle path.[4]

Mādhyamika posits two levels of truth, the 'supreme' (insight into emptiness) and the 'conventional' (insight into co-arising). Co-arising means that the elements of existence are contingent on one another in producing a given phenomenon, that a phenomenon is essentially a product of conditional causation. These two levels—the supreme and the conventional—are not irreconcilable: co-arising is possible because of emptiness, for without the emptiness of an essence in a given phenomenon, change, which characterizes phenomena, is impossible; and emptiness, on the other hand, is realized only through co-arising, that is in the realm of conceptual discrimination (*abhūta-parikalpa*) itself, in the realm of the constantly changing phenomena. Co-arising is the visual sign indicative of change which emptiness brings about. In this context then, the supreme does not denote absolute void, nor does the conventional denote a fixed state of existence. What the *kārikā* attempts to reveal is the notion that nothing can be produced without the elements of existence—the elements of co-arising—which are in themselves empty of a self-sustaining essence (*svabhāva*), that the absence of an essence in these elements makes co-arising possible.

The understanding of the correlationship between the supreme and the conventional is the 'middle', a principle which the popular *Heart Sūtra* describes as "form is emptiness and that very emptiness is form." The middle synthesizes the two extreme views as one organic entity. The term *Dharmadhātu* must now be redefined. *Dharmadhātu*, literally the 'world of the Dharma', is the embodiment of the middle. Though the term Dharma literally means 'that which one holds to be the truth' and generally refers to a given law or a principle, in Mahāyāna, it specifically refers to the middle path principle. *Dharmadhātu* refers to a world governed by the principle of the middle path, a principle devoid of the extremes. In Shingon, *Dharmadhātu* refers to the world of Mahāvairocana. Mahāvairocana is the creator of *Dharmadhātu*. (But the Shingon creator is emptiness, the source of co-arising. It is entirely different from the Brahmanic concept of the creator.)

Dharmadhātu is an object of philosophical investigation inasmuch as emptiness is related to ontological issues, but it provides itself with a source of practice inasmuch as it is related to the world of 'emptiness-performing' (*śūnyatāyām prayojanam*), the application of the insight into emptiness in the world of conventional reality, which Shingon requires as the progressive conditions to developing insight. This means that the conceptual understanding of emptiness has no validity whatsoever. It has validity only when that type of understanding is capable of implementing itself in the world of conventional reality. Implementation is the realm which reveals the *perfect* understanding of a given concept. Perfect understanding of emptiness is the practice of emptiness in the realm of the conventional. This correlation between theory and practice is important in Shingon, because Shingon is essentially a system of experiential philosophy: the doctrine provides the rational basis for bodhisattva practices and bodhisattva practices constitute the demonstration of the perfect understanding of that rationale. Shingon refers to the former as wisdom (*prajñā*), the latter compassion (*karuṇā*), one being contingent upon the other.

A question inevitably arises. Why must insight into emptiness be translated into practice? More specifically, why must wisdom be translated into compassion? Mahāyāna conceives emptiness as the supreme truth—the realm of non-discrimination, of pure consciousness—but supreme truth is theoretical truth. Practice verifies this theoretical truth. The ethical application of the correlationship between the supreme and the conventional is apparent: self-enlightenment (insight into emptiness) is contingent on enlightening others (insight into co-arising), since an insight into emptiness is an insight into the individual's intense awareness of his own contingency. Thus Mahāyāna contends that the enlightenment of self is the practice to enlighten others. There is no self-enlightenment without the enlightenment of others. The doctrine of emptiness provides the rational basis for the theory of universal enlightenment and the middle path principle clears away all forms of dichotomy and enables one to realize a world into which the opposites are completely dissolved and re-identified as the ever-changing entities of the unchanging organic whole—*Dharmadhātu*.

Through the meditational insight into *Dharmadhātu*, like a flash of lightning coming out of the vast reaches of space, Kūkai suddenly found himself in the instant eternity into which the past, present and future are dissolved, his consciousness expanding infinitely and encompassing all things within it. He realized Dharmadhātu, the world of *Dharmakāya* Mahāvairocana. He realized that he, the microcosm of *Dharmakāya* Mahāvairocana, is the Eternal Buddha. The purpose of the Shingon system of doctrinal evaluation and classification is to describe the development of the dimensions of the human consciousness, ultimately leading to the cosmic consciousness of *Dharmakāya* Mahāvairocana.

The *Hizō-hōyaku* explains the development of the human consciousness in ten stages—from the world of hells to the world of the Buddha—each stage inherent with the essence of Mahāvairocana. *Hizō* literally means the 'secret store'. It specifically refers to the doctrinal contents of the *Mahāvairocana* and *Tattvasaṃgraha Sūtras*. *Hōyaku* literally means the 'jewel key' and points to that which enables the opening of the secret store. Specifically, the 'secret store' is the ideal realm to be known, the 'jewel key' is the practice to realize that realm. The purpose of the *Hizō-hōyaku* is to reveal the development of the human consciousness and to ultimately unveil the 'true self', which is identified as *bodhicitta*, the enlightened mind. The stages described in the *Hizō-hōyaku* are outlined below in verses:

1) The Stage of the Goat Foolishly Transmigrating in the Six Destinies:

    The worldling, madly intoxicated, does not realize his own error;
    He is aware only of his appetites,
    Just like a goat.

2) The Stage of the Child Ignorantly Obsessed with Moral Precepts:

    Only because of circumstances, does he suddenly think of moderation;

Outline of the Ten Stages

1)	Foolish ignorant goat	Pre-humanistic: appetite and sex (worlds of hells, hungry-beings, beasts, and fighting-beings)	Worldly vehicles (the cycle of rebirth in the six destinies)
2)	Ignorant child of abstinence	Humanistic: Confucianism (world of men)	
3)	Fearless child	Trans-humanistic: Brahmanism and Taoism (world of gods)	
4)	Only-elements and no-self	Śrāvaka: direct disciple of the Buddha	Hīnayāna: arhats seeking self-enlightenment
5)	Plucking out karmic seeds	Pratyeka-buddha: the independent	
6)	Unconditioned compassion	Hossō (Fa-hsiang)	Mahāyāna: bodhisattvas seeking the enlightenment of self and others
7)	No-arising (*anutpāda*)	Sanron (San-lun)	
8)	One path (*Ekayāna*) to the Truth (*tathatā*)	Tendai (T'ien-t'ai)	
9)	No esesnce (*svabhāva*) in the ultimate	Kegon (Hua-yen)	
10)	Secret	Shingon	Buddhayāna: the all inclusive realm of Dharmakāya Mahāvairocana

Charity bursts forth in his heart,
Like a seed encountering the proper conditions.

3) The Stage of a Child Fearing Nothing:
A non-Buddhist, expecting rebirth in heaven, earns a short-lived peace;
Like a child or a calf,
Who depends upon its mother.

4) The Stage of One Affirming Only Elements and Negating the Self:
Understanding only the reality of dharmas and rejecting the self;
This description thoroughly contains the teaching of the goat cart.

5) The Stage of One Removing Karmic Seeds:
Understand the chain of causation and remove the seeds of ignorance;
Eliminating karmic seeds, he attains the fruit in silence.

6) The Stage of the Mahāyāna Adherent Who is Concerned about Others:
He becomes aware of all beings—this is the initial awakening of his great compassion;
He achieves insight into the nature of his mind through contemplating the errors of mental images,
By realizing mind-onlyness, his sense-objects are severed.

7) The Stage of One Who Realizes Non-arising:
He uses the eight negations to stop meaningless argument, and contemplates emptiness in one instant;
The mind is then still and markless and is at peace.

8) The Stage of One Realizing the Universal Path of Truth:
Because his mind is beyond dichotomy and is originally pure, he harmonizes the subject and object;
knowing this nature of mind, he is called Vairocana.

9) The Stage of One Realizing the Absence of any Essence within Ultimate Truth:
Water has no self-nature—waves are created only when water

meets wind;
Dharmadhātu cannot be the Ultimate: having been warned one should immediately forge ahead.

10) The Stage of One Glorifying the Secret School:
Revealed teachings dispel delusion, Shingon lays open the storehouse of the enlightened mind;
The secret jewel is now displayed, and the merit of all things is instantly realized.

These ten stages will be briefly examined.

2. The Ten Stages: The Dimensions of Encompassing

Pre-humanistic: The *Hizō-hōyaku* claims that the pre-humanistic vehicles stimulate appetite and sex and produce errors. These errors increase impure karmic seeds (action-potentials), and the accumulation of these seeds forces one to transmigrate within the six destinies (*gati*). The six destinies are the worlds of hells, hungry-beings, beasts, fighting-beings, men, and gods. The theory of the six destinies is probably pre-Buddhist. It is based upon the notion of karma, a belief that one's present action shapes one's future life. Transmigration (or rebirth) takes place within these six destinies. The Buddhist notion of liberation (*vimokṣa*) is intended to transcend the realm of the six destinies (*gatis*) by eliminating karmic seeds. Because sentient beings possess many kinds of karmic seeds and dwell in a variety of stations and sub-stations within the six destinies, the Buddha, who is the compassionate one, improvises skillful means to save them. The stages described below are what Kūkai conceived as the means.

Humanistic: This second stage deals with Confucian ethics and moral principles. The three principles—loyalty, filial piety, and obedience—which bind the relationship between the ruler and the ruled, parent and child, and husband and wife, respectively, and the five virtues—benevolence, justice, propriety, wisdom and fidelity—are emphasized. Men now begin to exercise moderation. But Kūkai calls this the stage of the ignorant child because the existential nature of man cannot be realized simply by observing established precepts and codified moral principles.

The World of Gods: This third stage deals with belief in supernatural beings, such as the gods of Brahmanism and Taoism. Interestingly, Kūkai placed religious pietism above Confucianism, whose social ethics were the established principles of the age, probably because he had been frustrated by the Confucian scholarship in which he had been trained. Interesting also is the fact that Brahmanic, Taoist and Shintō elements are found in abundance in Shingon, though Kūkai refers to this stage as that of the fearless child because Buddhism precludes belief in a supernatural being.

Śrāvaka: This fourth stage deals with the first of the Buddhist stages. A *śrāvaka*, literally a "hearer," meaning more precisely, a direct disciple of the Buddha (though later the term takes on the meaning of one who adhers to the tenets of early Buddhism, not the tenets of Mahāyāna), is one who seeks the path of his own liberation. The path of liberation is most succinctly dealt with in the *Abhidharmakośa*. Abhidharma is a compound meaning the "store" or "container" (*kośa*) of "things related or directed to (*abhi*) the Dharma." Dharma here refers to the four truths and *nirvāṇa*. The four truths are: life is painful, pain has its origin, the origin of pain must be eliminated, and there is a path to eliminate the origin of pain. *Nirvāṇa*, literally, "blowing out," means liberation from the elements which produce the pain of life (i.e. 'blowing out' human passions). The *Abhidharmakośa* deals with three major themes: the relationship between man and his world, which is described in terms of elemental force-factors (technically called dharmas); karmic transmigration, which is explained in terms of manifested (*vijñapti*) and unmanifested or latent (*avijñapti*) karma; and liberation which is brought about by eliminating misleading views and misleading thoughts. Let us now discuss these three themes.

In dealing with the relationship between man and his world, the text enumerates seventy-five *dharmas*[5] (not to be confused with Dharma, which is a general nomenclature for 'truth', 'law', or 'principle'), which are classified into five general categories: a) the conditioned (which is without form or function, such as space), and the conditioned, which consists of b) mind, c) form, d) mentals, and e) mind dissociated. Here we shall deal only with the conditioned *dharmas*. The mind refers to the accumulating agent of various experiences; form to the sense organs (eyes, ears, nose, tongue and body) and their respective sense fields (sight, sound, smell, taste and touch); mentals here means mental attributes (e.g. hate and greed, love and greedlessness, etc., the former group representing the wholesome dharmas and the latter the unwholesome); and mind dissociated are things neither of the mind nor of form but nevertheless things which have bearing upon the quality of the mind (such as the state of trance). Most significant, with reference to the five categories, is the interrelationship between the mind and the mentals, because the arising of mentals (e.g. hate) simply refers to the mind cognizing its object (the hated) through the sense organs (e.g. the eyes). But what, in fact, enables the mentals to arise and to disintegrate? It is karma.

Karma specifically refers to an action—influenced either by wholesome or unwholesome dharmas—and the subsequent arising of a consequence. The *Abhidharmakośa* explains the causes and results of an action in terms of manifested and unmanifested karma. The text claims that an impulse is manifested by or translated into either word-action or body-action, but the completion of a given action does not by any means mean the termination of the original impulse. When an impulse is manifested, a latent energy (or habit) of that impulse is deposited in the mind. As such, an impulse has the potential of being manifested in the future. For example, a killing-impulse does not disintegrate with the completion of the killing-act. The very act of killing in turn deposits the killing-seeds (the killing-potential) in the mind. The impulse—action—impulse feedback is what is commonly referred to as karma. Karma runs in an eternal cycle. Because it runs in cycle, it is referred to as karmic transmigration. The *Abhidharmakośa* holds that a sentient being transmigrates in the six destinies due to his own karma.

Man's liberation therefore is contingent upon freeing himself from this karmic cyclic force, a force which constantly contaminates his mind and brings about delusion. The contaminating elements are called *kleśa-dharmas*. *Kleśas* are of two general types: misleading views, which are misconceptions of phenomenal matters arising from a lack of proper reasoning power; and misleading thoughts, which are misconceptions of phenomenal matters derived from and rooted in the six senses. (For a complete list on misleading views and misleading thoughts, see p. 115–1 and –2.) Here it suffices to say that both refer to such *kleśas* as greed, hate and delusion. Misleading views refer to greed, hate and delusion which are acquired, and misleading thoughts refer to the same which are innate. The *Abhidharmakośa* maintains that misleading views can be eliminated by developing insights into the four truths through the practice of meditation, but that misleading thoughts can be eliminated only through the extinction of both mind and body because they are innate, that is, they are rooted in the six senses. For example, hate of the misleading view type can be eliminated if one comes to realize the causes and conditions which brought about that type of a mental, if he makes a rational effort to understand those causes and conditions, and if he eliminates those causes and conditions. But hate of a misleading thought type requires the complete extinction of the very elements which constitute existence—body and mind. The *Abhidharmakośa* further maintains that though misleading views are acquired, they are more powerful than misleading thoughts, and that though misleading thoughts are innate, they are less powerful than misleading views. But misleading views are easier to get rid of than misleading thoughts. Based upon misleading views and misleading thoughts, the *Abhidharmakośa* conceives two types of *nirvāṇa*, incomplete and complete. The former is a type of *nirvāṇa* which has eliminated misleading views, but not misleading thoughts; the latter is a type of *nirvāṇa* that has eliminated both misleading views and misleading thoughts.

In sum then, the *Abhidharmakośa* explains existence in terms of karmic cycle, which is conditioned by misleading views and misleading thoughts. In the context of that text, existence then essentially means karma, and liberation essentially means severance from karma. Insight into the four truths (which forms the theoretical basis for the development of the Abhidharma tradition of analyzing self into dharmas) is the initial step toward liberation. A *śrāvaka* therefore negates the reality of self (because it is essentially an aggregate of dharmas) and affirms the reality of *dharmas* (which shape and condition the self). But complete liberation, in the context of the *Abhidharmakośa*, means the extinction of both mind and body, as we have already established, because both mind and body are the accumulator and the repository of unwholesome dharmas. Thus the *Hizō-hōyaku* describes the *śrāvaka* vehicle symbolically as the 'goat cart' and conceives it as a lesser vehicle than a 'cow cart'. A 'cow cart' symbolizes a *bodhisattva* vehicle. A *bodhisattva* vehicle is conceived as superior because a *bodhisattva* seeks his enlightenment in the acts of enlightening others, by facing the realities of worldly problems, not retreating from them, the premise being that the *kleśas* of the world are the very materials of enlightenment, that without *kleśas* there is no enlightenment, that without them there is nothing to be enlightened.

Pratyeka-buddha: The fifth stage presents the *pratyeka-buddha*, a loner without a master, pursuing his method of self-liberation. He eliminates the source of karma by gaining insights into the law of cause and effect (*hetu-pratyaya*). As previously mentioned, Buddhism precludes the notion of a first principle, a first cause. Its theory of causation therefore is cyclic. The earliest theory consists of a three-phase-cycle: delusion (*kleśa*)—action (*karma*)—pain (*duḥkha*), as described below:

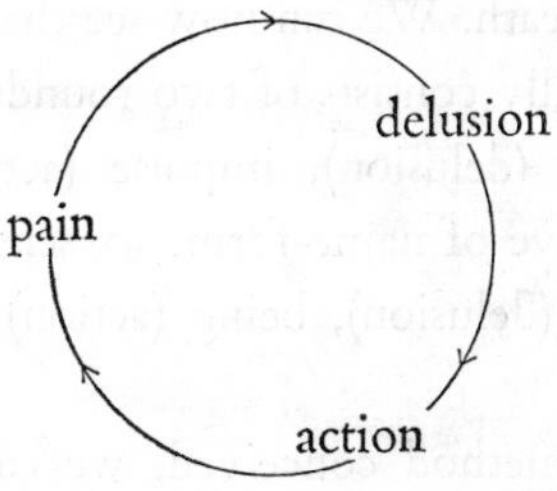

So, if one eliminates delusion, he eliminates action shaped by delusion; if he eliminates the delusion-shaped action, he eliminates the pain of life. A *pratyeka-buddha*, however, contemplates on the twelve-phase-cycle causation theory, which is an elaboration of the three-phase-cycle theory, as presented below:

The Twelve-phase-causation Theory

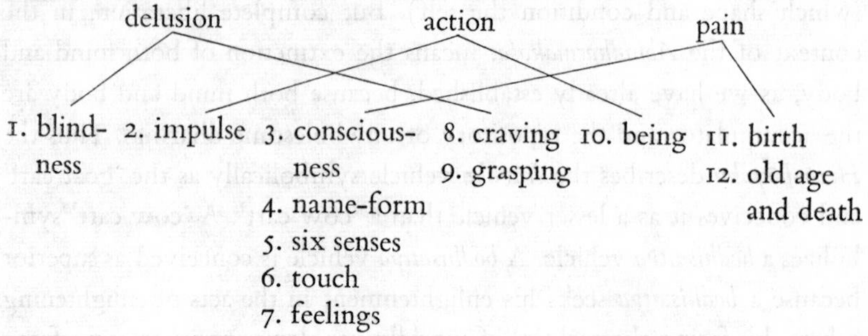

1) Blindness means ignorance, the basis of all delusions, imbedded with the false notion of the reality of self, the notion of clinging to the self; 2) impulse arises from blindness; 3) consciousness here refers to a wide range in the span of development of consciousness, beginning from 4) name-form, the embryonic state of the five aggregates (form, feelings, perceptions, impulses, and consciousness which produce designations—, "name" and "form"), and which develops into 5) the six senses at the time of birth, followed by the development of 6) the touch-sensation, and finally 7) feelings. Feelings stimulate 8) craving, and craving causes 9) grasping, both of which shape future 10) being, which is inherent with the element of blindness, and thus begins the cycle of 11) birth and 12) old age and death. We can now see that the twelve-phase-cycle causation theory actually consists of two rounds of the delusion-action-pain cycle: blindness (delusion), impulse (action), and consciousness (pain) which is inclusive of name-form, six senses, thouch and feelings; and craving-grasping (delusion), being (action) and birth, old age and death (pain).

Regardless of the method conceived, we can now see that both a *śrāvaka* and a *pratyeka-buddha* aim to realize self-liberation by eliminating their own *kleśas*. The stage of an arhat is the ultimate that a *śrāvaka* and a *pratyeka-buddha* attempt to realize. *Arhat* means one with supreme worldly wisdom. He is considered supreme because he has eliminated misleading views. An *arhat* is also defined as one worthy of receiving the offerings of others. He is considered worthy because he exemplifies enlightenment of a kind that a laity is thought incapable of realizing. Mahāyāna conceives an arhat to represent Hīnayāna. It criticizes Hīnayāna because Hīnayāna conceives two types of *nirvāṇa*, complete and incomplete. It is this notion—the two types of *nirvāṇa* leading to two types of world—which led to proposing a form of liberation that is highly unrealistic, completely divorced from empirical reality, that is "blowing out" human passions; to setting up a 'distance' between man and the Buddha and thereby distinguishing between the enlightenment of man and that of the Buddha; and to upholding the supremacy of the arhat—that is, holding that an arhat exemplifies enlightenment, that the laity simply represent the supporting entity of the arhat monastic institution—and not providing the laity the possibility of enlightenment within their present life.

The notion of two types of *nirvāṇa*, though treated in Abhidharma literature but by rule not in Mahāyāna literature, is not representative of the original teachings of Śākyamuni, since there is no mentioning of them in pre-Abhidharma literature, such as in the *Sutta-nipāta*, which most vividly describes the life and the sayings of the historical Buddha in a very positive manner. Though this text honors the ways of the monks, it does not speak of two types of *nirvāṇa*. It says, for example:

> Just as we attempt to control a snake's poison from spreading throughout our body, a monk controls his anger from spreading throughout his body; just like a snake abandons his old skin, a monk abandons [the notions of] "this" world and "that" world.[6]

The Abhidharma masters conceived two types of *nirvāṇa* probably out of sheer respect for Śākyamuni and for the arhats: one, complete, reserved only for Śākyamuni; the other, incomplete, for the arhats. The supposition underlying the two types of *nirvāṇa* is that the state of enlightenment realized by the historical Buddha cannot be realized by man during his life, that what can be realized during his life is a type of *nirvāṇa* reserved only for the professional, the monk, and even at that the highest a monk can expect to realize within his life is the state of arhat. The laity was expected to be guided by the monks, to lead a wholesome secular life, to dedicate themselves to supporting the monks, and to aspire for better rebirth in the future. However, notwithstanding Mahāyāna criticism, the notion of *nirvāṇa,* as entertained by the *śrāvakas* and *pratyeka-buddhas*—that is, "blowing out" human passions—seems more faithful to what the etymology of that term suggests. Hence, in referring to enlightenment, Mahāyāna generally employs the term "*bodhi*" (which actually means enlightenment and from which the term "buddha," the enlightened one, is derived) rather than "*nirvāṇa,*" probably because the latter smells of a state of extinction, a state of retreat and withdrawal, and probably also because the term "*bodhi,*" more so than "*nirvāṇa,*" offers a closer relation between the Buddha (who was a sentient being) and man (who is the seeker of "*bodhi*"), etymologically speaking. Even when Mahāyāna does employ the term '*nirvāṇa*', in the context of its own doctrine, the term does not mean the 'extinction' of body and mind. It generally refers to a state of tranquility and quiescence. But more often than not, it is spoken of with reference to the theory of the identity of *nirvāṇa* and *saṃsāra* (i.e. the realm of transmigration within the six destinies), a theory which claims that *saṃsāra* is the very material and the only available material to mankind to realize enlightenment, that enlightenment cannot be realized without *saṃsāra.* It is the theory of the identity of *nirvāṇa* and *saṃsāra,* based upon the doctrine of emptiness and co-arising as we shall subsequently see (under Sanron, this Chapter), which led to the development of the theory of universal Buddhahood.

But here we must exercise a degree of caution. Even though many pre-Mahāyāna schools, for example the Sarvāstivāda, presupposed that Buddhahood is a term exclusively reserved to describe the enlightenment of Śākyamuni, the Mahāsamghika, for example, also representing a pre-Mahāyāna school, did acknowledge the universal nature of Buddhahood. Nevertheless, it is a safe assumption to say that the mainstream of so-called Hīnayāna did make distinction between the enlightenment of the Buddha and that of man, between *nirvāṇa* and *saṃsāra,* and defined *nirvāṇa* as a state in which human passions were "blown out." Be as it may, here we are not necessarily concerned with etymological problems or with the problems of doctrinal distinction among pre-Mahāyāna schools. We are concerned with the problem related to actual human existence as experienced by Kūkai, for it is to this very problem that the *Hizō-hōyaku* addresses itself. The *Hizō-hōyaku* claims that the Abhidharma tradition of analyzing existence in terms of dharmas—though profoundly it may be meta-physically—is speculative, contributes to de-centralizing the human personality, and does not in fact offer enlightenment for all beings. Kūkai was interested in discovering a Dharma which portrays the human personality positively and dynamically, a type of personality capable of merging with the cosmic Buddha and of becoming the absolute master of the universe. It is through this kind of a Dharma that he attempted to establish the basis of human creativity and the ultimate dignity of all mankind. We shall now investigate the first of the Mahāyāna stages.

Hossō: This is the sixth stage. Hossō, derived from the Chinese Fa-hsiang, is the Chinese version of Yogācāra. Yogācāra means the practice of meditation. But Yogācāra developed into many sub-schools. Hossō is based upon Dharmapāla's (sixth century) *Vijñāptimātratā-siddhi*, translated by Hsüan-tsang in 659, though it is assumed that the translation contains many ideas of Hsüan-tsang and Kuei-chi (632–682), Hsüan-tsang's disciple, and on its commentary composed by Kuei-chi. Here we shall simply discuss two major ideas representative of Hossō: unconditioned compassion, which is compassion without discrimination, a theme articulated by all Mahāyāna schools; and mind-onlyness, a theme unique to Hossō which has had far reaching implications in the development of later Mahāyāna. These two ideas are co-related.

Compassion, a virtue certainly not absent in Hīnayāna, means sensitivity to human suffering, but in the Mahāyāna context, it also means a positive concern for the enlightenment of all beings. Enlightenment means the perfect cognition of truth. The purpose of Hossō meditation is to realize perfect cognition by turning (*parāvṛtti*) the mind from discrimination (*vikalpa*) to non-discrimination (*nirvikalpa*). Discrimination means fragmenting the world, based upon an arbitrary value concept; non-discrimination means unconditioned concern for all beings.

That which discriminates or does not discriminate is the mind. The purpose of Hossō meditation then is to eliminate discrimination and cultivate non-discrimination.

Hossō follows the Abhidharma tradition of enumerating *dharmas*. It identifies one hundred dharmas[7] and classifies them into five categories, of which the mind is the most important. The mind consists of eight levels of consciousness: 1) eye-, 2) ear-, 3) nose-, 4) tongue-, 5) body-, 6) *mano-*, 7) *manas*, and 8) *ālaya-vijñānas*. '*Vijñāna*' means consciousness. Etymologically, it is derived from '*vi*', "to discriminate"; '*jñā*', the root meaning "cognition"; and '*na*', "function." *Vijñāna* means cognition by discrimination. The first five consciousnesses are the perceptualizing elements; *mano-vijñāna* conceptualizes the perceived; *manas* measures, calculates, discriminates and thereby renders a value judgement on the conceptualized (*manas* is the ego); *ālaya* is the source of discrimination (which gives rise to the ego). But *ālaya* is not an absolute. Though it is the source of discrimination, it is actually the storehouse of the potentials (*vāsanā-bija,* the perfuming seeds) cultivated by the *manas*. In other words, the *manas-ālaya* relationship is cyclical, following the traditional karmic theory, that is, the perfuming seeds deposited in the *ālaya* shape the *manas*, while the *manas*, when it measures, calculated and discriminates the conceptualized, deposits its potentials in the *ālaya*. This simply means that unwholesome thought produces unwholesome action and unwholesome action in turn produces unwholesome thought. The function of the eight levels of consciousness is outlined below:

1) eye-*vijñāna* 2) ear-*vijñāna* 3) nose-*vijñāna* 4) tongue-*vijñāna* 5) body-*vijñāna*	first five *vijñānas*	instruments of perception
6) *mano-vijñāna*	sense center	instrument of conception
7) *manas*	thought center	instrument of discrimination
8) *ālaya-vijñāna*	consciousness-store	source of discrimination

To realize perfect cognition requires the transformation of *ālaya*, the source of discrimination, into *ādarśa-jñāna*. *Ādarśa* literally means 'mirror'. *Jñāna*, a term used in contradistinction to *vijñāna*, means wisdom. *Ādarśa-jñāna* refers to 'pure mind', a mind clear enough to reflect the world without distortion. When the *ālaya* is purified, *manas* is purified; when the *manas* is purified, the first six *vijñānas* are purified. Specifically, *manas*, whose function was to discriminate, is transformed into *samatā-jñāna*, the non-discriminating knowledge; *mano-vijñāna*, whose function was to conceptualize, is transformed into *pratyavekṣaṇā-jñāna*, the insight into the particular; and the first five *vijñānas*, whose function was to perceptualize, are transformed into *kṛtyānuṣṭhāna-jñāna*, perfect practice. 'Non-discriminating knowledge' means cognizing the world just as it is, without fragmenting it into arbitrary conceptual categories. 'Insight into the particular' means cognizing the parts as necessary entities of the whole (for there is nothing wrong with discriminating things provided that discrimination is free of bias). 'Perfect practice' means involvement in worldly issues and improvising methods to enlighten others. Perfect practice has the capability of doing this because it is liberated from the preconditioned notion of bias-discrimination. It is unconditioned. The transformation of *vijñānas* to *jñānas* is outlined below:

Vijñānas	*Jñānas*	*Jñāna Attributes*
ālaya	— *ādarśa*	mirror-mind (i.e. pure mind)
manas	— *samatā*	non-discrimination
mano	— *pratyavekṣaṇā*	insight to deal with the particulars of the world
first five	— *kṛtyānuṣṭhāna*	knowledge of putting that insight into practice

Thus transformation does not mean changing the world but rather changing the way of cognizing it, from discrimination to non-discrimination. The mind is capable of developing these two dimensions of cognition because it in itself is relative: it is a product of co-arising, it is not absolute. Hence Hossō claims that the external world is but a mental construction. The world of non-discrimination is the world of great compassion.

Sanron: This is the seventh stage. Sanron, derived from the Chinese Sanlun, is the Chinese version of Mādhyamika. The term means the Three Treatise School. The three refer to Nāgārjuna's *Mādhyamaka-kārikā*, his *Dvādaśamukha-śāstra* and Āryadeva's *Śata-śāstra.* Āryadeva was a disciple of Nāgārjuna. Among the three, the *Mādhyamaka-kārikā* is most important. Its opening verse states:

> I pay homage to the Buddha, the most supreme among the teachers,
> who has taught that [the nature of] co-arising,
> [which is]
> neither origination nor extinction,
> neither permanence nor impermanence,
> neither unity nor diversity,
> neither coming nor going,
> extinguishes meaningless arguments [*prapañca*].[8]

The series of negation, commonly referred to as the eight negations, is an exercise in circumscribing emptiness. That is, emptiness, circumscribed through the eight negations, brings about co-arising, and through co-arising one 'sees' emptiness. Co-arising is indeed emptiness and emptiness is co-arising. The complete awareness and understanding of this type of cognitive dimension constitutes insight into the middle path (*madhyamā pratipad*), which extinguishes meaningless arguments. The middle consists of:

> the middle of the two extremes;
> the middle which has eliminated the extremes;
> the absolute middle, which has eliminated the very notion of
> the middle as an antithesis of the extremes; and
> the conventional middle.

Though Mādhyamika employs a system of negative dialecticism to articulate its middle path doctrine, it is not a school of nihilism (*śūnyavāda*). It affirms empirical reality as the conventional middle. Nor is it a school of no thesis for its thesis is the middle.

The *kārikā* elaborates on the middle. Chapter 24, verse 18, states:

> What is dependent co-arising we term emptiness,

This serves as a designation
And is the same as the middle path.[9]

The verse reveals the middle path principle by positing two levels of thought: the realm of emptiness, which is called the 'supreme'; and the realm of co-arising, which is called the 'conventional'. The *kārikā* holds that co-arising is possible because of emptiness, that what co-arises, due to emptiness, is the visual sign of emptiness, and that insight into the organic relationship between the supreme and the conventional is the middle. The supreme and the conventional are the two aspects of reality. Insight into this kind of reality enables one to transcend dichotomies. The middle path doctrine articulates the principle of non-duality. It provids the basis for the theory of the identity of *nirvāṇa* and *saṃsāra.*

Though Sanron literally refers to the *Three Treatises,* it nevertheless relies heavily on the *Prajñāpāramitā.* It is from this literature that Sanron masters derive much of their thought and practice and attempt to resolve the perennial and paradoxical issue of the relationship between the subject and the object, the whole and the part, being and non-being, enlightenment and non-enlightenment, man and the Buddha. They see this relationship not as the opposite but the relative—one supplementing the other, the *raison-d'etre* of one contingent on the *raison-etre* of the other—of an organic whole, the *Dharmadhātu.* But in the Chinese development of Mādhyamika, what needs to be noted is the strong articulation on empirical practice, rather than on the mere apprehension of the noetic aspect of wisdom (*prajñā*). Hence, to the Sanron masters, enlightenment is not the goal. Practice is the goal, for practice is enlightenment. Practice is designed to realize one's inherent Buddha-nature. Based upon the theory of the non-duality of man and the Buddha, it presupposes that Buddha-nature is inherent. (Buddha-nature is the 'middle' expressed in soteriological terms.) It is the agent of integration between the seeming opposite, enlightenment and non-enlightenment, man and the Buddha. Buddha-nature is inherent and universal, but practice—the confrontation with the problems of empirical realities brought about through discursive thoughts and the means improvised to resolve those problems—

is necessary to be aware of one's own Buddha-nature. Thus, enlightenment is realized because of non-enlightenment. Non-enlightenment is the material for enlightenment. Without non-enlightenment, there is no enlightenment.

Sanron, employing Mādhyamika dialecticism and deriving much of its thought and practice from the *prajñā* literature, firmly established the doctrinal foundation for the domestication of Chinese schools of Buddhism, which articulate practice and which has had the greatest impact on the development of Japanese Buddhism. Japanese Sanron is an extension of Chinese Sanlun. Kūkai was initially a Sanron student. Sanron conceives emptiness as one great dynamic organism—space—compassing all things. Hence the *Hizō-hōyaku* says,

> The Great Space, boundless and silent, encompasses ten thousand images in its life-force; the Great Sea, deep and still, embraces thousand elements in its single drop. The all-embracing-one is the mother of all things. Emptiness is the source of conventional reality. Conventional reality is not real existence but it exists conventionally. Emptiness is not nothingness for it exists non-abidingly.
>
> Because form is no different from emptiness, it produces phenomena and eternally abides as emptiness; because emptiness is no different from form, it brings phenomena into extinction and eternally abides as form. Form is emptiness and that very emptiness is form. All dharmas are so likewise. What is there that is not?
>
> The water and the waves are inseparable, the gold and its marks are indistinguishable. Nothing is identical nor is anything different. This is the essence of the two truths, the middle. Realize the nature of emptiness without grasping it; and through the eight negations, transcend meaningless arguments.[10]

We shall now see the great impact that Sanron has had on the development of other schools of Mahāyāna developed in China.

Tendai: The eighth stage deals with Tendai, a Chinese school (T'ien-t'ai) which synthesizes all schools of Buddhism within the context of the

Lotus Ekayāna. Tendai provides instructions for meditation upon *tathatā*, the embodiment of emptiness and co-arising, the ultimate reality, in order to transcend the subject-object split (e.g. the knower and the known). It also emphasizes universal enlightenment.

Tendai follows the Mādhyamika line of thought (the middle), but it claims that any of the three levels of thought (emptiness, co-arising, middle) reveals the truth. That is, there is no co-arising without emptiness, co-arising is the state which reveals the nature of emptiness; co-arising is emptiness, emptiness is co-arising, and the organic relationship between the two—form is emptiness and emptiness is form—is the middle; the three aspects of truth can be seen in any one aspect and in any one aspect can be seen the three aspects. Tendai calls this the 'three-in-one' meditation (*isshin sangan*). But Tendai articulates another form of meditation more strongly, the 'three thousand worlds implicit in one instant thought' (*ichinen sanzen*). Three thousand worlds refer to the attributes of *tathatā*. This concept is analyzed under three categories: 1) ten stations of being, the model of which is derived from the *Avataṃsaka Sūtra;* 2) ten aspects of *tathatā*, the model of which is derived from the *Lotus Sūtra;* and 3) three worlds, the model of which is derived from the *Ta chih-tu lun.*

The ten stations of being are:

1) hells
2) hungry-beings
3) beasts
4) fighting-beings
5) men
6) gods
7) *Śrāvaka*
8) *Pratyeka-buddha*
9) *Bodhisattva*
10) Buddha

The first six are the stages within the six destinies, the following two, the *śrāvaka* and *pratyeka-buddha,* represent Hīnayāna, and the last two are Mahāyāna. Tendai presupposes that one station is inherent in any other station, so there are actually one hundred stations (ten times ten equals one hundred).

The ten aspects of *tathatā* are:

1) marks (external appearance)
2) nature (internal quality of what appears externally)
3) substance (the combination of marks and nature)[11]
4) potentiality (latent attributes)
5) function (the manifestation of latent attributes)
6) primary cause
7) secondary cause (the conditions which promote causes)
8) effect
9) retribution (the effect of the previous effect)
10) all complete (the sum total of the nine aspects of *tathatā*)

The ten aspects are implicit in each of the one hundred stations of being, thus producing the number one thousand.

The three worlds are: 1) sentient beings, 2) the physical environment which all sentient beings are dependent upon for their existence, and 3) the five aggregates (i.e. form, feelings, perceptions, impulses, and consciousness), the elements which condition the world view of all sentient beings (and which are also the karma-producing elements).

The Tendai world description consists of one hundred stations of beings, the ten aspects of *tathatā* which pervade the one hundred stations, which in turn are conditioned by the three worlds, thus producing three thousand worlds. But Tendai claims that these are not worlds distinct and apart from the mind. At any given instant, all three thousand worlds, or perhaps more, are implicit within one's mind. The mind conditions the world it cognizes. Tendai therefore claims that *tathatā* pervades from the lower realm of hell to the higher realm of the Buddha, that all these realms are of the mind. There is no sentient being without a Buddha-nature. (By implication, it also means that there is no sentient being without a hell-nature, though later, Tendai, under the influence of the *Awakening of Mahāyāna Faith*, articulates the theory of the inherent enlightenment of all beings.) Tendai is an existential philosophy—one's own beingness being contingent upon the state of beingness of others. Since this is the case, there can be no self-enlightenment without the enlightenment of others.

The 'three-in-one' is designed to develop insight into how a thing comes into being—by co-arising; the 'three thousand world implicit in one instant thought' is designed to develop insight into how a thing exists at a given instant—co-dependently. Both articulate existential awareness based upon Sanron.

Kegon: The ninth stage deals with Kegon, a Chinese school (Hua-yen) which synthesizes all types of Buddhist world view within the context of Kegon *Ekayāna,* which is the Kegon concept of *Dharmadhātu.* Kegon conceives four types of world:

1) The phenomenal, the world of co-arising;
2) The principle underlying phenomena, the world of emptiness;
3) The harmony between phenomena and principle, the world of the synthesis of the two; and,
4) The harmony between phenomena, the world of the syntheiss among the co-arising.

The last is most important because it represents the Kegon *Dharmadhātu.* This is a world in which all forms of dichotomy (e.g., being and non-being) are completely dissolved and a new dimension (the co-arising) unfolds itself, thus creating a dynamic cosmic harmony. It is from this dimension that Kegon sees and affirms the empirical world. Kegon describes that type of world in terms of the ten principles of causation, which are:

1) The co-arising of all elements at the same time to complete the whole. The whole is *tathatā.*
2) The complete blending of the 'one' (whole) and the 'many' (parts). For example, individual lights focused upon a stage create one immense light, the 'one' and the 'many' not obstructing each other, but instead supplementing one another.
3) The 'one' and the 'many' implicit in each other. In reference to the above example, each light retains its own identity as well as the essence of the light-totality focused upon the stage.
4) The co-identity of the 'one' and the 'many'. This implies that

neither is possible without the other, such as in the case of the 'one' and the 'many' being implicit in each other. Each supplements the other and thereby establishes its own identity.

5) The revealed and the unrevealed. Again the two are co-related, the 'one' being unable to exist without the other, as for example, the relationship between a seed and a sprout. The sprout reveals itself because of the seed, but the seed cannot exist without the sprout bearing fruit and finally producing the seed. Another illustration is a coin. Its two sides represent the revealed and the unrevealed.
6) The blending of all parts. This is the sum total of parts, each retaining its own identity and at the same time comprising the whole.
7) Indra's net, supposedly a net with jewels fastened at every intersection created by a knot, each jewel co-reflecting the images of another. This is a metaphorical description of the principles of the 'one' and the 'many' implicit in one another, and the co-identity of the 'one' and the 'many'.
8) The principles of co-identity and mutual penetration perceived through phenomenal reality. Co-identity means relativeness, such as in the case of the coin, where its two sides supplement one another. Mutual penetration is the Kegon term for co-arising and the blending of all elements. The two principles sum up all other principles. But it is through phenomenal realities that insight into these two principles is realized.
9) All time periods implicit within the one. The past, present, and future, and all subdivisions of the three time periods, are implicit in the immediate present, since the past is but a present reflection and the future a present anticipation.
10) Harmony between the primary and secondary causes. A seed is a primary cause of a fruit, while the earth, sun and moisture are the secondary elements. Harmony between the primary and the secondary is the condition which produces a desired end.

Kegon *Dharmadhātu* refers to the world of harmony among phenomena. It refers to the empirical world within which all forms of diversity are unified. The unifying principle is emptiness. Vairocana, the Kegon Buddha, is a symbolic representation of the Kegon world of perfect harmony, which in turn is the Kegon concept of ultimate reality. But Shingon claims that the Kegon *Dharmadhātu* is not the ultimate, because Kegon only points to that world. It does not reveal that world.

Shingon: The tenth and the final stage is Shingon. The previous stages revealed the *Kengyō* doctrines. This stage reveals the *Mikkyō* doctrine. The *Mikkyō* doctrine reveals the world of Mahāvairocana.

Let us now briefly review the contents of the ten stages before describing Shingon. The ten stages represent the path which Kūkai trod in his pursuit of truth. He rejected a type of life which was dictated by uncontrolled passion (the first stage); a life which was regulated by ethical systems, which were arbitrarily and externally imposed upon men, though such a life does tame men to control passion (the second stage); and a life in which one sees the worlds of gods, which were simply created by the minds of men who vainly aspired to heavenly paradise, though such a life does bring about a temporary relief from human anxiety (the third stage). He then probed into the worlds of the *śrāvakas* (the fourth stage) and *pratyeka-buddhas* (the fifth stage), who had developed a sophisticated system of analytical philosophy—which simply contributed to decentralize a personality and failed to cultivate a type of wisdom capable of gaining insights into the world of the middle. The middle synthesized all forms of dichotomy and revealed the organic world of *Dharmadhātu* into which all opposites were dissolved and re-identified as entities of the whole. It was this type of world in which he saw the final liberation of mankind. In dealing with Mahāyāna, therefore, Kūkai first discusses Hossō (the sixth stages)—a logical order of sequence inasmuch as karma remained the single outstanding issue throughout early Buddhism. But karma is completely absorbed into the stream of emptiness in Sanron (the seventh stage) and is re-identified as Buddha-nature. From Sanron, Kūkai plunges himself into the world of *Ekayāna* Tendai (the eighth stage), ever mindful of the existential significance of Mahāyāna. Thus the Tendai world of *tathatā*, encompassing all beings from those in hell to the buddhas, eventually evolves into the Kegon *Dharmadhātu* (the ninth stage), the ground from which Kūkai finally leaps into the world of *Dharmakāya* Mahāvairocana. Shingon is a school of Mahāyāna which attempts to reveal the world of *Dharmakāya* Mahāvairocana.

Chapter Three:
SHINGON DOCTRINAL CONCEPTS

1. The Three Enlightened-Body Theory

An understanding of the three enlightened-body theory is a prerequisite to the understanding of Shingon doctrine. This theory conceives the Buddha-body (*Buddhakāya*) from three distinct points of view: *Dharmakāya, saṃbhogakāya,* and *nirmāṇakāya*. A description of these three bodies first requires a definition of the term 'Buddha'.

The term Buddha (derived from *budh+ta*) refers to one who has attained enlightenment, that is, *bodhi* (derived from *budh+i*). The terms Buddha and *bodhi* are derived from the same etymological root. Buddha specifically refers to the one who possesses wisdom (*prajñā*) and exercises compassion (*karuṇā*). But here we must note that initially the term Buddha was a title reserved only for Śākyamuni, the historical Buddha (as was in the case of the Sarvāstivāda and many other but not all early splinter schools). It eventually came to be understood as the ideal image of mankind—in Mahāyāna—a concept which transcended the historical Śākyamuni and established enlightenment as a universal property. But the two—the historical Buddha Śākyamuni and universal enlightenment—are not unrelated. Śākyamuni became enlightened because he gained insight into the Dharma, that is, the truth concerning the nature of existence, which Buddhism defines as ever-changing (*anitya*), absent of a self-sustaining essence (*anātman*), and conditionally caused (*pratītya-samutpāda*). Thus, though Śākyamuni died as a historical personality, the Dharma is eternal and universal. There are therefore two general categories of the enlightened-body: enlightenment *per se*, which is the Dharma; and the historical personality, such as Śākyamuni, who was enlightened through his insight into the Dharma. Technically, the former is referred to as *Dharmakāya* and the latter *nirmāṇakāya.*

In the history of the development of Buddhist literature, the two enlightened-body theory appears in early sūtras, including early Mahāyāna *sūtras*—such as the *Prajñāpāramitā* and the *Saddharmapuṇḍarīka*—in which the two bodies are identified as *Dharmakāya* and *rūpakāya*, the former referring to a transcendental body and the latter referring to a physical body. Nagao Gadjin says,

> Until the time of the *Prajñāpāramitā Sūtra* and the time of Nāgārjuna, who developed the Mādhyamika philosophy based on the *sūtra*, only the twofold body of Dharma-body and Physical-body was conceived as a theory of the Buddha's body. It was in the philosophy of the Yogācāra school (or the Vijñāna-vāda school) represented by Asaṅga and Vasubandhu that the two-body theory developed until it was consummated into a three body theory.[1]

The development from the two to the three enlightened-body theory follows a logical sequence: the necessity for establishing an intermediary agent between *Dharmakāya* and *nirmāṇakāya*—an agent which must be inherent with the qualities of *Dharmakāya* and *nirmāṇakāya* but in itself is neither *Dharmakāya* nor *nirmāṇakāya*—in order to provide a logical justification in explaining the organic relationship between *Dharmakāya* and *nirmāṇakāya.* This intermediary agent is *saṃbhogakāya*, literally a 'rewarded-body', that is one who is 'rewarded' with the fruits of enlightenment as the result of having perfected *bodhisattva* practices. *Saṃbhogakāya* is the instrument through which the historical man realizes *Dharmakāya*, it is symbolic of the perfection of *bodhisattva* practices, and it is the instrument through which the Dharma penetrates the world of sentient beings. It is different from *Dharmakāya* in that it is not the Dharma *per se*—the truth in theoretical abstraction; it is different from *nirmāṇakāya* in that it is not a historically manifested body of truth—the truth conneived in the body of, say, Śākyamuni. Specifically, *saṃbhogakāya* is the means through which the historical man understands *Dharmakāya*, just like a mathematical symbol is a means to understand a given principle but is not the principle *per se*. As such, like *Dharmakāya* and unlike *nirmāṇākāya*, *saṃbhogakāya* is eternal and indestructible, and unlike *Dharmakāya* and like *nirmāṇakāya*, *saṃbhogakāya* is capable of communication with sentient beings. *Saṃbhogakāya* therefore is central to the understanding of the organic relationship between the two enlightened-bodies. It functions as a 'bridge' between *Dharmakāya* and *nirmāṇakāya*.

As Nagao has rightly pointed out, it is in Yogācāra that we see the three enlightened-body theory systematized, that is, the rational basis of this theory is found in the Yogācāra transformation (*parāvṛtti*) theory. Yogācāra presupposes a transformation—from a deluded mind to a non-deluded mind. The logical basis for this transformation is the middle path principle, the principle of dependent origination. This means that the mind is not an absolute entity. It is a repository of various elements by which it is conditioned, and the manner in which it is conditioned conditions the manner in which it cognizes the world, as, for example, a colored glass, which conditions the world which one cognizes. As such, transformation is possible, that is, the mind is capable of either cognizing the world of delusion or the world of non-delusion. But transformation, in the Yogācāra context, specifically refers to transforming a deluded mind to a non-deluded mind through meditation. Specifically, this meditation requires insight into what is technically referred to as the three *svabhāva* theory, a theory which explains the manner in which one cognizes the world—the nature of existence—from three different dimensions:

a) discriminating nature (*parikalpita-svabhāva*), that is cognizing the world by fragmenting it into conceptual categories based on an arbitrarily established value judgment;

b) relative nature (*paratantra-svabhāva*), that is cognizing that the elements of existence are empty of an eternal and absolute substance and thereby cognizing the world of dependent origination; and

c) true nature (*parinispanna-svabhāva*), that is cognizing the world of emptiness, i.e., gaining insight into Dharma *per se*.

The three axioms upon which the Yogācāra world-view is based presuppose, first of all, two diversified views—the Dharma *per se* and the empirical world. The former is what Mādhyamika refers to as the 'supreme' truth and the latter the 'conventional' truth. The human mind is capable of cognizing either dimension, since the mind is not an absolute entity but whose cognitive function is pre-conditioned by karma. Thus, the mind is capable of transformation: it can 'ascend', so to speak, to the level of 'supreme' truth, or it can 'descend' to the level of 'conventional' truth. The true nature of the mind is that it is 'relative', in that it is a conditioned product, not an absolute, unchanging, fixed product. As such, transformation takes place at the dimension of *paratantra-svabhāva*—within the context of the *ālaya. Ālaya* is *paratantra-svabhāva.*

The three enlightened-body theory is based upon the Yogācāra transformation theory, but whereas the former deals with the nature of the enlightened-bodies on a soteriological level, the latter deals with the nature of cognition on an epistemological level. Both, however, deal with the matter of transformation, with the intermediary—whether *saṃbhogakāya* or *paratantra-svabhāva*—as the focal point of the three axioms. Both are intended to enable liberation, the former through the understanding of the nature of *saṃbhogakāya,* and the latter through the understanding of the nature of cognition.

We have examined the three-enlightened-body theory and briefly compared it to the Yogācāra transformation theory as a means to provide a logical explanation of the former. But the three enlightened-body theory, as explained above, is a Mahāyāna property. Shingon interpretation is somewhat different. It is this difference that we must examine to understand the presuppositions underlying Shingon doctrine and practice. We shall first examine the Shingon concept of Mahāvairocana.

2. Mahāvairocana

Buddhism had its beginning in the enlightenment of Śākyamuni, A doctrine not based upon his personality therefore can be presumed to be outside the teaching of Buddhism. But the enlightened-body of Shingon is not Śākyamuni. It is Mahāvairocana. Yet Shingon identifies itself as Mahāyāna. This apparent contradiction is resolved by investigating the content of Śākyamuni's enlightenment. Though he was born and died as an historical personality, he became a Buddha through his insight into the Dharma. Shingon therefore claims that Śākyamuni is *nirmāṇakāya*, and Mahāvairocana, the Dharma *per se*, is *Dharmakāya*. The modifier '*Dharmakāya*' therefore precedes the term Mahāvairocana, i.e., *Dharmakāya* Mahāvairocana. Here we must note that though the term *Dharmakāya* is suggestive of a physical entity, it actually is another designation for Buddha-nature. Mahāyāna identifies Buddha-nature as the unconditioned and the unchanging, though it is shrouded with *kleśa*. Generally, Mahāyāna presupposes that Buddha-nature is inherent in all beings. *Dharmakāya* is the Shingon version of Buddha-nature and corresponds to the Hegelian notion of *absolute vernunft* or to what Spinoza referred to as *sub specie aeternitatis*.

Etymologically, Mahāvairocana is derived from the root '*virocana*', literally "shining upon, brightening, illuminating."[2] Rendered 'Ta-jih' in Chinese and 'Dainichi' in Japanese, Mahāvairocana in the Sino-Japanese context means the 'Great Sun'. Śubhākarasiṃha in his *Commentary on the Mahāvairocana Sūtra* explains the reason. He says:

> It eliminates darkness and illuminates all things;
> It enables the fulfillment of all works;
> It is the light which is neither created nor destroyed.[3]

The first line refers to wisdom, the second to compassion, and the third to eternal light, that is truth *per se*. The three are interdependent. Each attribute shall be explained categorically.

Wisdom. Derived from *prajñā*, 'wisdom', in the Mahāyāna context, essentially means right cognition. Right cognition means the understanding of emptiness as the ontological basis of existence. It is brought about by transforming the *vijñānas* (the first five plus the *mano-vijñāna*, *manas*, and *ālaya-vijñāna*, matters explained under 'Hossō') into their corresponding *jñānas*. But Shingon conceives of five categories of *jñānas:*
a) *Dharmadhātu-svabhāva-jñāna*, the all-encompassing wisdom (omnis-

cience) of *Dharmakāya* Mahāvairocana; b) *ādarśa-jñāna*, pure mind; c) *samatā-jñāna*, non-discriminating mind; d) *pratyavekṣaṇā-jñāna*, the insight to deal with the problems of sentient beings; and e) *kṛtyānuṣṭhāna-jñāna*, the knowledge to transform that insight into practice. The last four are attributes of the first.

The *Hizō-ki* describes the five *jñānas* through a metaphor about water, as follows:

a) *Dharmakāya-svabhāva-jñāna* is the nature of water *per se;*
b) *ādarśa-jñāna* cognizes all things like a clear body of water reflecting its surrounding form;
c) *samatā-jñāna* does not discriminate, like water flowing to all corners equally;
d) *pratyavekṣaṇā-jñāna* cognizes the attributes of reality, like a body of water reflecting the particular of its surrounding form; and
e) *kṛtyānuṣṭhāna-jñāna* translates insight into practice, like all things nurtured by water are capable of exhibiting vitality.[4]

Shingon also reveals the attributes of the five *jñānas* iconographically: *Dharmadhātu-svabhāva-jñāna* is Mahāvairocana, the central Buddha of the Shingon pantheon, who is surrounded by other Buddhas, each representing his own *jñāna* attributes, as outlined below:

Buddha	*Representative Type of Wisdom*	*Representative Type of Enlightenment*	*Dharmadhātu*
Mahāvairocana	*Dharmadhātu-svabhāva*	Dharma essence	*Dharmadhātu per se*
Akṣobhya	*Ādarśa*	Englightenment of self	Attributes of *Dharmadhātu*
Ratnasaṃbhava	*Samatā*		
Amitāyus	*Pratyavekṣaṇā*	Enlightenment of others	
Amoghasiddhi	*Kṛtyānuṣṭhāna*		

Mahāvairocana, the personification of *Dharmadhātu*, is the cosmic Buddha, endowed with the attributes of the four Buddhas:

Akṣobhya, the personification of *ādarśa-jñāna*, eliminates ignorance and illuminates all things. He is the Buddha who cultivates *bodhicitta*.

Ratnasaṃbhava, the personification of *samatā-jñāna*, reveals the Dharma to all men equally. He is the Buddha who preaches the Dharma.

Amitāyus, the personification of *pratyavekṣaṇā-jñāna*, is the Buddha whom sentient beings appeal to for realization of birth in the Pure Land. He is the Buddha of compassion.

Amoghasiddhi, the personification of *kṛtyānuṣthāna-jñāna*, manifests himself in the world of sentient beings and deals with the actual problems of mankind. He is the Buddha who provokes the realization of the Buddha's compassion.

Compassion. The second attribute of Mahāvairocana as described in Śubhākarasiṃha's *Commentary* is compassion. Here we must note that in Mahāyāna, wisdom is insight into the reality of human existence, such as the awareness of the bonds and impermanence of existence, and into methods for accomplishing the final liberation of all mankind. In contrast, compassion is an acute sensitivity to human suffering and the willingness to carry all beings to the realm of enlightenment. Compassion is the implementation of wisdom through skillful means. For this reason, wisdom and compassion are correspondent to each other, for there is no wisdom apart from compassion and no compassion apart from wisdom.

With this premise in mind, let us now briefly review the content of *Dharmakāya* Mahāvairocana:

Dharmakāya Mahāvairocana is the fundamental consciousness. By fundamental consciousness, we are referring to emptiness as the ontological basis of existence. So, in Shingon, *Dharmakāya* Mahāvairocana is sometimes described as *svabhāva Dharmakāya. Svabhāva* basically means 'essence', but here it actually means the "essence of an absence of an essence." It means emptiness. *Svabhāva Dharmakāya* refers to the essence of Mahāvairocana. But *Dharmakāya* Mahāvairocana does not exist apart from the minds of sentient beings. When the 'known-essence' (*svabhāva-Dharmakāya*) is reflected on (or cognized by) the minds of sentient beings, it takes the form of three *dharma*-bodies. Wisdom is manifested through these *dharma*-bodies. When wisdom is manifested, it is called compassion, since, as said before, compassion is the implementation (the manifestation) of wisdom through skillful means. The three wisdom-manifesting-compassion-dharma-bodies are described below:

a) *Saṃbhoga-Dharmakāya.* *Saṃbhoga* literally means the "rewarded," that is, one who is rewarded with insight into *Dharmakāya.* It represents one who has gained insight into the world of skillful means through which *Dharmakāya* can be understood. *Saṃbhoga-Dharmakāya* is of two kinds: *svasaṃbhoga-Dharmakāya,* one who enjoys the fruits of his own enlightenment; and *parasaṃbhoga-Dharmakāya,* one who directs the fruits of his own enlightenment to benefit others. *Parasaṃbhoga-Dharmakāya* refers to the *bodhisattva* in the *daśabhūmi* stages (see Chapter V-3 '*Daśabhūmi*').

b) *Nirmāṇa-Dharmakāya.* He is the historically enlightened one, such as Śākyamuni. *Nirmāṇa-Dharmakāya* expounds the Dharma to the *bodhisattvas* in the pre-*daśabhūmi* stages and to the *śrāvakas* and the *pratyekabuddhas,* improvising skillful means appropriate to the conditions of time and to the comprehension of a given audience.

c) *Niṣyanda-Dharmakāya.* *Niṣyanda* literally means "to flow." In Mahāyāna it means the "necessary consequence or result" (of perfect enlightenment). *Niṣyanda-Dharmakāya* refers to a buddha who transforms himself into forms appropriate to a situation and who enters the stations of the six destinies to enlighten their occupants.

The four Buddha-body theory (*svabhāva-Dharmakāya* and its three attributes) describes the implementation of wisdom, which is compassion. The following chart compares the Shingon four Buddha-body theory with the traditional Mahāyāna three Buddha-body theory:

Shingon Theory	*Traditional Theory*
Svabhāva-Dharmakāya (Mahāvairocana)	*Dharmakāya* (Enlightenment *per se*)
Attributes of *Dharmakāya* Mahāvairocana — *Sambhoga-Dharmakāya* — *Svasaṃbhoga-Dharmakāya* (Enlightenment of self); *Parasaṃbhoga-Dharmakāya* (Enlightenment of others)	*Saṃbhogakāya* (Means to enlightenment)
Attributes of *Dharmakāya* Mahāvairocana — *Nirmāṇa-Dharmakāya*; *Niṣyanda-Dharmakāya*	*Nirmāṇakāya* (Enlightener)

Eternal Light. The third attribute of Mahāvairocana as described in Śubhākarasiṃha's *Commentary* is Eternal Light. Eternal Light, a metaphor for truth, specifically refers to *tathatā*. *Tathatā* is described in terms of its three attributes:

a) the six elements, which are collectively the 'body' of wisdom, which eliminates ignorance and illuminates truth;

b) the four *maṇḍalas*, which are the 'marks' of that body, representing compassion; and

c) the three secrets, representing the 'functions' of this wisdom-based compassion.

These three attributes are dealt with in detail below:

3. *Tathatā*

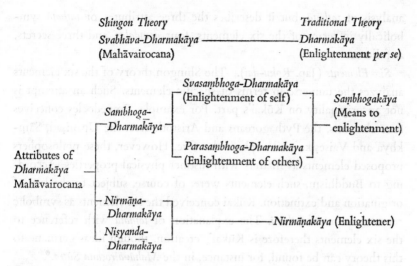

The *Awakening of Mahāyāna Faith*, a text attributed to Aśvaghoṣa (but in all probability a Chinese composition) and one of the major sources on which Shingon is based, says, "There is a Dharma which can arouse the roots of faith in Mahāyāna."[5] The text then goes on to identify the Dharma as *tathatā*, analyzing it in terms of its body, marks and functions. Shingon follows the tradition of the *Awakening of Mahāyāna Faith* in its analysis of *tathatā*, but it describes the three attributes of *tathatā* symbolically in terms of the six elements, four *maṇḍalas*, and three secrets, as follows:

Six Elements (Jap. *Roku-dai*). The Shingon theory of the six elements analyzes the universe in terms of specific elements. Such an attempt is not an originality on Kūkai's part. For example, Empedocles conceives four elements, the Pythagoreans and Aristotle five, the Upaniṣad, Sāṃkhya and Vaiseṣika philosophers also five. However, these philosophers proposed elements as matters with distinct physical properties. According to Buddhism, such elements were, of course, subject to the law of origination and extinction. Kūkai conceived the six elements as symbolic representation of *tathatā*. The explanation of *tathatā* with reference to the six elements therefore is Kūkai's creation, though ideas germane to this theory can be found, for instance, in the *Mahāvairocana Sūtra.*[6]

The six elements, treated in the *Sokushin jōbutsu-gi,*[7] are described below:

a) Earth: Symbolically represented by the syllable *A*, for *anutpāda* (non-origination), it means that *tathatā* is neither created nor destroyed. Thus, as the earth is the mother of all things, so is *tathatā* the source of co-arising. (Later we shall see this letter *A* employed as an object of meditation.)

b) Water: Symbolically represented by the syllable *VA* for the word '*vāc*' (voice or sound), it means that *tathatā* is beyond verbal description. Thus, as water in its natural form flows freely without being contained in any way, so is *tathatā* beyond conceptual categorization.

c) Fire: Symbolically represented by the syllable *RA* for the word '*rajas*' (passion), it means that *tathatā* destroys errors. Thus, as fire burns all things, so does *tathatā* burn up *kleśa*. (*Rajas* is the second *guṇa* in Sāṃkhya and denotes energy, dynamism, red, fire, etc.).

d) Wind: Symbolically represented by the syllable *HA* for '*hara*' (action), it means that *tathatā* is liberation. Thus, like wind moving about freely, so is *tathatā* endowed with complete freedom.

e) Space: Symbolically represented by the syllable *KHA* (space), it means that *tathatā* is without limits. It is universal, all pervasive, and omnipresent.

f) Mind: Symbolically represented by the syllable *HŪM* (perfect enlightenment), it means that the five attributes of *tathatā* described above are reflected upon the enlightened mind.

The first five are the material elements, and the sixth is the mind. Thus the six elements are reduced to mind (*citta*) and form/matter (*rūpa*). In other words, there is no mind apart from matter and no matter apart from mind, the perceiver and the perceived being interrelated. The two are the inseparable entities of *tathatā*, the Shingon concept of ultimate reality. Shingon is neither a school of dualism nor of non-dualism. Its logic follows that of Mādhyamika.

The six element theory is not only an analytical description of *tathatā*. It forms the basis of Shingon meditation, because Shingon claims that the understanding of the relationship between the six elements provides the key to understand the existential nature of man. In Shingon terms this correlationship is referred to as the harmony (i.e. the interfusion) of the six elements (Jap. *Rokudai-enyū*). Again, the theory of the harmony of elements is not an origination of Kūkai. The Chinese Ti-lun school postulated the theory of the harmony of the six 'marks'; Hua-yen, the harmony of the inexhaustible interfusion of elements; and T'ien-t'ai, the three thousand worlds implicit in one instant thought. Shingon follows the tradition of the concept of harmony developed in Chinese Buddhism. Though Taoist influence is apparent, this concept is not a diversion from Mahāyāna. Underlying the concept of harmony is the principle of co-arising, the principle of the interdependence of all elements. Emptiness enables co-arising. It is within the domain of emptiness that all forms of conceptual discrimination are dissolved and a new dimension (co-arising) unfolds itself; it is through this type of insight from which a Shingon practitioner recognizes the parts, each absent of an essence, interfusing with one another and contributing to create a dynamic cosmic harmony. *Tathatā* refers to this cosmic harmony. But Shingon is specific. It speaks of *tathatā* in terms of the six elements and maintains that the nature of the six elements—which intermingle in complete harmony with one another—constitutes the world itself, the first five representing the 'known' and the sixth the 'knower'.

The Four Maṇḍalas (Jap. *Shiman*). *Maṇḍala* in Edgerton's terms is a "circle, piece of ground specifically prepared in honor of a Buddha or saint (for him to sit on)."[8] Sometimes it is referred to as '*maṇḍa*', meaning "cream, best part, highest point, and the essence of things," while '*-la*' is a suffix meaning "possessed, support, and complete," according to Toganoo.[9] It specifically refers to the state of enlightenment illustrated by a graphic representation. The four *maṇḍalas*[10] are means to phenomenologically observe the six elements—the cosmic reality—from four different aspects. The four are:

a) *Mahā-maṇḍala.* '*Mahā*' means the universe or the whole, but here it encompasses the whole six elements representing tathatā. Thus, the *Mahā-maṇḍala* represents all states of existence within the world of *Dharmakāya* Mahāvairocana. These states of existence are described iconographically: the Buddha is surrounded by his companions (representing his attributes), the arrangement of which represents the contents of *Dharmakāya*. The following three *maṇḍalas* represent the three attributes of the *Mahā-maṇḍala*.

b) *Samaya-maṇḍala.* '*Samaya*' means "assembly, congregation, concourse."[11] Toganoo analyzes the term into '*sam*' meaning "universal, collective, whole" and '*aya*' meaning "to go."[12] In Shingon, *samaya* has a twofold meaning. From the viewpoint of the non-enlightened it means "to go to the realm of universal enlightenment," which is the realm of Mahāvairocana. (Here we must note that in spite of the Shingon theory of inherent Buddhahood, one must be enlightened to enlighten others.) From the viewpoint of the enlightened, *samaya* means 'to go to the realm of the collective suffering of mankind' because Mahāyāna enlightenment is contingent upon enlightening others. (Here we must note that enlightenment materials are found only in the realm of non-enlightenment, as symbolically expressed by the lotus—the lotus deriving the nourishment necessary for maintaining the purity of its existence from the slime of the environment in which it exists, being deprived of this slime there is no lotus.) Involvement in the non-enlightened realm requires not only the insight into enlightenment but also the improvising of skillful means to communicate that insight. Insight into enlightenment is wisdom. Wisdom means non-discrimination. Skillful means, which is compassion, is the method to communicate wisdom through discrimination. The *Samaya-maṇḍala* is a graphic representation of a variety of articles, such as swords, gems, the lotus, each representing a specific vow (compassion) of a Buddha to improvise skillful means. This is a vow-*maṇḍala*.

c) *Dharma-maṇḍala*. This *maṇḍala* is the embodiment of the Dharma (truth). It is designed to reveal the Dharma through the vehicle of letters, supposedly representing the 'voice' of *tathatā*. This does not mean that all Dharma-*maṇḍalas* represent a 'letter' *maṇḍala*. Sometimes these letters are replaced by buddhas and *bodhisattvas*. The *Dharma-maṇḍala* is also referred to as a *bija-maṇḍala*, a *maṇḍala* which shows the seeds (*bīja*) which produce all things. This is a truth-*maṇḍala*.

d) *Karma-maṇḍala*. *Karma* refers to the work of the Buddhas and *bodhisattvas*. It describes their efforts through the medium of sculpture. In Shingon, however, the *Karma-maṇḍala* is more often expressed as graphic representations, rather than by sculpture. (Angkor Vat and Angkor Tom in Cambodia and Boroboudour in Java are typical representations of the *Karma-maṇḍala*. The physical layout of the temple compound at the monastery on Mount Kōya, which is the Shingon headquarters in central Japan, is also an expression of the *Karma-maṇḍala*.) This is a work-*maṇḍala*.

Three Secrets (Jap. *San-mitsu*). The term 'three secrets' is derived from the Sanskrit '*tri-guhya*'. Specifically, the term refers to the three secret teachings of the Buddha revealed through the function of body (*kāya*), voice (*vāc*) and mind (*manas*) of *Dharmakāya* Mahāvairocana. A description of the three secrets requires some preparatory remarks. Because Shingon is based upon the *Ekayāna* premise of universal Buddhahood, it holds that man, just as he is, is the Buddha. Hence, ideally, there is no difference between the function of the Buddha (one who has realized *tathatā*) and man (one inherent with Buddha-nature); actually, however, man's Buddha-nature is covered by *kleśa*. This condition necessitates practice, if man is to realize his inherent Buddha-nature. From the standpoint of man, his aspiration to realize Buddhahood is described in terms of *tri-karma*, the three practices of man; from the standpoint of the Buddha, his desire to reveal *tathatā* to man is described in terms of *tri-guhya*, the three secret practices of the Buddha. The practices of man and of the Buddha are of three kinds: those performed by 'body', 'voice', and 'mind'. The merging of *tri-karma* and *tri-guhya* is realized through *adhiṣṭhāna*, (Jap. *kaji*), the instrument of integration between man and the Buddha. Shingon enlightenment therefore constitutes the merging of *tri-karma* and *tri-guhya* through *adhiṣṭhāna*, which is, specifically, the power (compassion) of (Mahāvairocana) Buddha that converges with the aspiration of man.

Adhiṣṭhāna is of three kinds: *mudrā*,[13] the finger sign; *dhāraṇi*, secret verses; and *yoga*, meditation. *Mudrā* is the instrument to realize the union of the bodies—*kāya-karma* and *kāya-guhya; dhāraṇi* is the instrument to realize the union of the voices—*vāk-karma* and *vāg-guhya;* and *yoga* is the instrument to realize the union of the minds—*manaḥ-karma* and *mano-guhya*. Kūkai therefore says, "*Adhiṣṭhāna* is the [union of the] Buddha's great compassion and the faith of all beings."[14] *Adhiṣṭhāna* is the means to realize integration between man and the Buddha as outlined below:

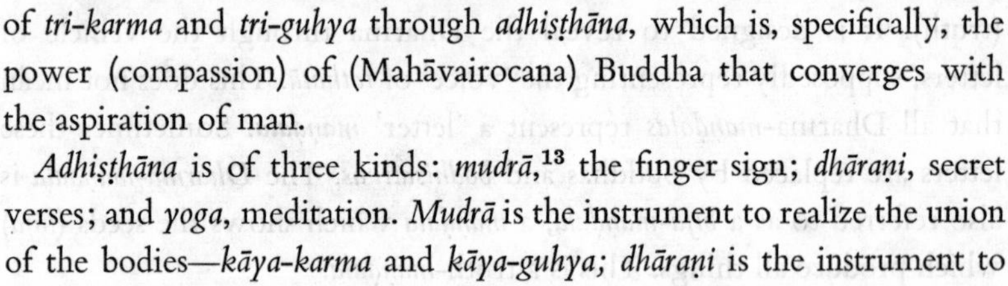

The three secrets indicate the process (i.e., the disciplines) involved in realizing *tathatā*, which is *Dharmakāya* Mahāvairocana, whose attributes are described by the six elements and the four *maṇḍalas*.

We have examined the three Buddha-body theory with reference to the three *svabhāva* theory, established that Mahāvairocana is *Dharmakāya*, and described *Dharmakāya* Mahāvairocana in terms of his three attributes

—wisdom, compassion and truth. Truth refers to *tathatā*. *Tathatā* was examined in terms of the six elements, which constituted the 'body' of Mahāvairocana, the four *maṇḍalas*, which constituted the 'marks' of Mahāvairocana, and the three secrets, which constituted the 'functions' of Mahāvairocana. *Adhiṣṭhāna*, which includes the practice of *mudrā*, *dhāraṇi* and *yoga*, was conceived as the instrument to bring about the integration of man and *Dharmakāya* Mahāvairocana. Shingon, however, conceives of another means to realize this integration—*A-ji* meditation—which we shall now examine.

4. *A-ji Meditation*

A-ji, derived from the Sanskrit *adi* meaning 'primordial', is a Japanese compound made up of '*A*', the basic vowel, and '*ji*' which means a letter. *A-ji* means the letter '*A*'. *A-ji* is also the object of meditation.[15] It is treated in detail in the *Mahāvairocana Sūtra* and in the *Bodhicitta Śāstra*.

The *Mahāvairocana Sūtra* says, "What is the *Mantra* Dharma? It is the teaching of the letter *A*."[16] *A-ji* symbolizes the *bīja* (seed) of *Dharmakāya* Mahāvairocana. '*A*' has two meanings in Sanskrit: it is a sign of negation, symbolizing emptiness; it is a sign of all-pervasiveness, symbolizing the source of all things. It is the embodiment of emptiness and co-arising. In '*A*' is contained the essence of the middle path. But meditation on a given letter is not an origination of Shingon, for it can be found also in non-Shingon literature. For example, the *Gaṇḍavyūha*[17] and the *Prajñāpāramitā*[18] *Sūtras* make reference to the "forty-two letter *dhāraṇīs*, beginning from "*A*," the *Ta chih-tu lun* says that the forty-two letters are the basis of all words,[19] and Sanlun and T'ien-t'ai describe the forty-two stages of *bodhisattva* practices in terms of forty-two letters. '*A*', symbolizing emptiness, is always conceived of as the source of all things.

In Shingon, '*A*' is the symbol for *Dharmakāya* Mahāvairocana. It is defined as the source of all things, emptiness of an essence, and non-origination. It is the source of all things because '*A*' represents the source of co-arising; it is emptiness because the essence contributing to co-arising is empty; it is non-origination because *tathatā* is the 'middle', that is, the absence of the two extremes, being and non-being. These three definitions represent the attributes of emptiness: the first describes its positive attribute, the second its negative, and the third represents the synthesis of the first two.

A-ji meditation is designed to gain three kinds of insight:[1] 1) that all dharmas arise due to conditions, and as such they are conventional designations; 2) that because they are conventional designations they are not true reality but empty of true reality; 3) and that true reality is the embodiment of being (revealed conventionally) and non-being (empty of an essence). In other words, *A-ji* meditation is designed to enable its practitioner to realize that reality is a flux, not to be conceived in any fixed conceptual categories. The middle is the cognitive dimension from which the being (co-arising) and its essential nature (emptiness) are realized as inseparable entities of total existence. The middle 'unfreezes' all forms of categorical concepts, negates extreme views (being and non-being), and enables the realization of ultimate reality which is *tathatā*. Hence Shingon claims that all things are distilled into '*A*' and from '*A*' emerge all things. But among the three definitions, the most fundamental is the third, 'non-origination' (Skt. *akāra-ādyanutpāda,* or in short *anutpāda,* literally "original non-production"). The Shingon term for this is *hompushō*. *Anutpāda* precludes the notion of the first principle or the first cause.

Because *anutpāda* is one of the fundamental concepts in Shingon, many commentaries have been written on it. The most representative of these is perhaps the writings of Kakuban (also known as Kōkyō Daishi, 1095–1143), the founder of neo-Shingon. He deals with the subject in considerable detail in his works, as for example the *A-ji hishaku* (The Secret Interpretation of *A-ji*), the *A-ji kan* (*A-ji* Meditation), and many others.[20] Kakuban's basic premise is that dharmas are due to the law of co-arising; as such they are essentially empty of an essence but are nonetheless conventionally real. The middle, which is the synthesis doctrine prominent in Mahāyāna literature, is Kakuban's rational basis for describing *anutpāda*. He says that *anutpāda* is synonymous with:

a) The mind (i.e. *citta*, the container of impressions and experiences): the embodiment of the cause of enlightenment, the roots of compassion, and the instrument to realize enlightenment.

b) *Dharmakāya:* the embodiment of *saṃbhogakāya* (one who has gained insight into emptiness) and *nirmāṇakāya* (one who reveals the nature of emptiness through skillful means);

c) The secret body (*kāya-guhya*): the embodiment of *vāg-* and *mano-guhya*, that is, the 'marks' and 'functions' of *tathatā*.

Kakuban attempted to portray the world of the union of all forms of diversity as conceived by the human consciousness, metaphorically. That is, because the union of diversity is based on the middle doctrine, union itself is a world beyond conceptual thought—such as being and non-being: it is beingness conceived through insight into the nature of co-arising; it is non-beingness conceived through insight into the nature of emptiness. Kakuban affirmed phenomenal reality but recognized the emptiness of dharmas which contributes to this type of reality-description. Kakuban also attempted to portray the world of the union, soteriologically. In this context, *anutpāda* is a realm of the non-creatable and the non-destructible; it is also the eternal realm because eternity is the non-creatable and the non-destructible. Hence *A-ji* is the source of all things and all things develop from it. Regardless of approaches to describe *A-ji*, '*A*' is the Shingon symbol for *tathatā*. It is *Dharmakāya*; *Dharmakāya* does not exist apart from man, for it is a world reflected upon the mind of man.

Why then did Kūkai formulate the six element theory of meditation? Historically, *anutpāda* is identified as a verbal symbol for marklessness (*alakṣana*), no essence (*asvabhāva*), and emptiness (*śūnyatā*), terms which characterize Mādhyamika. Kakuban's *A-ji* interpretation is a projection of Śubhākarasiṃha's thought, which follows the Mādhyamika dialectic pattern. But Kūkai had had to contend with the more positive world-description presented by the major schools of Chinese *Ekayāna*—represented by T'ien-t'ai and Hua-yen. He felt it necessary to articulate a more positive interpretation of the middle path doctrine. Hence, in addition to the *Mahāvairocana Sūtra*, which is Mādhyamika-oriented, he incorporated the *Tattvasaṃgraha Sūtra*, which is Yogācāra-oriented. From the latter he derived the doctrinal basis for the six element theory, the integration of the 'knower' and the 'known'. But the six element theory does not contradict the Mādhyamika thesis. Integration is possible because of co-arising, the central theme of Mādhyamika, because the mind itself is essentially markless, absent of an essence, and empty. As was previously mentioned, the *Mahāvairocana Sūtra* and *Tattvasaṃgraha Sūtra* are the two basic *sūtras* of Shingon. The former represents the Mādhyamika and the latter the Yogācāra doctrinal bases of Shingon. But following the model of the *Awakening of Mahāyāna Faith*, Kūkai incorporated the two major systems of Mahāyāna philosophy; and then he interpreted them symbolically, ever mindful of the soteriological mesasge of Mahāyāna, and conceived the six elements theory. Doctrinally, there is no difference whatsoever between the six element theory and *A-ji* meditation.

5. *Honji* and *Kaji*

We are now prepared to deal with the most crucial issue facing Shingon. Shingon is the doctrine which reveals the realm of *Dharmakāya* Mahāvairocana. It is also the teaching by *Dharmakāya* Mahāvairocana. The first needs no further explanation as it has already been explained, but the second does. The second issue revolves around the question concerning the form of *Dharmakāya* which reveals the secret doctrine. That is, though *Dharmakāya* Mahāvairocana was described as *svabhāva-Dharmakāya*, *saṃbhoga-Dharmakāya*, *nirmāṇa-Dharmakāya*, and *niṣyanda-Dharmakāya*, the specific question is which form of *Dharmakāya* reveals the secret doctrine? This question requires an examination of the terms *honji* and *kaji*.

Honji is a compound of *hon* and *ji*. *Hon* means 'fundamental'. *Ji* (not to be confused with *ji* in *A-ji*) literally means the 'earth', symbolically conceived as the source of all things. *Honji* literally means the 'fundamental ground' or the 'fundamental nature' of all things. It signifies the ground on which all things are dependent for their existence. *Honji* is frequently followed by another term, *suijaku*. *Suijaku* means the 'trace' or the phenomenal manifestation of the fundamental nature. *Kaji*, the Shingon equivalent of *adhiṣṭhāna* (a term already described) signifying the empirical instrument through which the fundamental nature is manifested, is the Shingon version of *suijaku*.

As a system of Japanese Buddhist thought, Chapter Sixteen of the *Lotus Sūtra* (in the Chinese translation) forms the basis for the development of the *honji-suijaku* theory. It speaks of the Eternal Buddha, who is conceived as *honji*, and the historical Buddha, who is conceived as *suijaku*, the emanation of the Eternal Buddha. In the course of Buddhism's coming into contact with Shintō deities, whom the masses worshipped, Japanese folk religion conceived buddhas and *bodhisattvas* as appearing in this world in the form of Shintō deities to save all beings. The buddhas and *bodhisattvas* were conveniently referred to as *honji* bodies and Shintō deities as the emanation of the *honji* bodies, i.e., *suijaku*, such as in the case of Hachiman, a Shintō deity. Thus, in the context of the history of Japanese religion, the *honji-suijaku* theory contributed to developing Buddhist-Shintō syncretism and provided the ground for the assimilation of Buddhist thought on a folklore level.

Historically, the term *honji-suijaku* is found in the *Iwashimizumonsho* (The Iwashimizu Letters), dated 937. But Murayama Shuichi refers to a passage, dated 698, in the *Zoku nihongi* (The Later Chronicles of Japan) in which he sees a semblance of a *honji-suijaku* phenomenon.[21] He warns, however, that it is necessary to investigate still earlier documents or religious phenomena to examine the beginnings of Shintō-Buddhist syncretism. Prince Shōtoku (d. 622) employs this term in his alleged composition, the *Shōman-gyō gisho* (The Commentary on the *Śrimālādevī-siṃhanāda-sūtra*),[22] though, as can be expected, the term, in the context of this text, is not associated with religious syncretism at all. It refers to the *bodhisattvas*, who represent the embodiment of the True Dharma and the emanation of the Eternal Buddha.

In Shingon, the *honji* body refers to the essential nature of *Dharmakāya*, that is *svabhāva-Dharmakāya*, while the *kaji* body refers to the manifested body, that is the *adhiṣṭhāna*-practitioner whose purpose is to realize the essential nature of *Dharmakāya*. Thus, we can see that the *honji-kaji* controversy, in the case of Shingon, stems from the interpretation of Mahāvairocana, the central issue on which Shingon schism took place. Śubhākarasiṃha's *Commentary on the Mahāvairocana Sūtra* says, "The *Bhagavān* is the Mahāvairocana, the essential nature of *Dharmakāya*."[23] It also says, "At this time the *Bhagavān*, because of his past compassion-vow, becomes mindful of this: 'If I were to dwell only in this [*honji*] realm, sentient beings would be unable to receive benefits; therefore, I dwell in the self-abiding, super-power of *adhiṣṭhāna samādhi*."[24] The first passage identifies Mahāvairocana as *honji*, the latter as *kaji*. Orthodox Shingon claims that *Dharmakāya* Mahāvairocana is *honji* (whose essential nature is *svabhāva-Dharmakāya*) and that his attributes (*saṃbhoga-Dharmakāya*, *nirmāṇa-Dharmakāya*, and *niṣyanda-Dharmakāya*) represent his *kaji* bodies. *Honji* is identified as the six elements, and *kaji* bodies as the 'marks' (the four *maṇḍalas*) and 'functions' (the three secrets) of *Dharmakāya* Mahāvairocana. But neo-Shingon claims that *Dharmakāya* Mahāvairocana *per se* is the embodiment of both *honji* and *kaji:* it presupposes that *svabhāva-Dharmakāya per se* is empty of body, marks, and functions, and that only through its attributes can the body, marks, and functions of *svabhāva-Dharmakāya* be revealed. The following chart outlines the orthodox and the neo-Shingon views on the *honji-kaji* issue:

Orthodox Shingon

Honji (essence)	*Kaji* (attributes)	
svabhāva-Dharmakāya (i.e., Mahāvairocana represented by the six elements, the attributes of which are the *ka-ji*-bodies.) →	*saṃbhoga-Dharmakāya*	— 4 *maṇḍalas*
	nirmāṇa-Dharmakāya	— 3 secrets
	niṣyanda-Dharmakāya	— 3 secrets

Neo-Shingon

Mahāvairocana

Honji (essence)	*Kaji* (attributes)
(which is without body, marks and functions)	(whose attributes consist of the six elements, 4 *maṇḍalas* and three secrets.)

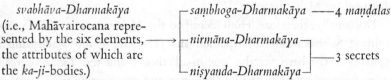

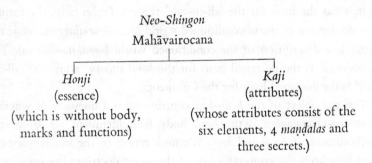

Many Shingon masters have taken part in the *honji-kaji* debate. Hōju's (1722–1800) *Himitsu innen kangen sōjō-gi* (The Meaning of the Secret Doctrine) is among the most interesting because it presents a synthesis of the two views.[25] He derives the basis for synthesis from the Kegon theory of 'all-in-one and one-in-all', which is one of the Kegon descriptions of *Dharmadhātu*. This theory sees the essence of *Dharmadhātu* ('one', i.e. the universal one) in the diversity ('all', i.e. the parts of the universal one) of forms, and the essence of the diversity ('all') in the all-encompassing *Dharmadhātu* ('one'). 'One' refers to emptiness, 'all' refers to co-arising. Though this theory contradicts the basis of Western philosophy (e.g. theories of dualism as presented by Anaxagoras, Plato and Aristotle), it bears distinct similarity to Spinoza's notion of *deus sive natura*. 'One-in-all' sees the essence of emptiness pervading all forms, and 'all-in-one' sees all forms integrated within the organic emptiness. At any rate, in the Shingon context, the 'one-in-all' is the basis of meditation to realize *prajñā*, while 'all-in-one' is the basis for the practice of compassion, the improvising of skillful means to communicate the 'one' essence to 'all'. The two are not distinct and apart. They are interdependent and non-dual. The six element theory is the Shingon's 'all-in-one and one-in-all' interpretation of the organic world of *Dharmakāya* Mahāvairocana.

Doctrinally, therefore, Hōju identified the *Mahāvairocana Sūtra* (transmitting Śubhākarasiṃha's tradition and representing the Mādhyamika system) as the basis for the 'one-in-all' theory and the *Tattvasaṃgraha Sūtra* (transmitting Vajrabodhi's tradition and representing the Yogācāra system) as the basis for the 'all-in-one' theory. Technically, the former is a description of the unconditioned world (*asaṃskṛta-dharma*), while the latter is a description of the conditioned world (*saṃskṛta-dharma*). The 'one-in-all' is the doctrinal basis for the *honji* theory, while the 'all-in-one' is the doctrinal basis for the *kaji* theory.

But the object of the *honji-kaji* controversy is a question of whether *svabhāva-Dharmakāya* is the *honji* body (enlightenment *per se*) or the embodiment of *honji* and *kaji*. We now return to the initial question, that is, who is the communicator of the secret doctrine: the *honji* body as orthodox Shingon maintains, or the *kaji* body as neo-Shingon maintains?

The *kaji* body theory destroys the basis of Shingon doctrine, since Shingon identifies the body of Mahāvairocana in terms of the six elements, his marks in terms of the four *maṇḍalas*, and his functions in terms of the three secrets, which, according to orthodox Shingon, are the manifested attributes of Mahāvairocana. Orthodox Shingon claims that *svabhāva-Dharmakāya* itself, not its attributes, possesses the capability to communicate. Nevertheless, the communicator (*svabhāva-Dharmakāya*) and the object to which the Dharma is communicated (sentient beings) are two different entities. Even with the assumption that the Dharma (*Dharmakāya* Mahāvairocana) is the communicator, the Dharma is the embodiment of enlightenment. The Dharma is beyond the reaches of sentient beings. Dharma reaches the realm of sentient beings only through *saṃbhogakāya* and *nirmāṇakāya* (and in the case of the four body theory, *niṣyandakāya*). But this is the *Kengyō* position, as held by Tendai. Neo-Shingon therefore recognizes that together with *honji*, *kaji* is also inherent in the Dharma. As it is apparent now, the intensity with which the *honji-kaji* controversy was debated essentially led Shingon doctrinal masters away from Kūkai's major thesis—the integration of man and *Dharmakāya* Mahāvairocana. The controversy centering on *honji* and *kaji*—the major issue which led to the orthodox and neo-Shingon schism—is based on a methodological premise which is contrary to the basic Shingon tenet.

Let us further elaborate. First, though the *honji-suijaku* represents a Buddhist theory of assimilation, as Alicia Matsunaga claims,[24] it is so only to the extent of interpreting the sophisticated philosophical content of Buddhism on a folklore level, which, incidentally, has its limitations. It cannot be employed to interpret the actual philosophical contents of Buddhism, such as the notions of emptiness and co-arising, which precludes the conceptual categories of either dualism or monism. Second, in Buddhism, *honji-suijaku* is a means to describe the attributes of the *bodhisattvas*, and as such, *kaji*, the instrument of integration between man and Mahāvairocana, is radically different in its content—philosophically as well as in the implementation of that philosophical thought in terms of practice—from what the *honji-suijaku* theory conceived on a folklore level attempts to do—an attempt in interpreting Buddhism on a folklore level. Hence, the arbitrary categories of *honji* and *kaji*, as these terms are understood in the context of folk religion, cannot be employed to describe the nature of Mahāvairocana, because, as said before, Mahāvairocana transcends all notions of dualism. The schism between orthodox and neo-Shingon is based upon this misconception. However, granting that Mahāvairocana transcends all notions of dualism, still is it possible for the *Dharmakāya per se* to reveal the Dharma? More specifically, is a personified Dharma, as is Mahāvairocana, a logical possibility in the context of Buddhist thought? Shingon *Mikkyū* responds in the affirmative, based on its supposition that *Dharmakāya*—the body of *Dharmadhātu*—is a living organism with distinct form, sound, and mind, in the same context that man, the microcosm of *Dharmakāya* Mahāvairocana, is a living organic entity. *Kengyō*, however, disclaims the *Mikkyō* theory of the personified Dharma.[27] The personified Dharma —*Dharmakāya* Mahāvairocana—and the integration of man with *Dhar-*

makāya Mahāvairocana are most succinctly dealt with in terms of the *Garbhakośadhātu Maṇḍala* and the *Vajradhātu Maṇḍala.*

CHAPTER FOUR
THE TWO *MAṆḌALAS*

1. Introduction

Tri-guhya, the three secret theory, is central to Shingon meditation. The objects of this meditation are the six elements, representing *tathatā*. Employing the traditional scheme of categorizing dharmas, that is form (*rūpa*) and mind (*citta*), Shingon conceives the first five of the six elements as form and the sixth as the mind. But it does not conceive form simply as material elements and the mind as that upon which ordinary mental awareness is reflected. Form is *ri* (Ch. *li*), the principle underlying all things, and the mind is *chi* (Ch. *chih*), that upon which the principle is reflected. Thus the first five elements—that is *ri*—represent that which ought to be known, that is the truth; while the sixth—that is *chi*—is the knower, that is the wisdom that has conceived the truth. The two, the known and the knower, are inseparable. The integration of the known and the knower is *Dharmakāya* Mahāvairocana, the personification of *tathatā* which is represented by the six elements. In *maṇḍala* terms, the known is the *Garbhakośadhātu Maṇḍala*, and the knower is the *Vajradhātu Maṇḍala*. They are the two basic forms of Shingon Mikkyō *Maṇḍala*. They are the specific objects of the *tri-guhya* meditation. The *gorin*, the five story-*stūpa*, or more specifically the *gorin-jōshin*, the five elements of the perfected body, provides by way of symbolism the rationale underlying the theory of the inseparability of *Garbhakośadhātu* and the *Vajradhātu*. The logical procedure to examine the Shingon *maṇḍalas* then is to first examine the *gorin* and then proceed to examine the *Garbhakośadhātu* and the *Vajradhātu*.

The *gorin* symbolically describes *tathatā* (in terms of the six elements), the *Garbhakośadhātu* (the known) reflecting upon *Vajradhātu* (the knower), and *Dharmakāya* Mahāvairocana (representing the union of the knower and the known) as described below:

The Five Elements of the Perfected Body

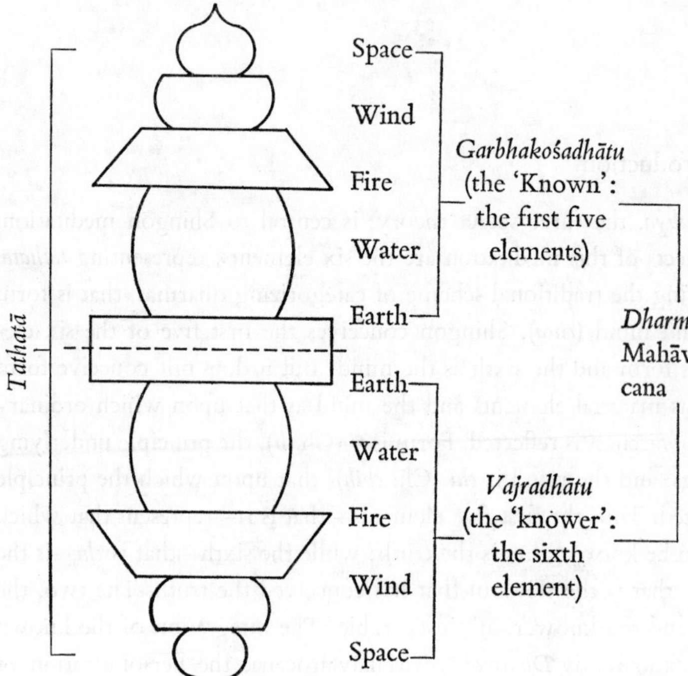

Dharmakāya Mahāvairocana is the personification of the Dharma, which is *tathatā*. The goal of Shingon *Mikkyō* is to perfect (i.e., to realize the essential nature of) the five elements represented by *Garbhakośadhātu* —which is reflected upon the sixth element, Vajradhātu—and to realize the integration of the known and the knower. One who realizes this union is *Dharmakāya* Mahāvairocana. Man is *Dharmakāya* Mahāvairocana. Kūkai therefore says, "The *sūtras* and *śāstras* conceal the secrets of the *mantra*-store. Without the use of pictures, they cannot be transmitted."[1] The *Garbhakośadhātu* and *Vajradhātu Maṇḍalas* are representations of the two aspects of the Dharma, which is *tathatā*, personified as

Dharmakāya Mahāvairocana. The *maṇḍalas* represent a layout depicting the secret doctrine, the integration of the known and the knower. Tucci therefore defines a *maṇḍala* as a "means or reintegration."[2]

In speaking of these two *maṇḍalas*, we are specifically referring to what is commonly known in Japan as the *genzu* (iconographic) *maṇḍala*, not a *maṇḍala* depicted verbally (such as the one in Śubhākarasiṃha's *Commentary*). The term *genzu maṇḍala* was probably introduced to Japan by Annen (d. 889 or 898) of Mount Hiei, the headquarters of the Tendai monastic system. Both the original composer and the manner in which the iconographic *maṇḍala* was introduced to China are unclear. One legend has it that the *Garbhakośadhātu Maṇḍala* was a painting by Śubhākarasiṃha of a world he saw in space, and that the *Vajradhātu Maṇḍala* was painted by Vajrabodhi under the instruction of the Buddha.[3] *Maṇḍala* is undoubtedly Indian in origin. Most likely the *maṇḍala* pantheon is a graphic projection of a southern Indian agrarian society of the Gupta Period.[4] But the style of the two *maṇḍalas* in question is Chinese. It is very probable that by the time of Hui-kuo, the Chinese Chen-yen master under whom Kūkai studied, many Chinese masters had either painted or had instructed professional artists to paint *maṇḍalas*. Kūkai introduced the tradition of the iconographic *maṇḍala* to Japan.

2. *The Garbhakośadhātu Maṇḍala* (Jap. *Taizōkai Mandara*, see Plate I)

The word *garbhakośa* consists of '*garbha*' and *kośa*. *Garbha* means "womb, embryo." Śubhākarasiṃha describes *garbhakośa* by comparing it to a mother's womb, which stores, protects and nurtures a child. Likewise, he further says, "*Bodhicitta* stores, protects and nurtures the seeds of the six elements."[5] '*Kośa*' means "store". '*Dhātu*' has a variety of meanings, such as "layer, stratum, element, sphere, region, world, body."[6] In short, *Garbhakośadhātu* represents the repository of truth, and is known in full as the *Mahā-karuṇā-garbhodbhava-maṇḍala*.[7] Ideas for the composition of this *maṇḍala* are drawn from the *Mahāvairocana Sūtra*. The *maṇḍala* is a graphic representation of the first five of the six

Plate I. *The Garbhakośadhātu Maṇḍala* (Taken from Sawa Takaaki *Mikkyō no bijitsu*, Tokyo: Heibonsha, 1964)

elements, the 'known'. It consists of twelve halls (see figure 1) with a total of 414 deities.[8]

The *Mahāvairocana Sūtra* says,

O Bhagavān, what is the cause of such a wisdom (*sarvajñāna*)? What are its roots? Vairocana Buddha speaks to Vajradhara, the Master of secrets. 'Excellent, excellent, Vajradhara! Excellent, excellent, Vajrapāni! You are asking the meaning of what I have

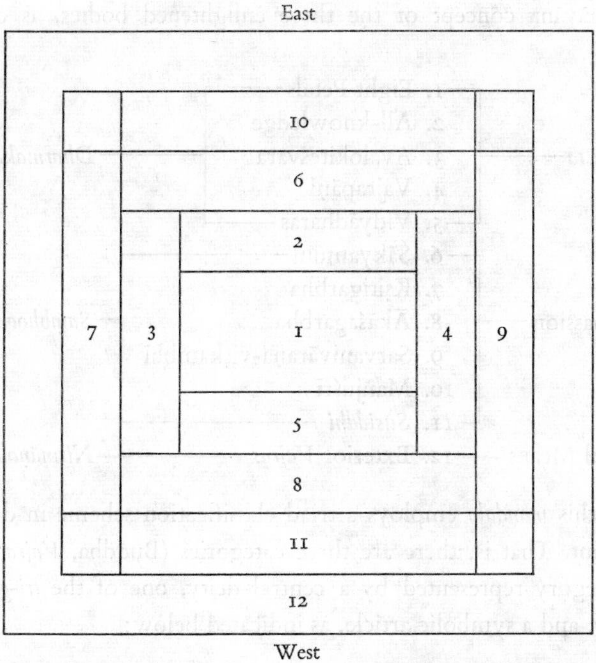

Figure 1. The twelve halls of the *Garbhakośadhātu* Assembly. 1) Eight Petals (Hachiyō-in), nine deities; 2) All-knowledge (Henchi-in), seven deities; 3) Avalokiteśvara (Kannon-in), thirty seven deities; 4) Vajrapāṇi (Kongoshu-in), thirty seven deities; 5) Vidyādharas (Jimyō-in), five deities; 6) Sākyamuni (Shaka-in), thirty nine deities; 7) Kṣitigarbha (Jizō-in), nine deities; 8) Ākāśagarbha (Kokuzō-in), twenty eight deities; 9) Sarvanivāraṇa-viṣkambhī (Jogaishō-in), nine deities; 10) Mañjuśrī (Monju-in), twenty five deities; 11) Susiddhi (Soshitchi-in), eight deities; 12) Exterior Vajras (Kongōgaibu-in), two hundred and five deities.

> said. Listen carefully and think with extreme care, I shall now explain it . . .' The Buddha says, '*Bodhicitta* is the cause, the great compassion is its root, and skillful means its end result.'[9]

The Buddha's response forms the basic concept for the composition of this *maṇḍala*, that is the improvising of skillful means—the compassion by which *bodhicitta* is cultivated. In Shingon, *bodhicitta*, compassion, and skillful means constitute the enlightenment trinity. It corresponds to the Mahāyāna concept of the three enlightened bodies, as described below:

Bodhicitta	1. Eight Petals 2. All-knowledge 3. Avalokiteśvara 4. Vajrapāṇi 5. Vidyādharas	*Dharmakāya*
Compassion	6. Śākyamuni 7. Kṣitigarbha 8. Ākāśagarbha 9. Sarvanivāraṇa-viṣkambhī 10. Mañjuśrī 11. *Susiddhi*	*Saṃbhogakāya*
Skillful Means	12. Exterior *Vajras*	*Nirmāṇakāya*

Thus this *maṇḍala* employs a triad classification scheme in describing its content. That is, there are three categories (Buddha, *Vajra*, *Padma*), each category represented by a central deity, one of the *tri-guhya*, an attribute, and a symbolic article, as indicated below:

General Group	*Deity*	*Tri-guhya*	*Attribute*	*Symbolic Article*
Buddha	Mahāvairocana	Body	Meditation	*Stūpa*
Vajra	Vajrasattva	Mind	Wisdom	Five-pronged *vajra*
Padma	Avalokiteśvara	Voice	Compassion	Lotus

The Buddha category includes the Eight Petals, All-knowledge, Śākyamuni, Mañjusrī, Vidyāharas, Ākāśagarbha, and Susiddhi—the halls running vertically through the center. The *Vajra* category includes Vajrapāṇi and Sarvanivāraṇaviṣkambhi, the two halls in the south. The *Padma* category includes Avalokiteśvara and Kṣitigarbha, the two halls in the north. Mahāvairocana is the central deity of the Buddha group, Vajrasattva of the Vajra group, and Avalokiteśvara of the *Padma* group. Vajrasattva and Avalokiteśvara, representing wisdom and compassion respectively, are emanations of Mahāvairocana. It is through them that *Dharmakāya* Mahāvairocana is revealed. Mahāvairocana is represented by the Eight Petals. Thus this hall is central and most significant among

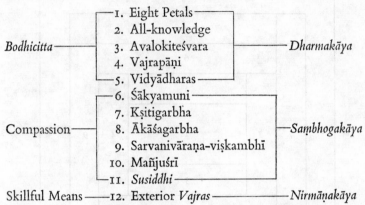

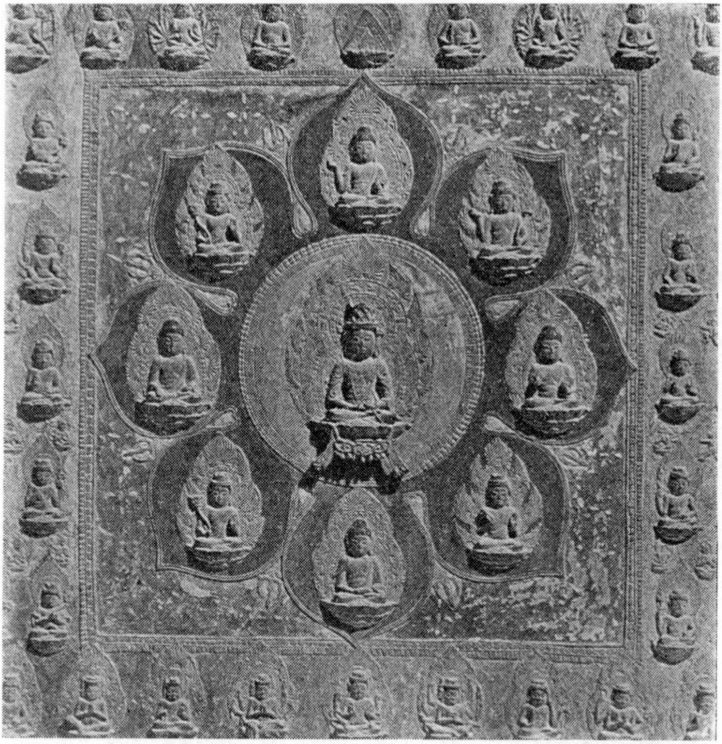

Plate II. The Hall of the Eight Petals (Taken from Sawa Takaaki *Mikkyō no bijitsu*, Tokyo: Heibonsha, 1964)

the twelve. It will be treated in detail. A brief description of other components will follow.

1) *The Eight Petals* (see Plate II). This hall represents the heart (*hṛdaya* or *citta*) or the core, and is the sign of: a) the four Buddhas, and b) the four attendant-*bodhisattvas*, all of whom emanate from the central Mahāvairocana. It is therefore also called the Hall of the Buddhas. Collectively, there are nine deities representing the nine *jñānas*. This hall is an iconographic representation of the Shingon concept of 'Buddhahood realized in the present body' (*Sokushin jōbutsu*, see Chapter V, Instant Buddhahood). Just as the *vijñānas* constitute the only available material to develop *jñānas*, so living beings are the only avialable materials to de-

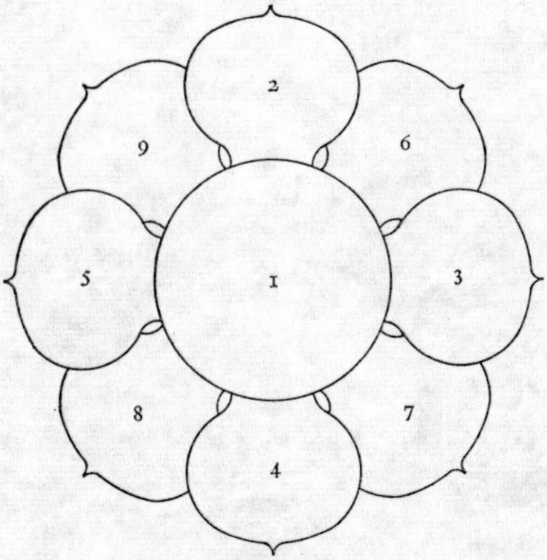

Figure 2. The nine deities of the Hall of the Eight Petals. Buddhas (who represent the realm of enlightenment): 1) Mahāvairocana, center; 2) Ratnaketu, east; 3) Saṃkusumitarāja, south; 4) Amitābha, west; 5) Divyadundubhimega-nirghoṣa, north. *Bodhisattvas* (who represent the stages of practice): 6) Samantabhadra; 7) Mañjuśri; 8) Avalokiteśvara; 9) Maitreya.

velop *buddhas*. It is in this context that Shingon claims that man is a potential *buddha*; it is upon this premise that it claims that man inherently possesses a buddha-mind (*buddha-citta*). Figure 2 shows the nine deities of the Hall of the eight petals.

A brief description of the five Buddhas and the four *bodhisattvas* is presented below:

Mahāvairocana portrays the *dharmadhātu-samādhi-mudrā*, right palm over left, with thumbs joined to form an oval. The five left fingers represent the five *jñānas*. This *mudrā* is the sign of non-duality, the integration of man and the Buddha. Light emitting from Mahāvairocana's body symbolizes the revelation of wisdom, spreading throughout the universe.

Ratnaketu portrays the charity (*dāna-*) *mudrā*, with his right hand opened and tilted, and the 'fearless' (*abhayadāna-*) *mudrā* with his left open and pointed up. '*Ratna*' means "jewels." Ratnaketu is one who offers wealth (Dharma) to all beings, according to their need, and protects them from harm and injury. He is therefore also called the '*Vajra* of Blessing and Longevity'. He corresponds to Akṣobhya of the *Vajradhātu Maṇḍala*.

Saṃkusmitarāja portrays the *abhayadāna-mudrā* in his right hand, indicating the spreading of compassion to all beings equally. He is therefore called the '*Vajra* of Equality'. He corresponds to Ratnasaṃbhava of the *Vajradhātu Maṇḍala*.

Amitābha portrays the Amita *mudrā*, left fingers on right, thumbs forming an oval, index fingers touching the thumbs to form circles. The three overlapping fingers symbolize the three elements (earth, water and fire) which conquer the three evils (*māras:* hate, greed, and delusion). Circles symbolize *nirvāṇa*. Amitābha is one who has extinguished *kleśa* and entered *nirvāṇa*. He is therefore called the '*Vajra* of Purity'. He corresponds to Amitāyus of the *Vajradhātu Maṇḍala*.

Divyadundubhimega-nirghoṣa portrays the evil (*māra*)-subduing, path *mārga*)-perfecting *mudrā*, left fist placed at the navel, opened right hand underneath it. He brings enlightenment to all beings of the universe by beating drums and startling them wherever they may be. He is also called the 'Immovable *Vajra*' or Acala. He corresponds to Amoghasiddhi of the *Vajradhātu Maṇḍala*.

These four Buddhas represent the four attributes of Mahāvairocana. The five Buddhas (the four plus Mahāvairocana) collectively represent the realm of enlightenment. In contrast, the four *bodhisattvas*—Samantabhadra, Mañjuśrī, Avalokiteśvara and Maitreya—represent the stages of practice (the cause-realm of enlightenment). Specifically, Samantabhadra represents the stage of awakening *bodhicitta*; Mañjuśrī, of cultivating *prajñā*; and Avalokiteśvara and Maitreya, of realizing *bodhi* and *nirvāṇa*, respectively.

The Hall of the Eight Petals represents the world of the five elements. The eleven other halls emanate from the Eight Petals.

2) *All-knowledge.* In the center of this hall is a triangle, representing *jñāna-mudrā*, the sign of Buddha-wisdom. With reference to the six

elements, the triangle represents fire. All-knowledge is realized by burning the four *māras*. Hence, *jñāna-mudrā* is variously referred to as the *mudrā* of all-knowledge, the *mudrā* of the knowledge of the *Tathāgatas*, and the mudrā of the state of all Buddhas. The two *śrāvakas*, pictured on the two sides near the peak of the triangle, are Uruvilvā-kāśyapa and Gayā-kāśyapa, symbolizing the conversion of the heretics to Śākyamuni's teaching, as related in the *Vinaya*, *Mahāvagga*, and other works. The triangle is the sign of Buddhahood. In contrast, *Bodhisattva* Mahāvīra, occupying the seat north and adjacent to the triangle, symbolizes the manifested action of the Buddhas. He is the *bodhisattva* who enlightens all beings. Because *jñāna* brings about the birth of the Buddha, the three 'Buddha-mothers' who symbolize this birth, also reign in this hall. These three are Buddhalocanā, Saptakoṭibuddhagavatā, and Mahāsukhāmoghatattvavagrā. This hall describes *Dharmakāya* Mahāvairocana emerging from the world of self-enlightenment to the world of enlightening others.

3) *Avalokiteśvara.* The *Bodhisattva* Avalokiteśvara possesses the power to respond to the plea of all beings. He is the central deity of this hall. The lotus, the sign of Avalokiteśvara, symbolizes the idea that pure mind is the original nature of man, though he lives in the world of *kleśa*. Avalokiteśvara's purpose is to communicate the lotus message to all beings through skillful means. Because he belongs to the Padma category, this hall is also referred to as the Hall of Padmapāṇi. In contrast to the Hall of All-knowledge, this is the Hall of the Great Compassion. These two halls represent the two aspects of Buddha-citta. Because the lotus message is directed to sentient beings, this hall corresponds to *pratyavekṣaṇā-jñāna*, the insight to deal with the particulars of the world.

4) *Vajrapāṇi.* Also known as *Bodhisattva* Vajrasattva, he is the central deity of this hall. He represents the wisdom with which *māra* is subdued and enlightenment is realized. Because Vajrapāṇi belongs to the Vajra group, this hall is referred to as the Hall of the *Vajra*. It is also known as the Hall of Vajrasattva. Whereas Avalokiteśvara represents the Buddha's great compassion, Vajrapāṇi represents the Buddha's inherent

wisdom. The Halls of Avalokiteśvara and Vajrapāṇi, representing the two attributes of Mahāvairocana, supplement each other. These two halls therefore occupy the two adjacent sides of the Eight Petals.

5) *Vidyādharas.* Vidyādhara is a compound formed from '*vidyā*', meaning "knowledge" (but here it specifically refers to *dhāraṇi* and *mantra*), and '*dhara*,' "that which holds or supports." *Bodhisattva* Vidyādhara therefore means one who possesses *jñāna*, the qualities of which are distilled into a secret formula (*mantra*) in order to subdue *māra* and to realize enlightenment, instantly. This hall describes the transformed body (*ādeśanācakrakāya*) of Mahāvairocana. Iconographically, this is represented by Prajñāpāramitā-*bodhisattva*, one who enlightens others.

6) *Śākyamuni.* Shingon sees Śākyamuni in various enlightened bodies. He is Divyadundubhimega-nirghoṣa-svabhāvakāya in the Eight Petals, but in this hall he is *nirmāṇakāya*, the historically manifested body of *Dharmakāya* Mahāvairocana. He is one of the teachers of the secret doctrine of Mahāvairocana.

7) *Kṣitigarbha.* Kṣitigarbha literally means the "womb of the earth." He is the central deity of this hall, representing firmness and indestructibility, profoundness and extensiveness. He gives birth to and nurtures all things, He represents the storehouse of truth. These truth-merits characterize *bodhicitta.* He is therefore the *bodhisattva* who has vowed to save all beings. It has previously been mentioned that Avalokiteśvara vowed to save all beings. Kṣitigarbha does what has not been done by Avalokiteśvara. Specifically he divides his body into six parts, sending these parts to save the beings of the six destinies. He does this during the period between Śākyamuni's enlightenment and the coming of the future savior, Maitreya. He therefore resides adjacent to the Hall of Avalokiteśvara.

8) *Ākāśagarbha.* Literally, the storehouse of space, he is the central deity of this hall and represents the *bodhisattva* of a wisdom as boundless as space, as his name indicates. He is adorned with jewels and holds a sword symbolizing wisdom in his right hand; in his left, he has a *cintāmaṇi,* a wish-fulfilling jewel, which symbolizes the fulfillment of that which a being desires. Whereas Mañjuśrī (to be subsequently de-

scribed) symbolizes wisdom *per se*, Ākāśagarbha is one who blesses all beings through the use of his wisdom.

9) *Sarvanivāraṇa-viṣkambhi.*[10] The name means "eliminating obstacles." This *bodhisattva* is the central deity of this hall and represents *jñāna* radiating from the Hall of Vajrapāṇi.

10) *Mañjuśri.* One of the attendants of Śākyamuni, he is the *bodhisattva* of supreme wisdom and is the central deity of this hall. Whereas Vajrapāṇi represented inherent wisdom, Mañjuśrī represents cultivated wisdom. That is, Mañjuśri's wisdom is designed to enable all beings to realize inherent wisdom.

11) *Susiddhi.* Meaning "perfection," here it means the perfection of Ākāśagarbha's work. This hall is therefore located adjacent to the Hall of Ākāśagarbha.

12) *The Exterior Vajras.* These deities, as a collective body, represent the world of the six destinies. Shingon holds that the destinies are entities of *Dharmakāya* Mahāvairocana and are the indispensible enlightenment-materials (because Mahāyāna enlightenment is contingent upon enlightening others). Iconographically, the deities of this hall function as the guardians of *Garbhakośadhātu Maṇḍala.*

One question might be asked at this time: Why do the east and west halls contain four rows (i.e., Mañjuśrī and Susiddhi are redundant)? The Shingon answer is that the triple formula is the Shingon-*maṇḍala* version of the three enlightened bodies (*Dharmakāya, saṃbhogakāya, nirmāṇakāya*), which can be elaborated into the four enlightened bodies, the addition being *niṣyandakāya*,[11] which enters the six destinies. In the case of the four enlightened bodies, the Exterior *Vajras* are *niṣyandakāya.*

In sum, the *Garbhakośadhātu Maṇḍala* consists of the central Hall of the Eight Petals, which is surrounded by three rows of halls each on its north and south, and four rows each on its east and west. The central theme of the *Mahāvairocana Sūtra*, which this *maṇḍala* depicts, is the triple formula. Hence, the Hall of the Eight Petals and its first surrounding row of halls (All-knowledge, Avalokiteśvara, Vajrapāṇi, and Vidyadhara) represents *bodhicitta;* the second row of halls (Śākyamuni, Kṣitigarbha, Ākāśāgarbha, Sarvanivārana-viśkambhī, Mañjuśrī, and Susiddhi) represents compassion; and the third (the Exterior *Vajras*) represents skillful means. *Garbhakośadhātu Maṇḍala* is an iconographic representation of the first five elements.

3. *The Vajradhātu Maṇḍala* (Jap. *Kongōkai Mandara*, see Plate III)

Vajra, as said before, means 'thunderbolt', 'weapon'. It is a "symbol of the indestructible and irresistible truth, hence applicable as an epithet to all things symbolizing this truth. By connotation it is masculine."[12] The *Śrāvakabhūmi* describes it as 'diamond-like'.[13] Śubhākarasiṃha's *Commentary* says, "Vajra represents fortitude and indestructibility [qualities which] characterize wisdom."[14] Ideas for the composition of the *Vajradhātu Maṇḍala* are drawn from the *Tattvasaṃgraha Sūtra*. The *Vajradhātu Maṇḍala* is the graphic representation of the sixth element, the 'knower'. It is also called the nine assembly *maṇḍala* because it consists of nine assemblies, containing 1,461 deities, as shown in figure 3.

5	6	7
4	1	8
3	2	9

Figure 3. The nine assemblies of the *Vajradhātu Maṇḍala*: 1) Karma, 1,061 deities; 2) *Samaya*, 73 deities; 3) Sūkṣma, 73 deities; 4) Pūja, 73 deities; 5) *Caturmudrā* or Four *Mudrā*, 13 deities; 6) *Ekamudrā* or One *Mudrā*, 1 deity; 7) Naya, 17 deities; 8) Trailokyavijayakarma, 77 deities; 9) Trailokyavijayasamaya, 73 deities.

The Karma Assembly is the central and most significant among the

Plate III. The *Vajradhātu Maṇḍala* (Taken from Sawa Takaaki *Mikkyō no bijitsu*, Tōkyō: Heibonsha, 1964)

nine assemblies. It will be treated in detail. A brief description of other components will follow.

1) *The Karma Assembly*. This is the central assembly. It is also called the 'basic assembly', because it is the Buddha's point of departure, as well as the Karma Assembly, because the function (karma) of the Buddha is to enlighten all beings. From the position of the non-enlightened, however, this is the terminal point of enlightenment; therefore, it is

also called the 'assembly of the perfect body', that is, the Buddha-body. Enlightenment means the actualization of the Buddha-body. Karma here means the Buddha's compassion. Compassion denotes improvising skillful means to enlighten all beings. Two methods have been improvised: *tri-guhya* meditation and the meditation on the five marks of Buddhahood. The former has already been examined. The latter requires a description. The meditation on the five marks of Buddhahood actually refers to the five stages of meditation to realize the Buddha-body. The five marks are:

a) penetrating (i.e. developing awareness of one's inherent) *bodhicitta*,
b) cultivating *bodhicitta*,
c) perfecting *vajra-citta* (i.e. perfecting the union of man and Buddha in one's mind),
d) realizing *vajra*-body (physical union),
e) supreme enlightenment (*anuttara-samyak-saṃbodhi*).

The *Bodhicitta Śāstra* explains the same five marks as follows:

a) seeing the moon (*bodhi*) through a thin cloud (*avidyā*),
b) clearing away that cloud,
c) becoming one with the moon,
d) realizing non-duality, and thereby
e) perfecting enlightenment.

The *Tattvasaṃgraha Sūtra* therefore says, "Your own body is the diamond (*vajra*) firm and indestructible."[15] This is the passage which Kūkai employs in his *Sokushin jōbutsu-gi* to explain the theory of Buddhahood realized in the present body.[16] The five marks of Buddhahood are stages of meditation to enable a practitioner to realize Buddhahood. *Tri-guhya*, in contrast, is a means to realize the interrelationship between man and the Buddha.

The overall structure of this assembly consists of the Great Circle, technically called the *Vajra* Circle, within which are the five sub-circles, technically called *vimokṣa* (liberation) circles. The *vimokṣa* circles are the seats of the Buddhas and their supporting *bodhisattvas*, and represent the five Buddha wisdoms. The *Vajra* Circle is surrounded by three

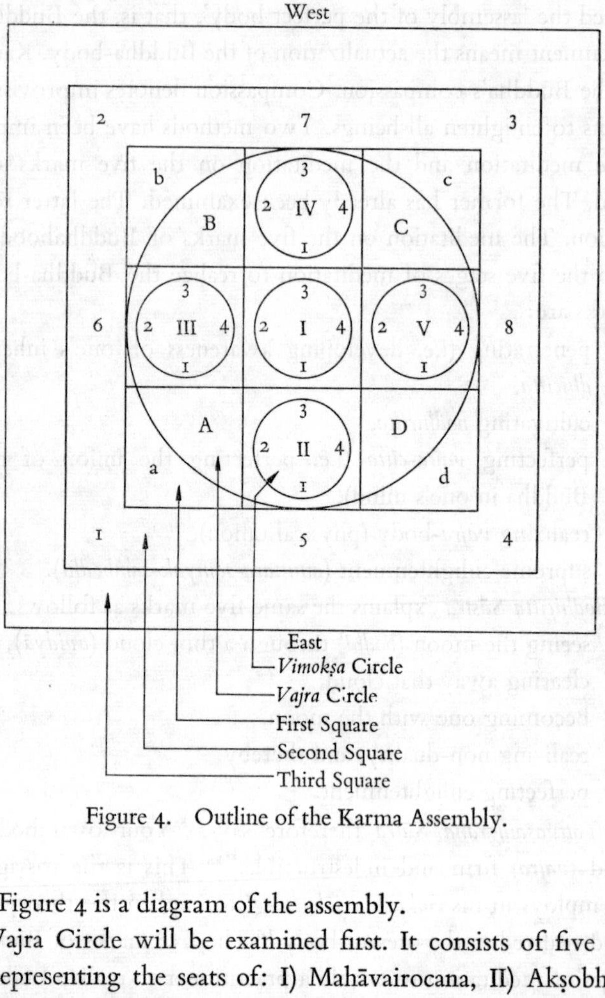

Figure 4. Outline of the Karma Assembly.

squares. Figure 4 is a diagram of the assembly.

The Vajra Circle will be examined first. It consists of five *vimokṣa* circles, representing the seats of: I) Mahāvairocana, II) Akṣobhya, III) Ratnasambhava, IV) Amitāyus and V) Amoghasiddhi. Each is described below:

The central *vimokṣa* circle is the seat of Mahāvairocana. On his sides are four *pāramitā* bodhisattvas (the *bodhisattva*-practice-perfection deities): Vajra (I-1), Ratna (I-2), Dharma (I-3), and Karma (I-4). These four *pāramitā bodhisattvas* are offered to Mahāvairocana by the four Buddhas (Akṣobhya, Ratnasambhava, Amitāyus and Amoghasiddhi). *Pāramitā* means "perfection." It was originally explained as a set of six qualities —charity, morality, patience, effort, meditation and wisdom. Four more qualities were subsequently added to the six—skillful means (*upāya*), vow (*praṇidhāna*), power (*bala*), and cognition (*jñāna*). The four *pāramitā* bodhisattvas mentioned above embody the virtues of the last four additions. In the Shingon context, skillful means refers to the manner in which merits (which one has accumulated by practicing the six *pāramitās*) are transferred to enlighten others. Vow means the resolution to practice the six *pāramitās* for the purpose of enlightening others. Power is that which enables one to cultivate the six *pāramitās* as instruments for enlightening others. Cognition means to comprehend the virtues of the six *pāramitās* as instruments to enlighten others. The four *pāramitās* originate in *prajñā*, the last of the six *pāramitās*. These four *pāramitās* give aid to and support the six. In the *Vajra* Circle, each of the four Buddhas, surrounding Mahāvairocana, is in turn encircled by four *prajñā bodhisattvas*, while Mahāvairocana is encircled by four *pāramitā bodhisattvas*. This arrangement expresses the relation between *prājñā-pāramitā* and the *four pāramitās*. The *prajñā bodhisattvas* offered by Mahāvairocana to his four Buddhas are described below:

The *vimokṣa* circle in the east is the seat of Akṣobhya. On his sides are his four *prajñā* bodhisattvas: Vajrasādhu (II-1), Vajrarāga (II-2), Vajrasattva (II-3), and Vajrarāja (II-4).

The *vimokṣa* circle in the south is the seat of Ratnasaṃbhava. On his sides are his four *prajñā bodhisattvas:* Vajrateja (III-1), Vajrahāsa (III-2,) Vajraketu (III-3), and Vajraratna (III-4).

The *vimokṣa* circle in the west is the seat of Amitāyus. On his sides are his four *prajñā bodhisattvas:* Vajradharma (IV-1), Vajratīkṣṇa (IV-2), Vajrahetu (IV-3), and Vajrabhāṣa (IV-4).

The *vimokṣa* circle in the north is the seat of Amoghasiddhi. On his sides are his four *prajñā bodhisattvas:* Vajrayakṣa (V-1), Vajrakarma (V-2), Vajrarakṣa (V-3), and Vajrasaṃdhi (V-4).

The five Buddhas are iconographic representations of the five wisdoms. Their respective *bodhisattvas* are the iconographic representation of practice, the implementation of wisdom. The five wisdoms represent what

Yogācāra (Hossō) referred to as the state of transformation from *vijñānas* to *jñānas*. Thus whereas the *Garbhakośadhātu Maṇḍala* depicted the triple formula of the *Mahāvairocana Sūtra*, the Karma Assembly, which is the basic assembly of the *Vajradhātu Maṇḍala*, depicts the five *jñānas*. Whereas the former maṇḍala employed the triad classification scheme to organize the deities of its pantheon, this *maṇḍala* employs a fivefold classification scheme as described below:

General Group	*Buddha*	*Jñāna*	*Vijñāna*	*Seat*
Buddha	Mahāvairocana (I)	*Dharmadhātu*	Ninth	Center
Vajra	Akṣobhya (II)	*Ādarśa*	Eighth	East
Ratna	Ratnasaṃbhava (III)	*Samatā*	Seventh	South
Padma	Amitāyus (IV)	*Pratyavekṣanā*	Sixth	West
Karma	Amoghasiddhi (V)	*Kṛtyānuṣṭhāna*	First five	North

Mahāvairocana is all-encompassing. The four remaining Buddhas are his attributes. Hence, *Dharmadhātu* encompasses all *jñānas*, the ninth *vijñānā* encompasses all *vijñānas*, the center encompasses all quarters. This is an iconographic representation of transformation—from *vijñānas* to *jñānas*.

Between the four *vimokṣa* circles are four female deities: Vajralāsī (A), Vajramālā (B), Vajragītā (C), and Vajranṛitā (D), who are the four *pūjā* (offering) *bodhisattvas* (of the interior, i.e. within the *Vajra* Circle) offered to Akṣobhya, Ratnasaṃbhava, Amitāyus, and Amoghasiddhi, respectively, by Mahāvairocana, indicating veneration, remembering that the four Buddhas are the emanation of Mahāvairocana.

In summary, the *Vajra* Circle consists of the five Buddhas, the four *pāramitā vodhisattvas*, the sixteen *prajñā bodhisattvas*, and the four *pūjā bodhisattvas*, making a total of twenty-nine deities.

The *Vajra* Circle is surrounded by three squares:

In the first square are the four *mahā-devis* (great deities), representing the four elements: fire (a), water (b), wind (c), and earth (d). They are called the four *Vajra* Circle-supporting deities. The fifth element, space, is represented by the *Vajra* Circle itself, and the sixth, mind, by the whole assembly.

In the second square are one thousand deities, representing the 'eternal present' (*bhadrakalpa*) *bodhisattvas*, revealed by the five Buddhas. In addition, in the four corners of the second square are: Vajradhūpā, incense (1); Vajrapuṣpā, flower (2); Vajrālokā, light (3); and Vajragandhā, perfume (4). These are the four female *pūjā bodhisattvas* (of the exterior, i.e., outside the Vajra Circle) offered to Mahāvairocana by the four Buddhas. Between the four female *pūjā bodhisattvas* are: Vajrāṇkuśa, hook (5); Vajrapāśa, rope (6); Vajrasphoṭa, chain (7); and Vajrāveśa, bell (8). These are the four *saṃgraha* (virtue-embracing) *bodhisattvas* offered to the four Buddhas by Mahāvairocana. The four Buddhas offer Mahāvairocana the virtues of benevolence; in turn, Mahāvairocana offers the four Buddhas the instruments to subdue *māra* to help them develop four kinds of virtue, which are: the offering of the Dharma and material things to benefit others (*dāna*); affectionate speech to invite all sentient beings to the realm of the Dharma (*priyavacana*); action—based on body, voice and mind—designed to benefit others (*arthakṛtya*); and the transforming of the body so that one can work with others and provoke their enlightenment on their own terms (*samānārthatā*). Thus, the four *pūjā bodhisattvas* (of the exterior) and the four *saṃgraha bodhisattvas* are collectively called the 'eight-pillar' *bodhisattvas*. They are the supporting elements of the *Vajra* Circle. The mission of the deities in this square is to enlighten all beings. Compassion is the means to enlighten them. Compassion is derived from *prajñā* and *samādhi*. *Prajñā* is represented by the sixteen *samādhi bodhisattvas*, i.e., the four *pāramitā bodhisattvas* of Mahāvairocana, the eight *pūjā bodhisattvas* (four interior and four exterior) of the five Buddhas, and the four *saṃgraha bodhisattvas* of the four Buddhas.

In the third square are the twenty guardian deities classified into five-heavens at the four quarters, as described below:

Heaven	*East*	*West*	*South*	*North*
Supreme	Nārāyaṇa	Āditya	Rākṣasa	Jaya
Space-dwelling	Kumāra	Candra	Vāyu	Vināyaka
Space-travelling	Vajrachinna	Vajrabhakṣaṇa	Vajravāsin	Vajramukha
Earth-dwelling	Brāhmaṇa	Ketu	Angi	Varuṇa
Beneath earth	Śakra	Piṅgala	Vaiśravaṇa	Yama

The function of these deities is to protect the *Vajra* Circle and its two encircling realms.

The *Karma* Assembly therefore is the basis of all other assemblies. It consists of the five Buddhas, sixteen *prajñā bodhisattvas*, and sixteen *samādhi bodhisattvas*, who collectively constitute the thirty-seven deities. Their mission is to reveal the Secret Buddha, Mahāvairocana. The thirty-seven deities are arranged in a chart below:

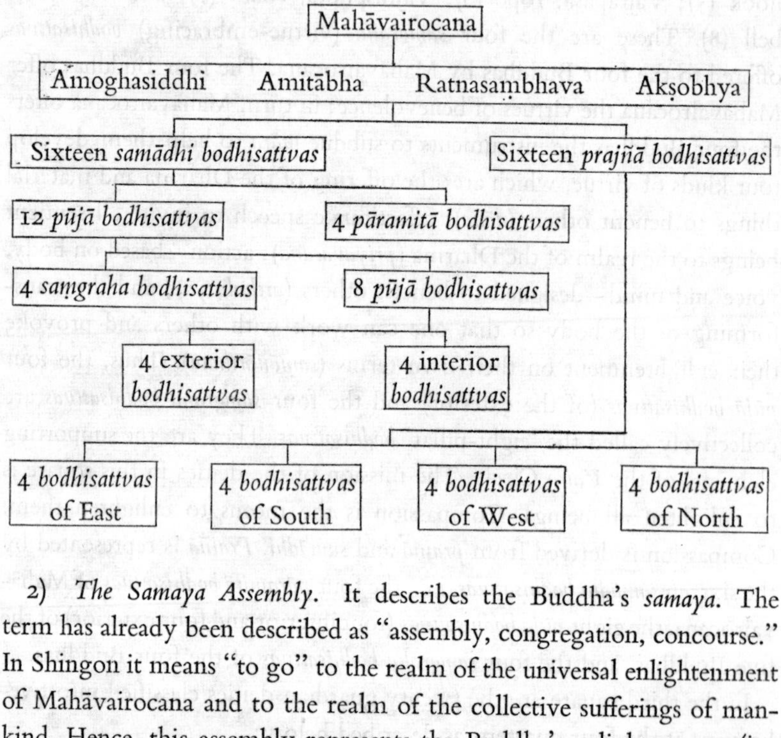

2) *The Samaya Assembly*. It describes the Buddha's *samaya*. The term has already been described as "assembly, congregation, concourse." In Shingon it means "to go" to the realm of the universal enlightenment of Mahāvairocana and to the realm of the collective sufferings of mankind. Hence, this assembly represents the Buddha's enlightenment (i.e. the vow to enlighten all beings).

3) *The Sūkṣma Assembly*. *Sūkṣma* means "fine, minute, subtle." Here it means the subtle wisdom of the Buddhas which is employed to enlighten all beings.

4) *The Pūjā Assembly*. *Pūjā* means "veneration, reverence, worship." Deities in this assembly offer articles to the five Buddhas, each article

representing a specific vow and each vow representing a specific method to enlighten all beings.

5) *The Four Mudrā Assembly*. *Mudrā* is a sign or seal. Here it refers to the finger signs of the Buddhas, representing their respective *jñāna*.

Let us pause here for a moment to review the contents of the four previous assemblies. The four previous assemblies described four specific attributes (*jñānas*) of *Dharmakāya* Mahāvairocana: *Mahā-jñāna* (the all-embracing *jñāna*), *samaya-jñāna* (the vow-*jñāna*), *Dharma-jñāna* (the *jñāna* expressed in words or letters) and *karma-jñāna* (the means-*jñāna*). The fifth assembly collects the attributes of the four previous assemblies. Hence, each of the *mudrās* of the four Buddhas represents one previous assembly. The relationship between the four Buddhas and their respective *jñāna* and *mudrā* is outlined below:

Buddha	*Jñāna*	*Mudrā*
Akṣobhya	*Ādarśa*	*Mahā-jñāna*
Ratnasaṃbhava	*Samatā*	*Samaya-jñāna*
Amitāyus	*Pratyavekṣanā*	*Dharma-jñāna*
Amoghasiddhi	*Kṛtyānuṣṭhāna*	*Karma-jñāna*

6) *The One Mudrā Assembly*. This represents the realm of *Dharmakāya* Mahāvairocana. The *jñāna*-fist-*mudrā*, (in full, the *jñānamuṣti-mudrā*), employed here, is the sign of the all-embracing Mahāvairocana.

Let us pause here again. The first for assemblies represented specific attributes of Mahāvairocana, the Four *Mudrā* Assembly collected the four assemblies into one. The One Mudrā Assembly synthesizes the four attributes of Mahāvairocana. The idea of four-assemblies-in-one or four *jñānas*-in-one is the Shingon way of expressing that all things are of Mahāvairocana and from Mahāvairocana emerge all things. In the *jñānamuṣti-mudrā*, the five left fingers symbolize the first five elements—four fingers are folded, while the index finger which symbolizes the wind element, points up, indicating life. The right fingers which represent the five *jñānas*, enwrap the left index finger, symbolizing that the elements of life are embraced by *Buddhajñānas*. One *mudrā* is the sign of non-duality (of man and the Buddha), the theoretical basis for realizing Buddhahood in the present body.

7) *The Naya Assembly.* This is the realm of Vajrasattva, representing *bodhicitta,* the emanation of Mahāvairocana as reflected on the mind of man. *Naya* means "path, method, or means" to enlightenment. In this assembly, Vajrasattva, occupying the central seat, is surrounded by the following four *bodhisattvas:*[17] Iṣṭavajra, Kelikilavajra, Rāgavajra, and Mānavajra, respectively, representing delusions derived from the four *kleśas*—lust, touch, craving, and conceit. These four *kleśas* are considered enlightenment material. That is, although the mind (*bodhicitta*) is inherently pure, it is enwrapped by the four *kleśas.* Therefore eliminating the four *kleśas* is the essential path to realize *bodhicitta.* The four bodhisattvas are forms of personified *kleśas,* the 'enlightenment materials,' symbolizing the kind of practice required to realize enlightenment.

8) *The Trailokyavijayakarma Assembly.* Trailokyavijayarāja, an incarnation of Vajrasattva, is the central deity of this assembly. Vajrasattva's virtue is compassion, but he reveals himself as Trailokyavijayarāja to subdue the three poisons (hate, greed and delusion). Trailokyavijayarāja, representing anger against evil, is three faced and three eyed to observe and detect greed, hate and delusion. He is surrounded by the fire of *prajñā* to burn *kleśa,* is equipped with tusks to cut off *kleśa,* has in his hands the *vajra* scepter, bow and arrows, rope and sword (which are the instruments to conquer evil). He tramples on the male demon Maheśvara with his left foot and the female demon Umā with his right.

9) *The Trailokyavijayasamaya Assembly.* Whereas the Trailokyavijayakarma Assembly described the physical activities of Trailokyavijayarāja, this assembly describes his vow (to enlighten all beings).

The Vajradhātu *Maṇḍala* is a graphic representation describing the methods by which the Buddhas and their supporting *bodhisattvas* attempt to enlighten all beings. The manner in which it has been described illustrates the 'effect-to-cause' (Buddha-to-man) process. By reversing the process, that is, by beginning from Trailokyavijayasamaya and terminating at Karma, we can similarly describe the 'cause-to-effect' (man-to-Buddha) process. In this case, the Trailokyavijayasamaya Assembly (9), the point of departure, is the station where a sentient being awakens to realize the compassion of the Buddhas and thereby becomes aware of his inherent *bodhicitta.* At the Trailokyavijayakarma Assembly (8), he eliminates *kleśa;* at the *Naya* Assembly (7), he realizes that *kleśa* are the very materials through which enlightenment can be realized; at the One *Mudrā* Assembly (6), he realizes that because *kleśas* are the materials to realize *bodhicitta,* man is potentially a Buddha; at the Four *Mudrā* Assembly (5), he realizes the four attributes of Mahāvairocana simultaneously; at the *Pūjā* (4), *Sūkṣma* (3), and *Samaya* (2) Assemblies, he realizes the four attributes individually; and at the *Karma* Assembly (1), he realizes Buddhahood. The *Karma, Samaya, Sūkṣma* and *Pūjā* Assemblies correspond, respectively, to the four *maṇḍalas*—the *Mahā, Samaya, Dharma,* and *Karma Maṇḍalas.* In short, the Four *Mudrā* and the One *Mudrā* Assemblies collect and synthesize, respectively, the four attributes of the four *maṇḍalas.* The *Naya* Assembly awakens *bodhicitta,* the Trailokyavijayakarma and Trailokyavijayasamaya Assemblies, respectively, enlighten others and self. To summarize, an outline is presented below:

Assembly	*Description*		
1. *Karma*	*Mahā-maṇḍala*	*Svabhāvacakrakāya*	*Tri-cakrakāya*
2. *Samaya*	*Samaya-maṇḍala*		
3. *Sūksma*	*Dharma-maṇḍala*		
4. *Pūjā*	*Karma-maṇḍala*		
5. Four *Mudrā*	Collecting four *maṇḍalas*		
6. One *Mudrā*	Synthesizing four *maṇḍalas*		
7. *Naya*	Awakening *bodhicitta*	*Saddharmacakrakāya*	
8. Trailokya-vijayakarma	Enlightenment of others	*Ādeśanācakrakāya*	
9. Trailokya-vijayasamaya	Enlightenment of self		

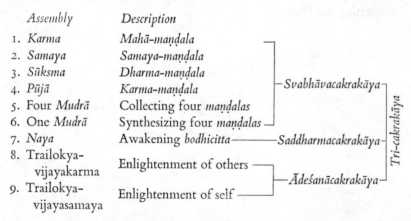

Shingon conceives three Dharma-wheel-bodies (*tri-cakrakāyas*): Mahāvairocana *per se* (*svabhāvacakrakāya*); the *bodhisattvas* representing the attributes of Mahāvairocana through compassion (*saddharmacakrakāya*); and the *bodhisattvas* representing the attributes of Mahāvairocana through compassionate anger (*ādeśanācakrakāya*). The first six assemblies represent *svabhāvacakrakāya,* the seventh *saddharmacakrakāya,* the eighth and ninth *ādeśanācakrakāya.*

4. Conclusion

Shingon *Mikkyō* is both a *mantra* school and a *maṇḍala* school. In Kūkai's own words, "The *maṇḍala* is the body of the secret teaching."[18] All that needs to be said of the Shingon concept of Buddha is contained within the *Garbhakośadhātu* and *Vajradhātu Maṇḍalas*. These two *maṇḍalas* identify the marks of *tathatā*, personify them into various types of enlightenment bodies (three or four), assign special signs or *mudrās* to them, and explain the nature of Mahāvairocana and his relation to man (i.e. the cyclic feedback between man and the Buddha). These *maṇḍalas* represent the Shingon ideal, which is the actualization of the eternal Buddha—*Dharmakāya* Mahāvairocana—within one's own body. It is in this context—in the context of "I-in-Buddha" and "Buddha-in-me"—that Shingon claims that the *Dharmakāya per se* is capable of communicating the Dharma.

CHAPTER FIVE

THE PATH TO BUDDHAHOOD

1. Initial Awakening

The two *maṇḍalas—Garbhakośadhātu* and *Vajradhātu*—are iconographic representations of Shingon doctrine. Shingon doctrine is a theoretical explanation of the identity of man and the Buddha based upon the supposition of inherent Buddha-nature. The theory of the identity of man and the Buddha, however, represents the 'ideal'. Actually, man is a sentient being whose mind is covered by *kleśa*. He becomes aware of his own Buddha-nature only when he has eliminated *kleśa*. The awareness that *kleśa* covers the mind and of the need to eliminate *kleśa* involves a frustrating experience, for such an awareness frequently leads one to realize his own limitations and the futility of efforts to overcome *kleśa*. This means then that prior to the conceptual formulation of the very idea of implementing theory into practice, prior to translating the 'ideal' into the 'real', we must deal with the problem of human will: the determination to fully understand theory and the commitment to implement that theory into practice. Practice takes on a significant religious dimension and becomes personally meaningful only when it is supported by this kind of will.

Here we must remind ourselves that though practice, in the context described above, specifically refers to the practice to eliminate one's own *kleśa*, the elimination of *kleśa* (e.g. hate) cannot be accomplished only through a realization of a new conceptual horizon (e.g. non-hate). Mental state does indeed shape action but action in turn shapes mental state. The perfection of a state of non-hate requires not only the elimination of the notion of hate but also the practice of non-hate. It is in this context that we speak of the importance of will, the determination to understand theory and the commitment to implement that theory into practice. Shingon refers to the awakening of this kind of will as 'awakening *bodhicitta*' (*bodhicitta-utpanna*). *Bodhicitta* means the 'thought of enlightenment'. We are now ready to discuss *bodhicitta* in more detail.

The awakening of *bodhicitta* takes place when one becomes aware of the futility of life calculated to satisfying the flesh and of the paradox involved in leading a wholesome life, and, most important of all, when one develops an intense desire, a determined will, to overcome this futility and paradox. This type of will presupposes that the nature of man is inherently pure, not defiled, that it is inherent with Buddha-nature. Awakening *bodhicitta* is based upon this kind of supposition. This supposition is important as it constitutes the basis of faith. So, what we have referred to as 'awakening *bodhicitta*' requires faith, the unconditional acceptance of the proposition that Buddha-nature is inherent in man. *Bodhicitta* and Buddha-nature then are synonymous. The awakening of *bodhicitta* is the realization of one's own Buddha-nature. Both require faith.

The *Bodhicitta Śāstra* describes the three attributes of *bodhicitta:* supreme truth, compassion and meditation.[1] Supreme truth refers to insight into emptiness, which is wisdom; compassion refers to the practice of emptiness, which is the implementation of wisdom on an empirical level; meditation refers to the internalized discipline required to cultivate wisdom and practice, both supplementing one another, for there can be no wisdom without practice and no practice without wisdom. In this context then, meditation is the agent of integrating wisdom and practice. We can now see that *bodhicitta,* as was in the case with Buddha-nature, represents the 'middle' expressed in soteriological terms. Here the term 'soteriological' involves an experiential connotation simply because inasmuch as it represents the 'middle', salvation is not understood within the limits of a noetic context. It is not simply a matter of apprehension. It is to be realized experientially, that is, it involves faith in the inherent 'good' in the essential makeup of man and the empirical demonstration, which is practice, of that inherent quality.

Faith essentially means belief (*śraddhā*) in and the perfect understanding (*adhimukti*) of Buddha-nature. But as an object of intellectual investigation, that is, as an object of discriminative conceptualization, Buddha-nature—being the 'middle'—does not exist. In fact it is not an object of intellectual investigation. Nevertheless, Buddha-nature is that which is sought by one who has become aware of the futility and paradox of life and has become deeply sensitive to the tragic problems of mankind. Kūkai therefore defines faith in Buddha-nature as "the awareness of the inherent quality within all men which can be discovered by penetrating beneath the consciousness level dominated by the 'seeds' of greed, hate and delusion."[2] The *Nirvāṇa Sūtra* says, "Buddha-nature is the great faith . . . Because all sentient beings are destined to realize it, we call it the universal nature of Buddhahood."[3] But this inherent and universal quality is real only to those who have come to understand the limits of the intellect in pursuit of an existential insight—the paradox one faces in pursuit of his authentic being. Shingon faith bears remarkable resemblance to what Friedrich E. Schleiermacher referred to as *schlechthinniges abhängigkeitsgefühl*, that is, that faith is beyond self-awareness, beyond the object of intellectualization. But though faith is beyond self-awareness, the self is the basis of discovering the authentic situation of one's own beingness; though faith is beyond the intellect, it is through the intellect that 'faith and undersatnding' are awakened.

How then is *bodhicitta*, which has been awakened in this manner, cultivated to maturation? In response to this question, Kūkai refers to the triple formula of the *Mahāvairocana Sūtra*, which says, "*Bodhicitta* is the cause; the great compassion is its roots; and skillful means is the end result."[4] This *sūtra* explains *prajñā*, the state of mind which cognizes supreme truth, by comparing it to a seed, which requires the condition to establish its roots and to produce fruit. *Bodhicitta* is the cause (seed) of wisdom, and compassion (i.e. practice) is the condition which enables that cause to bear fruit. *Bodhicitta* cannot be awakened without compassion, the conditioner which brings about Buddhahood. The triple formula articulates the theory of the primacy of practical reason (*primat der praktischen vernunft*). It is the Shingon version of what Schleiermacher referred to as *guterlehre*, the theory of good. In other words, though awakening *bodhicitta* is essential to practice, practice at the same time is the conditioner which cultivates the maturation of the awakened *bodhicitta*. What then constitutes practice?

2. Practice

The 'mind just as it is' is a phrase found in the *Mahāvairocana Sūtra.*[5] The term is synonymous to what the *Awakening of Mahāyāna Faith* refers to as 'inherent enlightenment'. The *Nirvāṇa Sūtra* calls it Buddha-nature, the *Prajñāpāramitā* literature calls it *prajñā*, the *Sukhāvatīvyūha* literature calls it Pure Land. In all these texts, the premise is that the 'original state of mind' is pure and undefiled. It becomes defiled because of *vijñānas*, the instruments that fragment the world into arbitrary conceptual categories. The realm perceived through *vijñānas* is therefore a delusion because *kleśa* is inherent in *vijñānas*. The original state of mind is revealed by eliminating *kleśa* and cultivating *bodhicitta*, the process of which is explained in terms of: a) three *kalpas*, b) six *nirbhayas*, and c) ten *bhūmis*. The first is designed to eliminate *kleśa* which covers *bodhicitta;* the second is designed to cultivate *bodhicitta* and to prevent its contamination by *kleśa;* the third reveals *bodhicitta*. The first two represent the Shingon theory of elimination (*shajō-mon*); the third represents the Shingon theory of revelation (*hyōtoku-mon*). What is eliminated is *kleśa;* what is revealed is *bodhicitta*. These three theories describe the process of the growth of *bodhicitta*. Each shall be described categorically.

a) *The Three Kalpas*. The term 'three *kalpa*' actually means an immeasurable duration of time (*tri-mahāsaṃkhyeya-kalpa*).[6] However, Shingon interprets the term as the three basic substances of the mind which grasp the unreal (*mithyā-graha*):[7] the crude (*sthūla*), the subtle (*sūkṣma*), and the most subtle (*prasūkṣma*). The *Awakening of Mahāyāna Faith* describes these three substances as follows: ignorance-based action, the perceiving, and the perceived. The first is the basis of the latter two, the character of the latter two being conditioned by the first. In Shingon, the first *kalpa* refers to the crude, the second to the subtle, and the third to the most subtle. Shingon, for that reason, does not conceive *kalpa* as a duration of time. It conceives it as the substance of delusion. This leads to a controversial issue which must be clarified before the Shingon concept of *kalpa* is described.

Disputes surrounding the abrupt versus gradual enlightenment are largely based upon the question of whether enlightenment is determined by the length of practice or not. According to Kūkai's system of doctrinal evaluation and classification, *Kengyō* affirms the *kalpa* (duration) requirement, though there is considerable dispute over whether Tendai and Kegon do.[8] Shingon theoretically presupposes inherent Buddhahood but in practice it nevertheless requires the *tri-guhya* meditation and claims that practice is the actualizing of the theory that man is inherently endowed with Buddhahood. In practice, therefore, there is no difference between Shingon *Mikkyō* and *Kengyō*, but the rationale involved in practice is different. More specifically, the two are different because of the interpretation of the term *kalpa*. As said before, Kengyō conceives *kalpa* as a duration of time. But *Mikkyō* conceives it as the substance of delusion, the premise being that enlightenment is not a matter to be realized in term of a duration of time. The Shingon interpretation of the three *kalpa* theory is described below.

The first *kalpa* corresponds to the delusion of grasping to the reality of self. This is a delusion because the self is empty of an essence (*pudgala-śūnyatā*). It is only a product of the five aggregates. According to Shingon, the *Śrāvaka* and *Pratyeka-buddha* (the fourth and fifth stages in Kūkai's system of doctrinal evaluation and classification) have transcended the first *kalpa* stage and have realized the emptiness of self.

The second *kalpa* corresponds to the delusion of grasping to the reality of dharmas. This is a delusion because dharmas are also empty of an essence (*dharma-śūnyatā*). According to Shingon, Hossō and Sanron (the sixth and the seventh stages) have transcended the second *kalpa* stage and have realized the emptiness of dharmas. Through the insight into emptiness, Hossō realized mind-onlyness and Sanron realized the middle-path.

The third *kalpa* corresponds to the delusion of grasping to ignorance (*avidyā*). This is the delusion of distinguishing dharmas in terms of the conditioned and the unconditioned. According to Shingon, Tendai and Kegon (the eighth and ninth stages) have transcended the third *kalpa* stage and have realized the synthesis of the conditioned and the unconditioned. Through this synthesis Tendai realized the realm of *tathatā*, while Kegon and Shingon realized the realm of *Dharmadhātu*.

The Shingon three *kalpa* theory, as it is now apparent, is a categorization of Buddhism into Hīnayāna, Triyāna and Ekayāna. Hīnayāna refers to the *śrāvaka* and *pratyeka-buddha* vehicles; Triyāna, literally the 'three vehicles', distinguishes the *śrāvaka, pratyeka-buddha*, and *bodhisattva* vehicles and claims the superiority of the *bodhisattva* vehicle; Ekayāna does not discriminate the three but encompasses all three within its all-embracing universal vehicle. In terms of Kūkai's ten stage doctrinal classification scheme, Hīnayāna refers to the fourth and fifth (stages before the fourth are pre-Buddhist), the *śrāvaka* and *pratyeka-buddha* vehicles; Triyāna refers to the sixth and seventh, the Hossō and Sanron; and Ekayāna refers to the eighth and ninth, Tendai and Kegon. These are *Kengyō* schools indicating *Kengyō* paths. The tenth, Shingon, is also Ekayāna but it is *Mikkyō*, not *Kengyō*. An explanation now follows.

Though Hossō (Yogācāra-vijñānavāda) and Sanron (Mādhyamika) form the two basic philosophical systems of Mahāyāna, Kūkai classified them below Tendai and Kegon. The former two present a world of synthesis, but they are nonetheless a synthesis based on the concept of the transformation of *ālaya* into *ādarśa-jñāna*—the transformation of the store of delusion to pure mind—in the case of Hossō, and insight into the eight negations in the case of Sanron. Both have yet to deal with the complex dimension of *Dharmadhātu*, the world of the infinite co-arising (continuity) of *dharmas* based on the doctrine of the emptiness of a *dharma*-essence. *Dharmadhātu* is a world of an organic living entity within which the *dharmas* absent of an essence continue to co-arise. Tendai and Kegon provide this infinite dimension. But Kūkai preferred the Kegon world of infinite interpenetration of *dharmas*, rather than the Mādhyamika-based Tendai description of three-truths (emptiness, co-arising, middle)-in-one type of a world-view.

Doctrinally, Kegon and Shingon are closely related. What distinguishes the two is the interpretation of *Dharmadhātu.* The *Kegon Sūtra* (*Avataṃsaka,* Ch. *Hua-yen*) describes *Dharmadhātu* (the realm of enlightenment) from the cause-realm, that is, it explains and establishes the causes to realize *Dharmadhātu,* as the case of the legendary Sudhana-śreṣṭhi-dāraka (literally, the merchant's son, who, in this text, is the 'seeker of truth') going through the fifty-two stages to realize enlightenment clearly demonstrates. This distinction is important. Shingon, unlike Kegon, does not speak of one becoming a Buddha (a concept which presupposes a duration of time), because it presupposes that one already is a Buddha, that inherent in him is Buddha-nature. Thus Shingon practice has meaning only to those who are aware of his Buddha-nature. It is not a practice to realize Buddha-nature. Shingon practice is the revelation of Buddhahood in a concrete context—the attributes indicated by the six elements, four *maṇḍalas,* and three secrets. We must now refer back to the gradual and sudden enlightenment theories. The process of enlightenment is gradual, but once enlightened, one realizes that that very moment is abrupt, sudden and direct—like a flash of lightning. Shingon enlightenment—consisting of the awareness of one's inherent *bodhicitta*—refers to the latter. Shingon therefore claims that Kegon, though of the highest among Kengyō schools, does not describe *Dharmadhātu* as concretely as does Shingon. Nevertheless, as mentioned before, Shingon, like Tendai and Kegon, is Ekayāna. Ekayāna transcends the three *kalpa* stages. One who has transcended the three *kalpa* stages realizes *Dharmadhātu,* the realm of the enlightenment of the Buddha. Hence, Śubhākarasiṃha's *Commentary on the Mahāvairocana Sūtra* says,

> If one transcends the three graspings in one's life-time, then in the present life he shall realize Buddhahood. Why should the duration of time be discussed?[9]

b) *The Six Nirbhayas. Nirbhaya* literally means "fearlessness." In Shingon it means mental peace. It is synonymous with *āśvāsa,* "to revive."[10] *Nirbhaya* means a state of awakening through freeing oneself from the bonds of *kleśa* and awakening to realize one's inherent *bodhi.*[11] The six *nirbhaya* theory analyzes the process of awakening. This process is explained in six progressive stages, each consisting of a *Kengyō* and *Mikkyō* interpretation as presented below:

Sannirbhaya, the stage of virtuous deeds. This is the fearless stage where one frees himself from the dictates of passion, develops a feeling for humanity, and observes moral principles. This is the pre-Buddhist stage. In Shingon it corresponds to a stage where the practitioner comes to realize the need to perform the *tri-guhya* meditation.

Kāya-nirbhaya, the stage of eliminating the impurity of the body. Here one realizes the Buddha-path, a realm beyond moral prinicples. One meditates on the impurity of the body, rids himself of body-*kleśa*, and realizes liberation from the delusion of grasping to the notion of the reality of self. This is the *śrāvaka* stage. In Shingon it corresponds to a stage where the *tri-guhya* practitioner visualizes his presiding deity.

Nairātmya-nirbhaya, the stage of realizing the emptiness of self. One who has liberated himself from the delusion of grasping to the reality of self now also liberates himself from the notion of possession (the *kāya-nirbhaya* and the *nairātmya-nirbhaya* eliminate the notions of the 'I' and 'mine', respectively). This is also a *śrāvaka* stage. In Shingon, it corresponds to a stage where the *tri-guhya* practitioner, who has perfected visualizing his presiding deity, is no longer obsessed by it.

Dharma-nirbhaya, the stage of realizing the emptiness of *dharmas*. Here one realizes that the five aggregates which make up the mind and body are in themselves empty of an essence. (*Kāya-nirbhaya* and *nairātmya-nirbhaya* dealt with the emptiness associated with self; *dharma-nirbhaya* deals with the emptiness of *dharmas*.) This is the *pratyeka-buddha* stage. In Shingon, it corresponds to a stage where the *tri-guhya* practitioner realizes that the presiding deity is empty of an essence and is markless (*alakṣaṇa*). Specifically he meditates and realizes that the deity is like a moon in the water, the image in a mirror.

Dharma-nairātmya-nirbhaya, the stage of emptiness of dharmas and self. Here one realizes liberation from all *dharmas*, gains insight into the world of emptiness, and conceives the world to be a mental construction. This is the stage of Hossō and Sanron. In Shingon it corresponds to a stage where the *tri-guhya* practitioner realizes that the presiding deity is a mark of one's own mind cultivated through meditation. (All other Buddhas and *bodhisattvas* are also marks; the term 'mark' in this context, should be interpreted as 'mental qualities'.)

Samatā-nirbhaya, the stage of unity (*sarva-dharma-svabhāva-samatā*). Here one no longer distinguishes between the supreme and the conventional, the mind (*citta*) and its attributes (*vijñānas*). It is the stage of the unity of diversity, since all dharmas are essentially interrelated because of the principle of emptiness and co-arising. This is the *Ekayāna* stage—Tendai, Kegon and Shingon. In Shingon the practitioner gains an insight into the source of the unity of diversity by realizing *anutpāda,* the original state of mind.

As previously mentioned, the three *kalpa* theory is designed to eliminate *kleśa* which conceals *bodhicitta,* while the six *nirbhaya* theory is designed to cultivate *bodhicitta.* The relationship between the three *kalpa,* six *nirbhaya* and Kūkai's ten stages is outlined below:

Three Kalpas	*Six Nirbhayas*	*Ten Stages*
First	*Sannirbhaya*	First Second Third
	Kāya- *Nairātmya-*	Fourth
	Dharma-	Fifth
Second	*Dharma-nairātmya-*	Sixth Seventh
Third	*Samatā-*	Eighth Ninth Tenth

3. *Daśabhūmi*

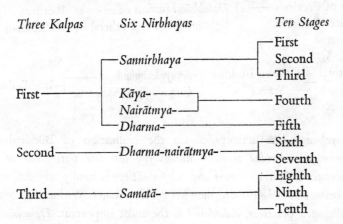

Mahāyāna is a *bodhisattva* doctrine. A Mahāyāna *bodhisattva,* as previously mentioned, is a "universal savior." He is interested in enlightening others as well as himself. The general classification of the *bodhisattva* stages, according to *Kengyō,* is as follows: a) ten stages of faith, b) ten stages of understanding, c) ten stages of practice, d) ten stages of transferring merit, e) ten stages of *bodhisattva per se* (*daśabhūmi*), and, f) the two Buddha stages, supreme enlightenment (*samyaksaṃbuddha*) and the most supreme enlightenment (*uttara-samyaksaṃbuddha*). These *bodhisattva* stages make a total of fifty-two, as outlined below:

Cause to Realize *Bodhisattvahood*	a) Ten Stages of Faith (in the Buddha, Dharma, and *Saṅgha*)		Faith
	b) Ten Stages of Understanding (emptiness)		Understanding
	c) Ten Stages of Practice (of enlightening self)		Practice
	d) The Stages of Transferring Merit (i.e. enlightening others)		Practice
Effect of Previous Practices (hence, *Bodhisattva* practices)	e) *Daśabhūmi* (union of enlightening self and others)		Realization (of *Bodhisattva*)
Sum total of cause and effect	f) Two Buddha Stages	*Samyaksaṃbuddha*	Buddhahood
		Uttarasamyaksaṃbuddha	Buddhahood

Samyaksaṃbuddha actually means the realization of Buddhahood. *Uttarasamyaksaṃbuddha* actually means the ultimate perfection of the practices to enlighten oneself and others. There is hardly any difference at all between *daśabhūmi* and the two Buddha stages. Within the context of *bodhisattva* practices, *daśabhūmi* is the most important. *Daśabhūmi* is a Mahāyāna term and a compound made up of '*daśa*', meaning ten, and '*bhūmi*', literally "earth." Earth signifies the producer and the container of wisdom, and the carrier and the nurturer of all beings. *Daśabhūmi* consists of stages designed to realize the union of self enlightenment and the enlightenment of others. It exemplifies *bodhisattva* practices. It is categorically described below:[12]

1) *Pramuditā*, the joyful stage. This is the stage of realizing Buddha-

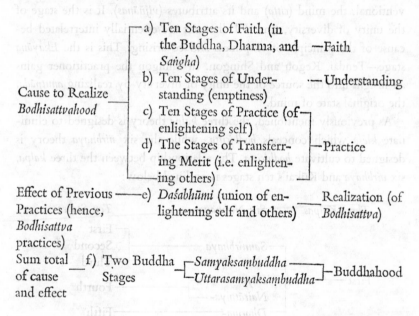

knowledge. Buddha-knowledge is realized by: a) severing misleading views, and b) gaining insight into emptiness.

a. Misleading views are:
   i) reality of self (*satkāya*)
   ii) extreme views (*antargrāha*) which consist of the notions of impermanence (*uccheda*) and permanence (*śāśvata*)
   iii) perverted views (*mithyā*) such as rejecting the law of cause and effect
   iv) the affirmation of the above three views (*dṛṣti-parāmarśa*)
   v) offense against morality (*śīla-vrata-parāmarśa*)
   vi) greed (*rāga*)
   vii) hate (*vyāpāda*)
   viii) delusion (*moha*)
   ix) conceit (*māna*)
   x) doubt (*vicikitsā*)

b. Gaining insight into emptiness means the realization of the emptiness of self and *dharmas*.

The stages enumerated below constitute a breakdown of items inherent in the first stage.

2) *Vimalā*, the immaculate stage. This is the stage of eliminating misleading thoughts. Misleading thoughts consist of greed, hate, delusion, conceit, and doubt. Though these five items have been enumerated under misleading views, the five items of the misleading view and of the misleading thought categories have roots in different sources. Misleading views are acquired, meaning that they are rooted in the power of human reasoning; misleading thoughts are innate, meaning that they are rooted in the sense organs and the sense fields. The former can be eliminated more easily than the latter, but has its roots in the latter. This is the stage where one eliminates misleading thoughts. Hence it is called the immaculate stage. Immaculate means purification. Purification (of the mind) is perfected here.

3) *Prabhākarī*, the light-giving stage. Light means *prajñā*. The cultivation of *prajñā* requires patience. Patience (*kṣānti*) is perfected here.

4) *Arciṣmatī*, the brilliant stage. *Prajñā* is intensified by eliminating

the residual elements of *kleśa*. Eliminating residual elements requires effort. Effort (*virya*) is perfected here.

5) *Sudurjayā*, the difficult-to-conquer stage. The union of supreme and conventional truths is realized. It is realized through meditation (*dhyāna*). *Dhyāna* is perfected here.

6) *Abhimukhī*, the *prajñā*-revealed stage. Meditation produces *prajñā*. *Prajñā* is perfected here.

7) *Dūraṃgamā*, the far-reaching stage. Far-reaching means improvising skillful means. This is the stage of putting *prajñā* into practice. Skillful means (*upāya*) is perfected here.

8) *Acalā*, the immovable stage. Immovable refers to a vow. The vow (*praṇidhāna*) to enlighten all beings is perfected here.

9) *Sādhumatī*, the unerring-effect stage. The vow must be supported by a power which translates it into the actual practice of enlightening all beings under all conditions, at all times, and without error. Power (*bala*) is perfected here.

10) *Dharma-meghā*, the dharma-cloud stage. The wisdom perfected in the previous stages reveals itself equitably and universally, giving joy to all beings, like a cloud appearing after a drought. This is the stage of the perfect cognition of reality (*Dharmadhātu*).

Whereas *Kengyō* regards *daśabhūmi* as the cause-stage to Buddhahood, Shingon's interpretation of it consists of two general theories: a) practice, and b) inherent.

a) The practice theory consists of two types: *a kleśa*-eliminating theory, and a *bodhicitta*-revealing theory. The first theory holds that though the elements of grasping (crude, subtle, and most subtle) have been eliminated in the pre-*daśabhūmi* stages, the basic ignorance (*avidyā*) which obstructs a practitioner from realizing *bodhicitta*—the 'grasping atom'—still needs to be eliminated stage-by-stage. The second theory presupposes that the three elements of grasping have been eliminated at the pre-*daśabhūmi* stages; it does not speak of a 'grasping atom'. It conceives the first stage of *daśabhūmi* to be the basis of self-enlightenment and the stages which follow as those implementing the knowledge acquired through self-enlightenment for the benefit of others. The first is designed to eliminate the elements (*kleśa*) concealing *bodhicitta*, the second to reveal the merits of one's own *bodhicitta*. Both theories conceive *daśabhūmi* in stages.

b) The inherent theory is based upon the notion that all things are implicit in one. This notion, again, is not an original idea of Kūkai. It is Ekayāna. The *Śrimālādevīsiṃhanāda-sūtra* claims that all facets of morality are implicit in the *bodhisattva* practice of enlightening others, Tendai claims that three thousand worlds are implicit in one instant thought, and Kegon speaks of the theory of 'all-in-one'. In Japan, schools of Kamakura Buddhism articulated the same theme: Zen claims that the three disciplines (*śīla*, *samādhi*, *prajñā*) are implicit in Zen and develops Zen discipline, Pure Land claims that all practices are implicit in faith and develops a 'one-directed' faith in the Buddha Amitābha, and Nichiren claims that all knowledges are implicit in the Lotus Dharma and develops the *daimoku* (the chanting of the title of the *Lotus Sūtra*) formula. The Shingon inherent theory presupposes that *bodhicitta* is inherent in the practitioner. As such, it does not conceive *daśabhūmi* to be stages of practice. The numeral ten, following the Kegon tradition, is interpreted as inexhaustible. *Daśabhūmi* therefore is interpreted as the manifestation of the inexhaustible merits of *bodhicitta*. Implicit in this theory is the idea that the first embodies all other stages, that all stages are implicit in the first. Hence Shingon speaks of '*shoji soku goku*', "the first as the final."[13] Reference is to the *bodhicitta*, the repository of inexhaustible merits.

The practice theory (inclusive of the *kleśa*-eliminating and *bodhicitta*-revealing theories) and the inherent theory are both based upon a positional difference in viewing man and enlightenment. The practice theory presupposes that man is inherently defiled and prescribes stages to remove man's *kleśa* and to reveal his *bodhicitta:* it involves a gradual method to realize enlightenment; it sees enlightenment from the sphere of man. The inherent theory presupposes that man is inherently enlightened: it does not reject the validity of the practice theory; it considers practice a necessary means to realize one's inherent inexhaustible merit; it sees enlightenment from the sphere of the enlightened one.

Daśabhūmi is modeled upon the six perfection (*pāramitā*) theory. The six are developed into ten in the *Prajñāpāramitā* literature. *Daśabhūmi* corresponds to the ten *pāramitās*. The six *pāramitās* are: charity (*dāna*), morality (*śīla*), patience (*kṣānti*), effort (*virya*), meditation (*dhyāna*) and wisdom (*prajñā*). In its *Ekayāna* context, *prajñā* embraces all other *pāramitās*. That is, *prajñā* is meditation, the source which perfects charity. Charity is not the mere offering of material goods; it is, as the *Śrimālādevīsiṃhanāda -sūtra* says, "the giving of body, life, and possessions to spread the Dharma."[14] As such, charity is the external (social) manifestation of *prajñā* in a most dynamic way. A guide line is provided for that purpose—charity must be directed by morality and supported by the virtuous of patience and effort. *Prajñā* therefore embodies the five *paramitās* as shown below:

Elements inherent in prajñā

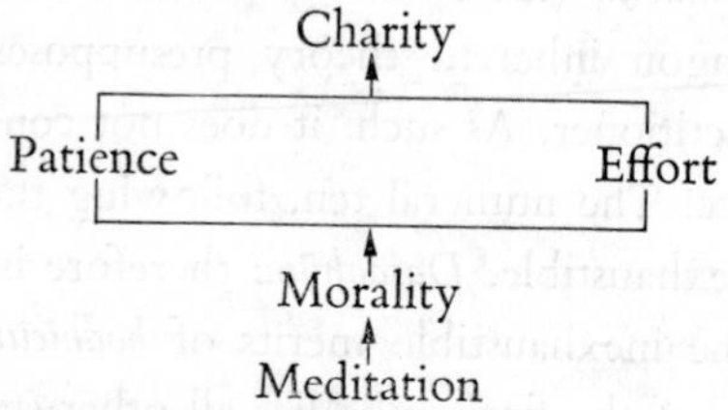

Prajñā embodies the five *pāramitās*, and the six *pāramitās* (*prajñā* plus the five) are expanded into ten. The four additional *pāramitās* are descriptive items of *prajñā:* 7) skillful means (*upāya*), 8) the vow to enlighten all beings (*praṇidhāna*), 9) the power to enlighten all beings (*bala*), and 10) the perfect cognition of reality (*jñāna*). Shingon identifies the first five *pāramitās* (charity, morality, patience, effort, and meditation) as items of self-cultivation; the last four (skillful means, vow, power, and perfect cognition) as instruments to benefit others. Some items overlap but the first five of the ten are internalized disciplines, the last four are external expressions of the first four. All *pāramitās* are implied in the sixth, *prajñā*.

4. The Organic Relation between the *Pāramitās* and *Daśabhūmi* and Shingon's Interpretation of the *Daśabhūmi*

The six *pāramitās*, ten *pāramitās*, and *daśabhūmi* are paths designed to realize Buddhahood through self cultivation and to implement that which has been cultivated to benefit others. The relationship between the six *pāramitās* and the *daśabhūmi* is outlined below:

Basic Three-stage Path to Enlichtenment	*Six Pāramitās*	*Daśabhūmi*
Understanding		1. *Pramuditā* (Joyful Stage)
Practice	Five *Pāramitās* (Accumulating merit)	2. *Vimalā* (Immaculate Stage)
		3. *Prabhākarī* (Light-giving Stage)
		4. *Arciṣmatī* (Brilliant Stage)
		5. *Sudurjayā* (Difficult-to-conquer Stage)
		6. *Abhimukhī* (*Prajnā*-revealed Stage)
	Dāna Pāramitā (Transferring merit)	7. *Dūramgamā* (Far-reaching Stage)
		8. *Acalā* (Immovable Stage)
		9. *Sādhumatī* (Unerring Effect Stage)
Realization		10. *Dharmameghā* (Dharma-cloud Stage)

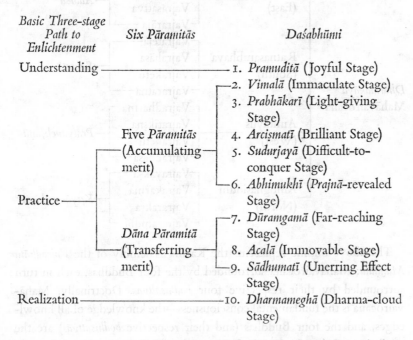

Insofar as the itemized description of the *daśabhūmi* is concerned, there is no difference whatsoever between *Kengyō* and *Mikkyō*. What distinguishes the two is the interpretation of *daśabhūmi per se: Kengyō* conceives *daśabhūmi* as graded stages of practice; Shingon *Mikkyō* conceives it as the embodiment of a variety of virtues, not stages to eliminate something (such as *kleśa*) or to gain something (such as *prajñā*). Hence it is the realm of enlightenment—*Dharmakāya.* Enlightenment is described iconographically: the four Buddhas (Akṣobhya, Ratnasaṃbhava, Amitāyus, and Amoghasiddhi),[15] each with his four attending *bodhisattvas* (totalling sixteen), represent the four attributes (*jñānas*) of *Dharmakāya* Mahāvairocana. The following chart is an outline of the iconographic model of the Shingon version of the realm of enlightenment—the *Dharmakāya.*

	Four Buddhas	*Sixteen Bodhisattvas*	*Four Jñānas*
Dharmakāya Mahāvairocana	Aksobhya (East)	Vajrasādhu, Vajrarāga, Vajrasattva, Vajrarāja	*Adarśa*
	Ratnasambhava (South)	Vajrateja, Vajrahāsa, Vajraketu, Vajraratna	*Samatā*
	Amitāyus (West)	Vajradharma, Vajratīkṣna, Vajrahetu, Vajrabhaṣa	*Pratyavekṣaṇā*
	Amoghasiddhi (North)	Vajrayakṣa, Vajrakarma, Vajrarakṣa, Vajrasaṃdhi	*Kṛtyānuṣṭhāna*

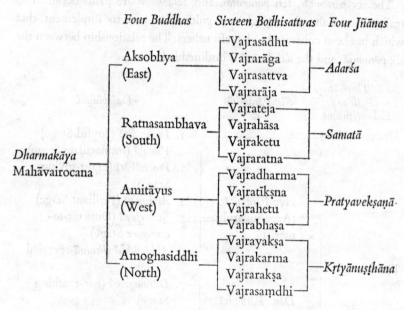

The above outline represents the Karma Assembly of the *Vajradhātu Maṇḍala:* Mahāvairocana surrounded by the four Buddhas, each in turn surrounded by their respective four *bodhisattvas.* Doctrinally, Mahāvairocana is the fundamental consciousness—the knowledge of all knowledges, and the four Buddhas (and their respective *bodhisattvas*) are the attributes of this fundamental consciousness (that is, *ādarśa-*, *samatā-*, *pratyavekṣaṇā-*, and *kṛtyānuṣṭhāna-jñānas*). The four Buddhas and their *bodhisattvas* are an iconographic representation of the attributes of *Dharmakāya* Mahāvairocana. Shingon employs the traditional *daśabhūmi* schema as a method to describe the contents of *bodhicitta,* the instrument upon which truth is reflected. *Daśabhūmi* in Shingon reveals the content of *bodhicitta.* But since Shingon presupposes that the awareness of *bodhicitta is* 'awakening' (the cause-realm), that enlightenment is the realm of *Dharmakāya* Mahāvairocana (the result-realm), and that the first *daśabhūmi* stage is really the final stage, it holds that the awareness of *bodhicitta* (the cause-realm) is enlightenment (the result-realm). Hence, the first *daśabhūmi* stage encompasses all *daśabhūmi* stages. It is not the first of many stages to realize a goal. It is the goal.

5. Summary on Practice

A summary on practice essentially means a summarization of the process of cultivating *bodhicittta*. The following chart summarizes that process in terms of: 1) the triple formula (Kūkai's version placed in parenthesis), 2) the six *nirbhaya* theory, 3) Shingon's ten stage classification, 4) the three *kalpa* theory, and 5) the *daśabhūmi* stages.

An Outline of Practices to Cultivate Bodhicitta

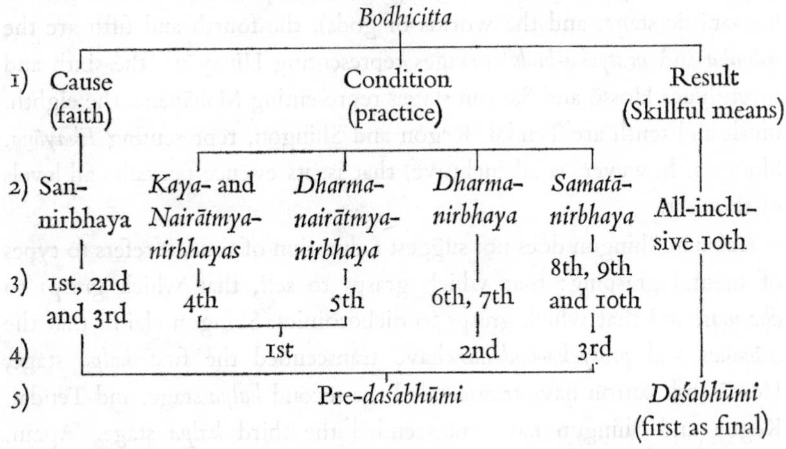

The triple formula of the *Mahāvairocana Sūtra*, the six *nirbhaya* theory, Shingon's ten stage classification, the three *kalpa* theory, and the *daśabhūmi* are means to explain that *bodhicitta* is inherent in all beings. The cultivation of *bodhicitta* then essentially means the awakening of the inherent *bodhicitta*.

Kūkai's version of the triple formula is that the awakening of *bodhicitta* (through faith) is the cause of enlightenment, that the practice of compassion is the condition which nurtures that cause which leads one to enlightenment, and that improvising skillful means to implement that compassion is the end result of that enlightenment.

The six *nirbhaya* theory shows the process of awakening to realize enlightenment, beginning from meditation, visualizing one's own presiding deity, not being obsessed with that deity, being aware of the emptiness of that deity, realizing that a deity is but a mental construction, and developing insight into the original state of mind.

The ten stage classification is based upon the six *nirbhaya* theory. The former is an elaboration of the latter. That is whereas the six *nirbhaya* theory is based upon an Indian religious model (i.e. on the *Mahāvairocana Sūtra*), the ten stage classification deals with both Indian and Chinese religious models. Hence, in the ten stage classification, the first, second and third are pre-Buddhist stages (that is, the pre-humanistic stage, the humanistic stage, and the worlds of gods), the fourth and fifth are the *śrāvaka* and *pratyeka-buddha* stages representing Hīnayāna, the sixth and seventh are Hossō and Sanron stages representing Mahāyāna, the eighth, ninth and tenth are Tendai, Kegon and Shingon, representing *Ekayāna*. Shingon, however, is all-inclusive, that is, its essence pervades all levels of thought.

Kalpa in Shingon does not suggest a duration of time, it refers to types of mental grasping: that which grasps to self, that which grasps to *dharmas*, and that which grasps to dichotomies. Shingon claims that the *śrāvakas* and *pratyeka-buddhas* have transcended the first *kalpa* stage, Hossō and Sanron have transcended the second *kalpa* stage, and Tendai, Kegon and Shingon have transcended the third *kalpa* stage. Again, Shingon is all-inclusive, its essence pervades all levels of *kalpa*.

Daśabhūmi is the *bodhisattva* practice stage. But Shingon claims that all *bodhisattva* stages are inherent in the first *daśabhūmi* stage, *pramuditā*, the stage of realizing Buddha knowledge. As such, it holds that the first nine of the ten stage classification are pre-*daśabhūmi* stages because they have not yet developed the theory that the first stage embodies all other stages. This does not mean that Shingon rejects other Mahāyāna-Ekayāna interpretations of *daśabhūmi*. It recognizes the validity of their interpretations, but because it holds to the triple formula theory—that improvising skillful means to implement compassion is the end result of enlightenment—it claims that all stages of *daśabhūmi* are inherent in the first stage of *daśabhūmi*. What Shingon means essentially is that one who has gone through the practices of the *daśabhūmi*, stage by stage, and has reached the final stages, then realizes that all stages are inherent in the first stage. The practice-stage theory is gradual and inductive, while the inherent theory is direct and intuitive.

So, in terms of the triple formula, skillful means is the ultimate result of the awakening of *bodhicitta*. 'Result' means that Shingon meditation has its validity only when the discipline cultivated within it is implemented to benefit all beings. In terms of the six *nirbhaya* theory, the ten stage classification, and the three *kalpa* theory, Shingon, which is the all-inclusive doctrine, is the final blooming of *bodhicitta*. In terms of the *daśabhūmi*, the first stage embodies all the other stages. These theories have their origin in India, but Kūkai's interpretation of them is unique in itself. It is most succinctly revealed in his ten stage classification. The tenth, the Shingon stage, is an expository account of the theory that *bodhicitta* is inherent within the practitioner at all stages and at all times, and as such any one stage is capable of awakening bodhicitta. Kūkai neatly syncretized systems of thought developed in India and China and articulated his own theme—that Buddhahood or *bodhicitta* (the terms are synonymous, in that the awakening of bodhicitta is the realization of Buddhahood) is inherent in all beings.

6. Instant Buddhahood: The Union of Man and *Dharmakāya* Mahāvairocana

Mahāyāna literature reveals the nature of Buddhahood. Mahāyāna practices are disciplines to achieve Buddhahood, and the goal of Mahāyāna is the realization of Buddhahood. However, questions as to whether Buddhahood consists of a theoretical or a factual possibility, a mental realization or an actual physical attainment, a state limited to Śākyamuni or a universal one shared by all men, a past possibility, a present possibility or a future possibility—these have been discussed and argued for centuries among Buddhists in Asia. The history of the development of Buddhist thought has been in large part a history of the evolution of the concept of Buddhahood.

In India, after the death of Śākyamuni, Buddhahood was conceived as a possibility limited only to Śākyamuni. His immediate disciplies, no matter how great their intellectual and spiritual capacities may have been, did not dare to even consider the possibility of attaining the state of mind realized by their master. Reverence to Śākyamuni eventually gave rise to deification, transcending his historical personality, and later, to the development of the theory of the universal body of enlightenment, *Dharmakāya*. The theory of universal Buddhahood paved the way for the development of the theory of inherent Buddha-nature. Universal Buddhahood was a subject that was discussed in India for many centuries, as Mahāyāna literature extant either in Sanskrit or in Tibetan and Chinese translations—such as in the *Lotus*, *Nirvāṇa*, *Vimalakīrti*, and *Śrimālādevīsiṃhanāda Sūtras*—attests. The Chinese and Japanese Buddhists accepted this theory, but they were not satisfied to interpret it merely as the possibility of one becoming a Buddha, an idea which presupposes a duration of time and a process of becoming. Instead they emphasized that universal enlightenment means the recognition of the inherent property of enlightenment in all sentient beings. This means that all beings are in themselves, as they are, the embodiment of enlightenment. They are substantially the Buddha.

Implicit in the notion of universal enlightenment is the Mādhyamika theory of non-duality: the compound metaphor of the lotus and the mud most succinctly reveals the notion that there is no enlightenment apart from non-enlightenment; Kegon speaks of the non-duality between mind and *Dharmadhātu;* Zen claims that the mind—just as it is—is that of the Buddha, no distinction being made between man and Buddha; Pure Land holds that one who has accumulated merit must transfer it for the benefit of others to perfect enlightenment, making no distinction between *nirvāṇa* and *saṃsāra;* and Shingon developed the theory of *sokushin-jōbutsu*, that the "body, just as it is, is that of the Buddha." The *Sokushin jōbutsu-gi* states.

1) The six elements, without obstruction,
can only be realized through *yoga;*
2) The four *maṇḍalas* are inseparable;
3) The three secret *adhiṣṭhānas* are practiced
and immediately Buddhahood is realized.
4) The multitude of jewels co-reflecting their images in Indra's net,
is like all phenomena reflecting within the human body;
5) The wisdom of Vajrasattva lies inherent within all beings;
6) The mind and its attributes are nothing beyond dust;
7) Each of these [the mind and its attributes] possesses the five
jñānas which are without limit
8) The five *jñānas* are the true wisdom,
because of the power of *ādarśa-jñāna* (Buddhahood).[16]

The first three lines describe the attributes of *tathatā*, that is, the six elements (body), four *maṇḍalas* (marks), and three secrets (functions). The fourth line describes the harmony of the three attributes by employing the Kegon world-description model. The last four lines provide the *raison d'etre* of the 'instant Buddha' theory: the fifth says that the wisdom of Vajrasattva, representing *bodhicitta*, is inherent in all beings; the sixth line, that the mind (*ālaya*) and its attributes (*vijñānas*) are the sources of delusion (*kleśa*); the seventh, that *vijñānas* are the wisdom (*jñāna*) materials free of *kleśa*, for without *vijñāna* there is no *jñāna*. The seventh line deals with *parāvṛtti*, the transformation from *vijñāna* to *jñāna;* hence, the eighth line says that *ādarśa-jñāna* (the *ālaya*-transformed pure consciousness) is inherent in the consciousness (*vijñāna*) of all sentient beings. In summation, *jñāna* is the material of Buddhahood and *vijñāna* is the material of sentient beings; but *jñāna* is the transformed material of *vijñāna.* Hence Buddhahood-substance (or Buddha-nature) is inherent in all beings.

The *Sokushin jōbutsu-gi* elaborates upon these verses. It describes how the identity of man and the Buddha can be realized instantaneously through the practice of *tri-guhya* meditation. The *Ihon Sokushin jōbutsu-gi* (The Later *Sokushin jōbutsu-gi*)[17] provides the rationale underlying the 'instant Buddha' theory by classifying Buddhahood into three general categories:

a) *Rigū-jōbutsu*, literally, "principle-inherent Buddhahood." This theory holds that from the standpoint of '*ri*' (the principle underlying phenomena), man is essentially a Buddha. It presupposes that man, whether enlightened or not, consists of the six elements, four *maṇḍalas*, and *tri-guhya;* that his body is the *Garbhakośadhūtu Maṇḍala;* and that his mind is the *Vajradhātu Maṇḍala.* Therefore man, just as he is, is *Dharmakāya Mahāvairocana. Rigu-jōbutsu* is the Shingon version of what Plato referred to as '*noesis*'.

b) *Kaji-jōbutsu*, literally, "*adhiṣṭhāna-Buddha*"—the empirically realized Buddhahood. This theory presupposes that the mind of man is covered by *kleśa*. Hence, despite the fact that man inherently is a Buddha, Buddhahood is a realm to be realized *a posteriori*—the actual (man) and the ideal (Buddhahood) integrated through the instrument of *adhiṣṭhāna. Kaji-jōbutsu* affirms the theory of instant Buddhahood but requires practice to realize it.

c) *Kendoku-jōbutsu*, '*ken*' meaning "to reveal," '*doku*', "to acquire." *Kendoku-jōbutsu* means to acquire (Buddhahood) by revealing its inherent nature in the mind of man.

In sum, *rigu*, the principle to be known, is the cause of Buddhahood; *kaji*, the practice to realize Buddhahood, is the conditioner of Buddhahood; and *kendoku*, the union of principle and practice, is the actualization of Buddhahood. The term *sokushin jōbutsu* therefore has three levels of meaning. On the *rigu* level, it refers to the Buddha as the ideal image of man; on the *kaji* level, it requires practice; and on the *kendoku* level, it refers to the Buddhahood inherent in all beings. These are not three distinct approaches to Buddhahood, for the first two are dependent upon one another to realize the third. *Rigu* provides the doctrinal premise for practice; *kaji* provides evidence of the validity of that premise; *kendoku* is the goal of Shingon practitioners. Shingon is a combination of the gradual and abrupt methods to enlightenment: it is gradual inasfar as a practitioner is concerned; it is abrupt inasfar as the enlightened one is concerned. It is a doctrine which has incorporated the Mādhyamika notion of emptiness and non-duality and the Yogācāra notion of transformation from *vijñāna* to *jñāna*, culminating in the *sokushin jōbutsu* theory.

The term *sokushin jōbutsu* has been rendered as 'instant Buddhahood' in the absence of a better translation. However this translation needs to be qualified. The term 'instant' suggests a time element; the term 'Buddhahood', in contrast to 'sentient beings', suggests the existence of a distinct body. No such implication is involved in *sokushin jōbutsu*. Ideally this theory presupposes that there is neither a process of transformation nor a duration of time, neither a difference of identity nor of substance, between man and the Buddha. In Shingon man is the Buddha, just as he is. He is *Dharmakāya* Mahāvairocana. He is the *Dharmadhātu*.

EPILOGUE

Philosophizing is a process of reawakening ourselves to our own authentic human situation. In this process Western existentialism is extremely critical toward categorically fixed systems of philosophy; for inasfar as the existential nature of man is concerned, it must be understood in a state of flux. Jaspers therefore says, "A philosophy of systems is, as a man, like someone who builds a castle, but lives next door in a shanty."[1] The authentic human situation cannot be adequately described or understood within the context of a given conceptual category. It must be understood experientially. For what is involved in such an awakening is not necessarily the affirmation of a new conceptual horizon but the realization of a new socio-religious configuration of man. This very issue has been the problem of fundamental concern to Buddhists throughout the centuries.

What the Buddhists aim at is *mokṣa,* liberation from the fundamental sufferings of mankind. They seek *nirvāṇa. Nirvāṇa* is a realm which one realizes after having exhausted all human efforts at rationalizing the nature of human existence and having awakening to the authentic human situation—that the nature of existence is not a fixed one but involves an intense awareness of one's own contingency and the realization of ultimate freedom. But inasfar as *nirvāṇa* is related to the human situation (*saṃsāra*), *nirvāṇa* is a realm involved in the conventional; inasfar as the human situation is related to the awakening of man (*nirvāṇa*) by exhausting the rational, the human situation deals with the supreme. Mahāyāna sees *nirvāṇa* and *saṃsāra* as one organic entity, not as opposites. The Mahāyāna *weltanschauung* involves the identity of *nirvāṇa* and *saṃsāra.* But what is the theoretical basis for the identity of *nirvāṇa* and *saṃsāra*. This subject leads us to examine the Yogācāra system of 'mind-onlyness' (*citta-mātra*), often referred to as the Vijñaptimātratā.

The term 'mind-onlyness' means that all things are of the mind (*manomaya*) and from the mind (*manoja*) and only the mind 'becomes'. *Citta-mātra* does not imply the changing of the world *per se* but the changing of the manner in which we cognize the world. Within that context, *citta-mātra* implies that existence cannot be adequately understood within a given conceptual category but within a flowing stream, in a flux. But in the analysis of the mind, it was said that in the root of the *vijñānas*—the instruments through which one cognizes the world—is the *ālaya*, which stimulates the forces of grasping. But is the *ālaya* a fixed, unchanging entity? No. The Vijñaptimātratā system acknowledges two opposing realms inherent in the nature of the *ālaya*, the realm of true nature (*tattva*) and the realm of discriminating nature (*vikalpa*). The problem now is to describe in concrete terms how these two opposing realms are related to one another, because if true nature and discriminating nature are totally unrelated, the *citta-mātra* theory has no relevance whatsoever in elucidating the nature of human existence. Let us now elaborate by making specific reference to the Vijñaptimātratā literature.

The *She tai-cheng lun*, Paramārtha's Chinese translation of Asanga's *Mahāyāna-saṃgraha*, calls the *ālaya* the 'basic *vijñāna*,' "the basic 'substance' which discriminates."[2] But is it possible for the *ālaya*, the repository of the seeds of discrimination, to transform itself into *prajñā*-wisdom, the quality of which is non-discrimination? This is essentially what we mean when we speak of the co-relationship between true and discriminating natures. The Vijñaptimātratā system deals with this particular subject in terms of the three *svabhāva* theory (which we have briefly dealt with in Chapter III). Let us review this theory. This theory analyzes the nature of things cognized by the human consciousness into: the discriminated (*parikalpita-svabhāva*), the relative (*paratantra-svabhāva*), and true reality (*parinispanna-svabhāva*). *Parikalpita-svabhāva* means the nature of discriminative cognition—the grasping to those things which are essentially absent of an essence (*svabhāva*). *Paratantra-svabhāva* means the nature of things cognized through an understanding of the law of conditional causation—that all things are conditionally caused and exist co-dependently, that all phenomena are therefore relative. *Parinispanna-svabhāva* means the nature of perfect cognition—that is, insight into tathatā, the ultimate reality. Hence, Vasubandhu's Commentary on the *Mahāyāna-saṃgraha* says, "*ālaya-vijñāna* is *paratantra-svabhāva*. All *vijñānas* preceding it are *parikalpita-svabhāva*."[3] But discriminating nature and paratantra-svabhāva are not of the same quality. How can unrelated qualities be identified as one? He elaborates:

> because it [the nature of discrimination] arises according to the conditions of its own perfuming seeds [*vāsanā-bija*], it is dependent upon conditions and cannot self-exist. If it comes into being, it disintegrates at an instant and is never in control of itself. Therefore it is called *paratantra-svabhāva*.[4]

In the Vijñaptimātratā system, the discriminated and the relative are accepted without question as the co-dependents. In other words, whether one sees a contradiction between the discriminated and the relative or not, depends on whether one considers the relative an antithesis of discrimination or the very nature of discrimination. The fact is that the relative involves the element of co-dependence as Vasubhandu has rightly pointed out: it gives rise to phenomena and it is the ground of human existence. This means that although individuality (the discriminated) is dissolved into the stream of dependent causation (the relative), it is this very stream which becomes the 'substance' of individual existence.

We might now be able to understand in more concrete terms what *citta-mātra* means. If we were to seek the source which produces discrimination and grasping, the phenomena of which are reflected on the mind through the instruments of the *vijñānas*, we must penetrate beyond the surface of the empirical self, into the *ālaya*. But if the *ālaya* is not a permanent substance but an impermanent non-substance whose nature is determined by its perfuming seed, which in turn is dependently caused, the *vijñānas* must then be of a kind quite different from that which are rooted in an autonomous, independent and fixed source of grasping. The *ālaya* in fact is not autonomous and not independent. But if the *ālaya* is absent of an essence, the *manas* loses its own basis in asserting its own quality. The *vijñānas*, therefore, should not be considered the instruments of grasping rooted in the *ālaya* but co-dependently existing with the *ālaya*. Hence, when we say that the *ālaya* is the source of discrimination, what we actually mean is that the very 'substance' of discrimination is conditionally caused. As such, the discriminated and the relative are not substantially opposite qualities but are co-involved, co-dependent, and interwoven in the makeup of their own respective nature: the relative nature (*paratantra-svabhāva*) enables discrimination, the discriminating nature (*parikalpita-svabhāva*) itself is due to the nature of the relative.

The theory that the discriminated and the relative are co-involved, co-dependent and interwoven, casts light upon our understanding of the essential nature of conditional causation. And only in the context of the *ālaya*, the basic discriminating body, can this essential nature be brought into clear focus. Thus various modes of existence are nothing more than the conditioning of the *vijñāna* following the law of conditional causation. Asvabhāva's *Commentary on the Mahāyāna Saṃgraha* therefore rightly points out that "All elements of existence are produced by conditional causation due to the nature of *citta-mātra*."[5] Dharmapāla, in his *Vijñaptimātratā-siddhi*, clarifies this issue.

Dharmapāla identifies two processes of causation inherent in the relative, namely, contamination (*saṃkleśa*) and purification (*vyavadāna*).[6] The process of causation by discrimination is referred to as contamination; the process of causation by non-discrimination is referred to as purification. Thus underlying cognition, within the context of the relative, are found the realms of discrimination and true reality. This means —taking the empirical cognition-subject as a point of reference—that we find, first of all, the cognition-object (the discriminated), but as the cognition-subject gradually ascends, so to speak, and becomes purified, we see the cognition-object simultaneously evolving to the realm of true reality. It is not clear whether Dharmapāla conceived such processes, but the fact that he had conceived the element of conditional causation inherent in the relative and the fact that he had distinguished two processes of causation within it seems to imply that he did. If so, does such an explanation have any validity in elucidating the existential nature of man?

Because the relative refers to the cause-making-condition-nature, illusions are not in themselves the relative. Illusions are due to this relative nature, as we have already established. It then follows that because all things are conditionally caused, there can be no modes of being independently existing: discriminating nature is *parikalpita-svabhāva;* discrimination-free nature is *parinișpanna-svabhāva.* This means then that the three modes of existential nature (*parikalpita-*, *paratantra-*, and *parinișpanna-svabhāva*) point to the same nature, conditional causation or the relative. What is different is the position from which the nature of existence is pointed. If we were to conceive the three modes of being as independent realms we could not come to understand the underlying relationship between *parikalpita-svabhāva* and *paratantra-svabhāva,* nor could we explain the development of the dimensions of our encompassing *parikalpita-svabhāva* through *parinișpanna-svabhāva* within the structural totality of the human consciousness. Thus as the Mādhyamika elucidated the fact that that which is conditionally caused should not be understood in terms of opposites, so likewise does the Vijñaptimātratā system elucidate the fact that 'only the mind becomes' through the understanding of the principle of conditional causation as the basic ground of being. We can now see that insight into *paratantra-svabhāva* enables us to encompass the worlds of the discriminated and the non-discriminated. And that insight provides us with the rational basis to understand the nature of the *ālaya.* But how is *citta-mātra* related to Shingon?

The quest for an existential insight begins from probing into the nature of the human consciousness. Buddhists call the consciousness the "*citta.*" It is a variation of '*citra*', meaning "various, different, manifold."[7] The human consciousness is the repository of various seeds of experience collected as the result of karma. Kūkai described the human consciousness—empty of remorse, controlled by passion and greed, and undeveloped beyond the satisfaction of the flesh—as follows:

In the triple world [i.e., the six destinies],
Madmen do not know their madness;
Among those from the four births [mammals, birds, fish and gods],
The blind are unaware of their blindness.
Birth, birth, birth and birth,
They are blind at the beginning of birth;
Death, death, death and death,
They remain blind even at death.[8]

Nevertheless, man is capable of introspecting the nature of his own being (the *citta*) and of penetrating the authentic self. Kūkai discovered that the world of the devil and of hellish beings, as well as the world of truth (*tathatā*) do not exist apart from *citta*. They are in fact the construction of the *citta*. Furthermore, most significantly, the *citta* is absent of its own essence, thus enabling it to construct the worlds. A mind absent of an essence is technically called '*acitta*',[9] which D. T. Suzuki rendered as '*mushin*', the mind of no-mind.[10] *Acitta* is the authentic self. Shingon calls it *bodhicitta*. Whether it is called *acitta* or *bodhicitta*, this state of mind absent of an essence, like an undistorted mirror, is capable of right cognition, because it is absent of the trappings of preconceived notions which stimulate discrimination and grasping. *Bodhicitta* is in fact the embodiment of the insight into the emptiness of an essence in the human mind; it is therefore capable of penetrating a realm which transcends dichotomy (such as discrimination and non-discrimination) and thereby liberates the mind from all forms of delusions (the trappings of preconceived notions); and, as such, it enables one the complete freedom of action—the practice of emptiness (*śūnyatāyām prayojanam*), which is the implementation of theory into practice.

A *bodhisattva* is possessed of this kind of insight. Specifically, he realizes non-discriminative wisdom while coursing from *parikalpita-svabhāva* to *parinişpanna-svabhāva;* and he realizes discriminative wisdom while coursing from *parinişpanna-svabhāva* to *paratantra-svabhāva*. There is nothing wrong with discrimination, provided that it is absent of a preconceived bias. Bias arises when one cognizes the world, the nature of which is *paratantra-svabhāva*, through a deluded mind, a mind which does not cognize the world as *paratantra-svabhāva*. The world cognized through a deluded mind is the world of *parikalpita-svabhāva*. A bias-free-discriminative wisdom, cultivated while coursing from *pariniṣpanna-svabhāva* to *paratantra-svabhāva*, is essential for a *bodhisattva* to deal constructively with the problems of the empirical world. Let us now delve further into what we mean by non-discriminative wisdom and discriminative wisdom and see how these two types of wisdom are correlated and how they are related to practice.

Non-discriminative wisdom refers to inherent wisdom and discriminative wisdom refers to acquired wisdom. Inherent wisdom is a type of wisdom which characterizes that of a Buddha. It is therefore also called *Buddha-citta*. On the other hand, acquired wisdom is a *bodhisattva* wisdom. It forms the basis of *bodhisattva* practice. *Bodhicitta*, a term employed to refer to the enlightened mind of a sentient being and which gives rise to *bodhisattva* practice, is rooted in *Buddha-citta*. In other words, a *bodhisattva*, in the Mahāyāna context, is a sentient being whose *bodhicitta* has been aroused. As such, he is the practitioner—the implementor—of *Buddha-citta*. *Buddha-citta* is also called Buddha-nature. Buddha nature is inherent in all beings, if we were to accept the proposition that all beings maintain the potential, that is *bodhicitta*, to realize enlightenment. Proof of this proposition is revealed through practice, that is, *bodhisattva* practice. It is in this context that faith is conceived as the basis of *bodhisattva* practice. Faith here means the unconditional acceptance of the proposition that all beings maintain the potential to realize enlightenment. Enlightenment, in this case, refers to insight into Mahāyāna Dharma. Mahāyāna Dharma is the composite of wisdom and compassion, the former referring to the insight into emptiness and the latter referring to the practice of emptiness. Practice of emptiness means the application of the insight into emptiness in dealing with empirical matters, specifically, the elimination of all notions associated with the self as an entity of reality. The grasping to the notion of reality of self breeds greed, hate and delusion. Hence, the practice of emptiness simply means the elimination of ignorance (*avidyā*), which breeds the elements of greed, hate and delusion, in the process of dealing with actual empirical matters.

We have seen in terms of the three *svabhāva* theory that insight into one's inherent Buddha-nature involves the process of development of the dimension of human consciousness from *paratantra-svabhāva* to *parinişpanna-svabhāva*, while practice, the implementation of that insight, involves development of the dimension of human consciousness from *parinişpanna-svabhāva* to *paratantra-svabhāva*. *Bodhicitta*, the nature of which is *paratantra-svabhāva*, is the embodiment of this no-beginning, no-ending cyclic progression, between insight and practice. What is important to note here is that this kind of insight—insight into *paratantra-svabhāva*—enables us to encompass the opposites and to identify them as one, as for example in the case of the identity of truth and delusion (as described in the *Lotus Sūtra*), of the pure and the impure (as described in the *Sukhāvatīvyūha Sūtra*), of *nirvāṇa* and *saṃsāra* (as described in the *Nirvāṇa Sūtra*), of inherent non-discriminative wisdom and acquired discriminative wisdom (in Yogacāra). *Paratantra-svabhāva* likewise provides us with the rational basis to understand the Shingon theory of the integration of man and *Dharmakāya* Mahāvairocana, for this integration is brought about within the context of *bodhicitta*. The term identity conceived within the context of *paratantra-svabhāva* does not mean mathematical identity. It means the relative, relative in the sense that the opposites are the necessary and supplementary entities of an organic whole. The organic whole is *Dharmadhātu*. *Dharmakāya* Mahāvairocana is *Dharmadhātu*, the embodiment of emptiness which brings about the phenomena of co-arising. Man is the microcosm of *Dharmakāya* Mahāvairocana.

We can now see that the Buddha conceived by Kūkai was not the historical Buddha. Why was this so? Kūkai was not concerned with the theoretical issue of a past Buddha (e.g. Śākyamuni) or a future Buddha (e.g. Maitreya). He was concerned with the actualization of Buddhahood in the present body, the container of *kleśa*, disturbed by the pains and tragedy of life. Drawing much of his ideas from Mahāyāna, such as the theory of the identity of *nirvāṇa* and *saṃsāra*, and expressing such ideas symbolically, he systematized the theory of 'instant Buddhahood'—I-in-Buddha and Buddha-in-me—a theory which, in my view at least, is based upon *citta-mātra*, a theory which awakens us to realize that the human consciousness is capable of infinite expansion (I-in-Buddha) and infinite extraction (Buddha-in-me), simply because it is absent of an essence, and simply because its nature is *paratantra-svabhāva*. As such, man, just as he is, is substantially a Buddha, a realm realized experientially through *bodhisattva* practice, the practice of emptiness. Shingon is a system of religion in that it emphasizes faith. But it also provides the basis for humanistic concern because it emphasizes universal Buddhahood and thereby most strongly articulates the dignity of all beings. But most important of all is the fact that Shingon is a Mahāyāna school of Buddhism which has incorporated the philosophical tenets of Mādhyamika and Yogacāra, describes the realm of integration of man and Dharmakāya Mahāvairocana—the cosmic Buddha—symbolically, and articulates an experiential approach to realize that realm. Shingon Mikkyō remains a 'secret' only to those who are incapable of understanding the true nature of existence but no longer remains so to those who have understood that nature.

NOTES

ABBREVIATIONS:

T. *Taishō shinshū daizō-kyō* (The *Taishō Tripiṭaka* in Chinese), ed. and comp., Takakusu Junjirō, Watanabe Kaigyoku, et al. Tokyo: Taishō issaikyō kankō-kai, 1924–34.

Z. *Zokuzō-kyō* (The *Zokuzō Tripitaka* in Chinese), ed. and comp., Maeda Eun, Nakano Tatsue, et al. Kyoto: Kyoto zokyō shoin, 1905–12.

K. *Kōbō daishi zenshū* (Collected Works of Kōbō Daishi), ed. and comp., Sofū senyō-kai. Tokyo: Yoshikawa Kōbunkan, 1910 (first print).

M. *Mikkyō dai-jiten* (Mikkyō Encyclopedia), ed. and comp., Matsunaga Shodō. Kyōto: Naigai Press. Vol. 1, 1931, Vol. 2, 1932, Vol. 3, 1933 (first print).

CHAPTER ONE: THE INDIAN FOUNDATION OF TANTRIC BUDDHISM

1 Sir Monier Monier-Williams. *A Sanskrit-English Dictionary*. London: Oxford University Press (New Edition), 1951, p. 1241c.

2 Benoytosh Bhattacharya. *An Introduction to Buddhist Esoterism*. Varanasi: Chowkhamba Series Office (Second Edition), 1964, p. 15.

3 Matsunaga Yūkei. "Tantric Buddhism and Shingon Buddhism," *The Eastern Buddhist* (New Series). Kyōto: The Eastern Buddhist Society, Vol. II, No. 2, Nov., 1969, p. 1.

4 *Ibid.*, p. 6.

5 See for example the citations in *Digha-nikāya* (*Āgama*), *T.* 1. 1, p. 84, *Majjhima-nikāya, T.* 1. 26, p. 724, *Four Division Vinaya, T.* 22. 1428, p. 754.

6 Iwamoto Yutaka. *Bukkyō nyūmon* (Introduction to Buddhism). Tōkyō: Chūkō shinsho (32), 1964, pp. 134–35.

7 I-ching. *Shi-yu ch'iu-fa kao-seng chüan* (The Biography of Eminent Monks who Sought the Dharma in the Western Region), *T.* 55. 2066, p. 1.

8 Ennin. *Nyūtō shingu seikyō mokuroku* (New Catalogue of Buddhist Works in T'ang), *T.* 55. 2167, p. 1086.
9 I-ching. *Kao-seng chüan*, *T.* 51. 2066, p. 7.
10 Contained and cited in Fei-cho. *San-pao kan-ying yao-lueh lu* (A Catalogue of Brief Essays concerning the Monks' Response to the Three Jewels), *T.* 51. 2084, p. 383.
11 Toganoo Shōun. *Himitsu bukkyō-shi* (History of the Secret School of Buddhism). Kyōto: Naigai Press, 1933 (first print), p. 17.
12 *Z.* 15. 8 (see preface).
13 *Z.* 1. 36. 1, p. 272. For details on Bolora, see Hsüan-tsang. *Ta-T'ang shi-yu chi*, *T.* 15. 2087, p. 884.
14 Toganoo. *Himitsu bukkyō-shi*, pp. 35–6.
15 Yamada Ryūjo. *Bongo butten no sho bunken* (Buddhist Sanskrit Sources). Kyōto: Eiraku-ji shoten, 1958, p. 163.
16 Matsunaga. *The Eastern Buddhist*, p. 8.

CHAPTER TWO: THE SHINGON SYSTEM OF DOCTRINAL EVALUATION AND CLASSIFICATION

1 *Hizō-hōyaku*, *T.* 77. 2426, p. 263a.
2 *Ibid.*, p. 263c.
3 *Un-ji gi*, *T.* 77. 2430, p. 405a.
4 The Chinese translation of the *Mādhyamaka-kārikā* (Chapter 24, Verse 18), *T.* 30. 1564, p. 33b.
5 For a complete list of the seventy-five dharmas, see Richard H. Robinson, "Classical Indian Philosophy, Part I," *Chapters in Indian Civilization*, comp. and ed., Joseph W. Elder, Madison: Department of Indian Studies, 1967, p. 167.
6 *Suttanipāta*. I. 1.
7 *Chapters in Indian Civilization*, p. 188.
8 *Mādhyamaka-kārikā*. *T.* 30. 1564, p. 1.
9 See note no. 4, above.
10 *Hizō-hōyaku*. *T.* 77. 2426, p. 370b.
11 The Chinese term '*t'i*', loosely translated as "substance," is commonly employed in contrast to '*hsing*' (appearance) and '*yung*' (function). '*T'i*' refers to the combination of marks (appearance of things) and the nature (of those things). It does not refer to *svabhāva*.

CHAPTER THREE: SHINGON DOCTRINAL CONCEPTS

1 Nagao Gadjin, "On the Theory of Buddha-body (*Buddha-kāya*)," *The Eastern*

Buddhist, Vol. XI, No. 1, May, 1973, p. 30.

2 Sir Monier Monier-Williams, *A Sanskrit-English Dictionary*, p. 983b.

3 This is an abridged translation. For the complete, in the original, see Śubhakārasiṃha's *Commentary on the Mahāvairocana Sūtra*, *T.* 39. 1796, p. 579a. (The *Taishō* gives I-hsing as the composer of this *Commentary*. Actually, it was dictated by Śubhakārasiṃha and recorded by I-hsing, though it is possible to assume that many of the ideas contained in it are I-hsing's.) For a detail description of the term 'Mahāvairocana', see *Kongōchō giketsu*, *T.* 39. 1798, p. 808, and *Dainichi-kyō giketsu*, *K.* 1, p. 636. Watanabe Shōkō discusses the relationship between Virocana and Vairocana. See his "Virocana and Vairocana—A Prolegomena," *Mikkyō-gaku mikkyō-shi ronbun-shū* (Studies of Esoteric Buddhism and Tantrism), comp. and ed., Nakano Gishō. Kyōto: Naigai Press, 1965, pp. 371–390.

4 *Hizō-ki*, *K.* 2, p. 10.

5 *Awakening of Mahāyāna Faith*, *T.* 32. 1666, p. 575b. The most recent English translation of this text is by Y. S. Hakeda (Columbia University Press, 1967.) The Commentary on this text, referred to as *Shaku makaen-ron* in Shingon, was introduced to Japan by Kaimin of Yakushi-ji in 779. Although alleged to be composed by Nāgājuna, the authenticity of this *Commentary's* author was disputed from the time of its introduction. Kūkai, seemingly undisturbed by such arguments, made frequent reference to it in composing many of his works (e.g. *Hizō-hōyaku*, *Nikyō-ron*, etc.). As a matter of fact, there is hardly any text composed by Kūkai that does not make reference to it. The great influence that this *Commentary* has had on Shingon can be seen by the fact that many studies on it were produced by Shingon masters. For example, *Shaku makaen-ron shiki* by Shinken (1259–1322), *Shaku makaen-ron kotanzaku* by Junkei (1260–1308), *Shaku makaen-ron sho* by Ukai (1345–1416), *Shaku makaen-ron kanchū* by Gakugen (1619–1743), etc. Morita Ryūsen's *Shaku makaen-ron no kenkyu* (Kyōto: Fujii benseidō, 1935) is perhaps the most comprehensive study on this *Commentary* done in recent decades. As it is apparent, studies on the *Shaku makaen-ron* are interpretive accounts of the *Awakening of Mahāyāna Faith* from the Shingon point of view.

6 *Mahāvairocana Sūtra*, *T.* 18. 848, p. 9b. See the verse which describes *tathatā*. Similar lines can also be found in *ibid.*, pp. 13, 19, 31, 38, etc.

7 Kūkai explains the theory of the six elements in full in his *Sokushin jōbutsu-gi*, *T.* 77. 2428, pp. 381c–82c.

8 Franklin Edgerton, *Buddhist Hybrid Sanskrit* (Vol. II. Dictionary). New Haven: Yale University Press, 1953, p. 416.

9 Toganoo Shōun. *Mandara no kenkyū* (Studies on the *Maṇḍala*). Kyōto: Naigai Press, 1927, pp. 1–2. This is possibly the most comprehensive study on the

maṇḍala in any modern language today. A selected bibliography on the *maṇḍala* is provided on pp. 519–32.

10 Ideas germane to the theory of the four *maṇḍalas* can be found in texts which Kūkai makes reference to. For example, the *Mahāvairocana Sūtra*, *T.* 18. 848, p. 44a, *Prajñāpāramitā-naya Sūtra*, *T.* 19. 1004, p. 610, and others. Kūkai's interpretation of the four *maṇḍalas* is treated in detail in his *Sokushin jōbutsu-gi*, *T.* 77. 2428, pp. 382c–83a, his *Hizō-hōyaku*, *T.* 77. 2426, pp. 363a–b, *ibid.*, 373a, and others.

11 Edgerton. *Buddhist Hybrid Sanskrit Dictionary*, p. 565.

12 Toganoo. *Mandara no kenkyū*, p. 263.

13 Basic forms of Shingon *mudrā* are classified into twelve *añjali* (i.e. non-fist mudrās) and four (sometimes six) fist *mudrās*. See the *Mahāvairocana Sūtra*, *T.* 18. 848, p. 24, and Śubhakārasiṃha's *Commentary*, *T.* 39. 1796, p. 714. The origin and development of *mudrās* are treated in considerable detail in Toganno, *Mandara no kenkyū*, pp. 469–89.

14 For details on *adhiṣṭhāna*, see *Hizō-ki*, *T.* (Zuzō-bu I), p. 36, *Dainichi-kyō kaidai*, *K.* 4, p. 686, and others.

15 For a comprehensive bibliography on '*A-ji*' meditation, see *M.* I, pp. 17c–20a.

16 *Mahāvairocana Sūtra*, *T.* 18. 848, p. 10.

17 *Gaṇḍavyūha Sūtra* (i.e. *Mahā-vaipulya-buddha-avataṃsaka-sūtra*), *T.* 9. 278, p. 765.

18 *Mahā-prajñāpāramitā-sūtra*, *T.* 8. 223, p. 256.

19 *Ta chih-tu lun*, *T.* 25. 1509, p. 408.

20 For an interpretive account of Kakuban's *A-ji* meditation in modern Japanese, see Kusuda Ryōkō, *Shingon mikkyō seiritusu katei no kenkyū* (A Study on the Evolution of Shingon *Mikkyō* Thought). Tōkyō: Sankibo, 1969, pp. 201 ff. For Kakuban's reform movement, see Matsunaga Yūkei, *Mikkyō no rekishi* (History of *Mikkyō*). Kyōto: Heiraku-ji shoten, 1969, pp. 224–228.

21 *Nihon bunka jiten* (Dictionary of Japanese Culture), comp. and ed., Kawasaki Yasuyuki, Morisue Yoshiaki, Wakamori Tarō. Tokyo: Asakura shoten, 1964, pp. 666–667 (*honji-suijaku*).

22 Shōtoku Taishi. *Shomangyō-gisho* (Commentary on the *Śrimālādevīsiṃhanāda-sūtra*), ed. by Saeki Jōin. Tokyo: Morie shoten, 1939, p. 7a.

23 Śubhakārasiṃha's *Commentary*, *T.* 39. 1796, p. 580.

24 *Ibid.*, p. 598.

25 A summary of Hōju's idea on '*honji-kaji*' is presented by Takagami Kakushō, *Mikkyō gairon* (Outline of *Mikkyō*). Tōkyo: Dai-ichi shobō, 1942, pp. 158–161.

26 Alicia Matsunaga, *The Buddhist Philosophy of Assimilation*. Vermont and Tōkyō: Sophia University and Charles E. Tuttle, Co., 1969, pp. 1–3.

27 Ui Hakuju and Miyamoto Shōson, eminent Japanese Buddhologists, challenged the Shingon theory of the personified Dharma. See Ui, *Bukkyō hanron* (I). Tōkyō: Iwanami shoten, 1947 (first print), pp. 90–91. See also Nasu Seiryū, "Dainichi-kyō no kyōshi ni tsuite" in the *Chizan Gakuhō* (Journal of Chizan Studies). Tōkyō: Kin'yō-sha, No. 66, Feb., 1954, pp. 2–23, in which he answers the challenges of Ui and others and defends the Shingon position.

CHAPTER FOUR: THE TWO *MAṆḌALAS*

1 *Goshōrai mokuroku*, *K.* 1, p. 95.

2 Giuseppe Tucci. *The Theory and Practice of the Maṇḍala* (trans., Alan Houghton Brodrick). London: Rider and Co., 1961, pp. 21–48.

3 *M.* 1, p. 477c.

4 Miyasaka Yūshō, "Indo no mikkyō" (Tantric Buddhism in India) in *Kōza bukkyō* III. Tōkyō: Daizō shuppan, 1959, pp. 206–07.

5 Toganoo. *Mandara no kenkyū*, p. 65.

6 Sir Monier Monier Williams. *A Sanskrit-English Dictionary*, p. 513c.

7 Toganoo. *Mandara no kenkyū*, p. 63.

8 The *Mahāvairocana Sūtra* and Śubhakārasiṃha's *Commentary* cite thirteen halls. Toganoo claims that the twelve-hall concept (as employed in the *Garbhakośadhātu Maṇḍala*) is a Japanese device. See Toganoo, *Mandara no kenkyū*, p. 102.

9 *Mahāvairocana Sūtra*, *T.* 18. 848, p. 1b–c.

10 Sarvanivāraṇa-viṣkambhī does not appear in the *Maṇḍala*. Several contrasting view have been expressed by *Mikkyō* masters to explain this. Toganoo claims that in the process of transcribing verbal *maṇḍala* into *genzu maṇḍala*, Sūryaprabha, who appears in the lower end portion of the Hall of Kṣitigarbha, and Sarvanivāraṇa-viskambhī, who is seated adjacent to him, were interchanged. See Toganoo, *Mandara no kenkyū*, pp. 175–77.

11 Gonda Daisōjō. *Mandara tsūge*. Kyōto: Heigosha, 1919, p. 35.

12 *Buddhist Texts Through the Ages*, ed. and comp., Edward Conze, I. B. Horner, David Snellgrove, and Arthur Waley. New York: Harper and Row, 1964, p. 321.

13 In full, the *Śrāvakabhūmi* says, "For what reason is it [i.e., that *samādhi*] called 'diamond-like'? As follows: the diamond, being among all other gems, such as the *maṇi*, pearl, *vaiḍūrya* jewel, *śaṅkhasilā* jewel, and coral, chief, best, most hard, most firm, scratches those others and is not scratched by other gems. In just the same way, this *samādhi*, being among all learned *samādhis*, chief, best, most hard, most firm, overcomes all corruptions and is not overcome by productive corruptions. Therefore it is called diamond-like." (Translated

by Alex Wayman in his *Analysis of the Śrāvakabhūmi Manuscript*. Berkeley: University of California Press, 1961, p. 134.)

14 In full, the *Commentary* says, "*Vajra* is like the wisdom or reality [*Dharmakāya*]; it surpasses all speeches and practices [*marga*]; it is that which is conditioned; it is not manifested dharma; it has no beginning, middle, or end; it is inexhaustible and cannot be destroyed; it parts from all defilements and is unchangeable and indestructible." See Śubhakārasiṃha's *Commentary*, *T*. 39. 1796, p. 580a.

15 *Tattvasaṃgraha Sūtra*, *T*. 18. 875, p. 329a.

16 *Sokushin jōbutsu-gi*, *T*. 77. 2428, p. 381c.

17 Names of these *bodhisattvas* vary according to texts. The *M* presents an outline which gives the corresponding names used in various texts. See Vol. I, p. 629a–c. Regardless of how the names are presented, these four *bodhidattvas* are the personification of four types of *kleśa*. For detail concerning each of the *bodhisattvas*, see *M*. III, p. 2218b (for *Iṣṭa-vajra*), *M*. I, p. 437b and *M*. II, p. 1387b (for *Kelikila-vajra*), *M*. I, p. 3a (for *Rāga-vajra*), and *M*. III, p. 2091b–c (for *Māna-vajra*).

18 *Hizō-ki*, *T*. (Zuzō-bu I), p. 44.

CHAPTER FIVE: THE PATH TO BUDDHAHOOD

1 *Bodhicitta Śāstra*, *T*. 12. 374, p. 535b.

2 *Sammaya kaijō*, *K*. I, p. 133.

3 *Nirvāṇa Sūtra*, *T*. 12. 374, p. 556c.

4 *Mahāvairocana Sūtra*, *T*. 18. 848, p. 1b–c.

5 *Ibid.*, p. 1c.

6 For detail, see *Ta-chih-tu lun*, *T*. 25. 1509, p. 120.

7 The Shingon concept of *kalpa* and its *tri-kalpa* interpretation are derived from the *Mahāvairocana Sūtra*. For detail, see Śubhakārasiṃha's *Commentary*, *T*. 39. 1796, p. 600.

8 Shinshō (1186–1242), Dōhan (1178–1252), Shōken (1307–1392), and Yūkai (1345–1416) maintained that all *Kengyō* schools (including Tendai and Kegon) affirmed the traditional *kalpa* theory; Raiyū (1226–1304) and Unshō (1614–1693) believed that Tendai and Kegon did not.

9 Śubhakārasiṃha's *Commentary*, *T*. 39. 1796, p. 600.

10 *Ibid.*, p. 605.

11 For further detail, see the *Mahāvarrocana Sūtra*, *T*. 18. 848, p. 3. Also see Śubhakārasiṃha's *Commentary*, *T*. 39. 1796, p. 605.

12 For an English source on the *daśabhūmi*, see Har Dayal. *The Bodhisattva Doctrine in Buddhist Sanskrit Literature*. London: Kegan Paul, 1932. For Chinese

canonical sources, see *Shih-ti lun*, *T.* 26. 1522, and *Ta-ch'eng i'chang*, *T.* 44. 1851. For a modern Japanese work, see Terada Masakatsu, *Kegon-gyō jūji-bon*. Kyoto: Hōzōkan, 1961.

13 The notion of 'first as final' is derived from Subhakārasiṃha's *Commentary*, *T.* 39. 1796, p. 578c.

14 *Śrimālādevīsiṃhanāda Sūtra*, *T.* 12. 353, pp. 218c–19a.

15 The idea of portraying enlightenment in terms of sixteen *bodhisattvas* is derived from Śubhakārasiṃha's *Commentary*, *T.* 39. 1796, p. 605.

16 *Sokushin jōbutsu-gi*, *T.* 77. 2428, p. 381c.

17 *Ihon sokushin jōbutsu-gi*, *K.* 4, p. 10.

EPILOGUE

1 Karl Jaspers, *Reason and Existenz*. London: Routledge and Kegan Paul, 1956, p. 26.

2 Ui Hakuju, *Shōdaijō-ron no kenkyū* (Studies on the *Mahāyāna-saṃgraha*), Vol. II (Text). Tokyo: Iwanami shoten, 1955 (second print), p. 5.

3 Vasubandhu, *Commentary on the Mahāyāna-saṃgraha* (tr. by Paramārtha), *T.* 31. 1598, p. 163c.

4 *Ibid.*, p. 186b.

5 Asvabhāva. *Commentary on the Mahāyāna-saṃgraha* (tr. by Hsüan-tsang), *T.* 31. 1598, p. 399b.

6 Dharmapāla. *Vijñaptimātratā-siddhi*. (I have used the "Shindō" edition for this part of research.) See *Jōyuishiki-ron*, ed. Saeki Jōin, Vol. II. Ōsaka: Shosō-gaku seiten kankō-kai, 1940, pp. 14 ff.

7 Monier Monier-Williams. *A Sanskrit-English Dictionary*, p. 396a.

8 *Hizō-hōyaku*, *T.* 77. 2426, p. 263.

9 Vasubandhu. *Triṃśikā* (tr. by Hsüan-tsang). *T.* 31. 1586 (verse 29), p. 60.

10 Suzuki Daisetsu. *Mushin to iu koto* (Vol. 7, *Suzuki Daisetsu Zenshū*). Tōkyō: Iwanami shoten, 1968, p. 115.

REFERENCE

This is a selected and annotated bibliography on contemporary Shingon studies with primary consideration given to book length sources, most of which are in Japanese, only a few in Western languages. Essays have been omitted simply because there are over 50,000 of them related to Buddhist studies published in academic journals in Japan from the late nineteenth century to 1971. Over 27,000 essays appeared between 1931 and 1955, during a span of twenty-four years, and over 9,000 essays appeared between 1956 and 1971, during a span of fifteen years. Roughly some 500 essays on Shingon doctrine were written in the course of the last ten years. Many of these essays warrant serious attention, but to review them systematically constitutes a major project in itself.

Despite the great interest in Shingon studies shown by Japanese Buddhologists, Shingon is a field of Buddhist studies that has hardly been touched upon by Western scholars. With the exception of Hakeda's *Kūkai: Major Works* and Tajima's *Etude sur le Mahāvairocana-sūtra*, there is no comprehensive study either on Kūkai, his thought, or texts upon which his thought is based. There is still no comprehensive and structured study on Shingon doctrine. Only few Western sources can be cited in this reference.

This reference is primarily intended to introduce basic Japanese secondary materials on Shingon for the benefit of Western Japanologists interested in Shingon studies. As such, primary works included in the *Taishō Tripiṭaka* and in the Shingon canons are omitted.* Interpretive studies on those works are included. Entries are classified into topic categories.

I. Shingon Bibliography

1 *A Bibliography on Japanese Buddhism*. Comp. and ed. by Bandō Shōjun, Hanayama Shōyū, Satō Ryōjun, et al. Tōkyō: CIIB Press, 1958. For Shingon titles, see pp. 81–90. Entries in this bibliography were compiled without scholarly discrimination and are limited to Western sources. Unannotated.

---

* Canonical sources on Kūkai's major works and classical commentaries on those works are already provided by Yoshito S. Hakeda, *Kūkai: Major Works*, pp. 281–283.

2 *Bukkyōgaku kankei zasshi ronbun bunrui mokuroku*. (A Catalogue of Essays in Buddhist Studies). Comp. and ed. by the Committee on the Collection of Essays on Buddhist Studies of Ryūkoku University. Kyōto: Nagata bunshōdō, 1972. Contains a total of 9,103 titles related to Buddhist studies which appeared in Buddhist academic journals and periodicals in Japan from 1956 to 1971. For titles related to Shingon, see nos. 4277–4448, pp. 218–225. Unannotated.

3 *Bukkyōgaku kankei zasshi ronbun bunrui mokuroku*. (A Catalogue of Essays in Buddhist Studies). Comp. and ed. by Satō Tetsuei. Kyōto: Hyakka-en, 1961. Contains a total of some 27,000 titles related to Buddhist studies which appeared in Buddhist academic journals and periodicals in Japan from 1931 to 1955. For titles related to Shingon, see pp. 247–306. Unannotated.

4 Hakeda, Yoshito S. *Kūkai: Major Works*. New York: Columbia University Press, 1972. For titles of major composition by Kūkai, see pp. 281–283; for titles concerning the life and thought of Kūkai, see pp. 283–287. Unannotated.

5 *Kaitei zōhō: bukkyō ronbun sō-mokuroku*. (A General Catalogue of Essays in Buddhist Studies: New Edition). Comp. and ed. by Tsuboi Tokkō and Kanayama Masayoshi. Tōkyō: Taikandō shoten, 1935. Contains a total of 14,223 titles related to Buddhist studies which appeared in Buddhist academic journals and periodicals in Japan from late nineteenth century to 1935. For titles related to Shingon, see nos. 13,121–13,332, pp. 673–683. Unannotated.

6 *Kitagawa, Joseph M. Religion in Japanese History*. New York: Columbia University Press, 1960. Offers a general bibliography on Japanese religion, including Shingon, in both Japanese and Western languages (pp. 373–456). Unannotated.

7 *Kōbō daishi kankei bunken mokuroku*. (Bibliography on Kōbō Daishi). Comp. and ed. by Kōya-san: Koya-san University Library, 1960. This useful and important bibliography presenting works related to the life and work of Kōbō Daishi (Kūkai) has had only limited distribution. Unannotated.

8 *Kōya-san kankei bunken mokuroku*. (Bibliography on Studies related to Kōya-san.) Comp. and ed. Kōya-san: Kōya-san University Library, 1961. This useful and important bibliography offering works related to Kōya-san scholarship has had only limited distribution. Unannotated.

9 *Mikkyo kankei shuyo shoseki mokuroku*. (A Catalogue of Major Works Related to Mikkyō). Comp. and ed. by Ōyama Jinkai (in mimeograph). This useful bibliography containing titles related to major works on Shingon, both classic and modern, extracted from the card catalogue of Kōya-san University Library compiled by a civil service official of the Bureau of Religious Affairs, the Ministry of Education, Tōkyō has had only limited distribution. Unannotated.

10 "Shingon-shū kankō tosho mokuroku." (A Catalogue of books published by the Shingon school). Comp. by Hashimoto Kaizen in the *Kōya-san no kenkyū* (Essays by specialists of Kōya-san Monastery), (a Special Research Edition), comp. by Ōyama Kōjun. Kyōto: Naigan Press, 1936, pp. 1–38 (appendix). Excellent bibliography on Shingon works published from the late nineteenth century to 1936. Unannotated.

II. Mikkyō Encyclopedia and Chronological Table of Shingon History

1 *Mikkyō dai-jiten.* (Mikkyō Encyclopedia). Comp. and ed. by Matsunaga Shōdō. Kyoto: Naigai Press. Vol. I, 1931; Vol. II, 1932; Vol. III, 1933. An indispensable source for serious studies on Shingon, this work includes entries on Shingon technical terms, personalities, classical works, etc. Topic index, an index on Shingon Sanskrit terms, and a Japanese alphabetical index are provided. This is the standard and most authoritative Shingon encyclopedia currently available.

2 *Shingon-shū nenpyō.* (A Chronological Table of the History of Shingon). Comp. by Moriyama Shōshin. Tokyo: Shingi Shingon-shū shūmu-*d*hō, 1934. A convenient chronological table with source reference. A useful reference for a historical study of Shingon.

III. *Collected Works on Shingon and Kōbō Daishi* (Kūkai)

1 *Bunka shijō yori mita Kōbō Daishi den* (The Life of Kūkai—from the Perspective of Cultural History). Comp. and ed. by Moriyama Shōshin. Tokyo: Kokusho kankō-kai, 1973 (new print). (First print, 1934.) This collection of essays critically examines most of the available sources related to the life of Kūkai. The best critical source for those interested in a serious research on the life of Kūkai. Highly recommended.

2 *Kōbō Daishi chosaku zenshū* (The Collected Works of Kōbō Daishi). Comp. by Hasuo Kanzen. Kyoto: Rokudai shimpō-sha, 1935. The most popularly employed collection of biographies of Kūkai. But the data this work employs are uncritically accepted and no distinction is made between history and legend. This collection is a revision of *Kōbō Daishi godenki* (Biographies of Kōbō Daishi) published in 1921.

3 *Kōbō Daishi denki shūran* (Compendium of the Biographies of Kōbō Daishi). Comp. and ed. by Miura Akio. Tokyo: Morie shoten, 1934 (first print). (New print, 1970). Works related to the study of Kūkai are arranged according to the period of composition. A convenient source of reference.

4 *Kōbō Daishi sho deshi zenshū* (Collected Works of the Disciples of Kōbō Daishi). Comp. and ed. by Hase Hoshū. Kyōto: Rokudai shinpō-sha, 1942 (first print). (1974, new print). Excellent source to investigate Kūkai through

the records written of him by his disciples.

5 *Kōbō daishi zenshū*. (Collected Works of Kōbō Daishi). Comp. and ed. by the Center of *Mikkyo* Cultural Study of Kōya-san University. Tokyo: Yoshikawa kōbunkan, 1910 (first print). (Subsequently, it was published in 1934–35, and 1965. Additional works are included in each successive print.) It includes Kūkai's works contained in the *Taishō Tripiṭaka* (as well as in other Japanese canons compiled in recent decades), modern Japanese translations of Kūkai's works, and classical commentaries on his works. Excellent reference source.

6 *Mikkyō-gaku Mikkyō-shi ronbun-shū* (Essays on *Mikkyō*: Doctrine and History). Comp. and ed. by the staff of Kōya-san University. Kyōto: Naigai Press, 1965. Collection of essays on Shingon and related fields by both Japanese and Western scholars. A very useful reference to those interested in examining specific issues and problematics on Shingon.

7 *Shingon-shū zensho* (The Collected Works of the Shingon School). Comp. and published by Kōya-san: Kōya-san University, 1934. The most comprehensive collection of works primarily on Shingon doctrine. Highly recommended.

8 *Zoku Shingon-shū zensho* (The Later Collected Works of the Shingon School). Comp. and ed. by Nakagawa Zenkyō. Kōya-san: Kōya-san University, 1973. This collection supplements the *Shingon-shū zensho* and is primarily a collection of Shingon rituals. The complete collection has not been published as of this date. Highly recommended.

IV. Recent Works on the Life of Kūkai

1 Hakeda, Yoshito S. *Kūkai: Major Works*. New York: Columbia University Press, 1972. For the "Life of Kūkai," see pp. 13–60; for the "thought of Kūkai," see, pp. 61–100. This is the most comprehensible work on Kūkai in any Western language.

2 Miyasaki Ninshō. *Shin Kōbō daishi den* (A New Biography of Kōbō Daishi). Tokyo: Daihōrin-kaku, 1967. An excellent interpretive work on the life of Kūkai in good modern literary Japanese for the popular reader.

3 Watanabe Shōkō and Miyasaka Yūshō. *Shamon Kūkai* (Sramana Kūkai). Tokyo: Chikuma shobō, 1967. The best among modern works on the life of Kūkai for the popular reader. Flashing insights by the authors make this an extremely enjoyable and interesting book to read, even for those engaged in a serious historical study of Kūkai.

V. Shingon Doctrine and History

1 Kanayama Bokushō. *Shingon Mikkyō no kyōgaku* (Shingon *Mikkyō* Doctrine).

Kyōto: Naigai Press, 1944. Though written in a pre-war Japanese literary style, this is a good work by an eminent Shingon scholar and practitioner. It deals with the historical development of Shingon doctrine, cites passages from primary sources but do not specifically identify them. One of the useful secondary reference works for those interested in serious research on the historical development of Shingon thought.

2 Katsumata Shunkyō. *Mikkyō no nihon-teki tenkai*. (The Japanese Development of Mikkyō). Tōkyō: Shunju-sha, 1970. One of the best in recent Shingon publications. This work deals with the history of the development of Shingon thought, cites reference, and indicates considerable sophistication in handling basic source materials.

3 Kusuda Ryōkō. *Shingon Mikkyō seiritus katei no kenkyū*. (A Study on the Development of Shingon *Mikkyō*). Tōkyō: Sankibo, 1964. One of the most comprehensive and carefully researched works on Shingon ever published in recent years. In addition, this work contains adequate reference for those interested in serious research. Highly recommended.

4 Matsunaga Yūkei. *Mikkyō no chie*. (The Wisdom of *Mikkyō*) (in the Shōwa bukkyō zenshū Series, No. 6. 6). Tōkyō: Kyōiku shinchō-sha, 1973. Excellent introductory book on Shingon for the popular reader.

5 ——. *Mikkyō no rekishi*. (History of *Mikkyō*). Kyōto: Heiraku-ji shoten, 1969. This book deals with the historical development of Tantric tradition from India to Tibet, China to Japan. The author makes reference to a variety of up-to-date Japanese and Western sources as well as classical sources in Sanskrit, Tibetan and Chinese. It is carefully documented and is the best historical treatment of the history of Tantric Buddhism as it spread from India to East Asia. Highly recommended.

6 Miyasaka Yūshō. *Mikkyō-teki seimei no shibo*. (The Quest for the Eternal Life of *Mikkyō*) (in the *Shōwa bukkyō zenshū*, No. 6. 1). Tōkyō: Kyōiku shinchō-sha, 1967. This is a collection of Miyasaka's essays which are designed to enhance Shingon and to interpret Shingon's social and ethical values today. It is Shingon described by its devotee and scholar in a sincere manner.

7 Miyasaka Yūshō and Umehara Takeshi. *Seimei no umi: Kūkai* (The Sea of Life: Kūkai) (in the *Bukkō no shisō* Series, No. 9). Tōkyō: Kadokawa shoten, 1969. A good introductory book on Shingon, the theme of which is the eternal life of Mahāvairocana as conceived by Kūkai.

8 Morita Ryūsen. *Himitsu bukkyō no kenkyū* (A Study on *Mikkyō* Buddhism). Kyōto: Rokudai shinpō-sha, 1935. This is essentially a study on Shingon doctrine and considered one of the best on Shingon published in pre-war Japan.

9 Nagaoka Keishin. *Sokushin jōbutsu no michi*. (The Path to 'Buddhahood

Realized in the Present Body'). Tōkyō: Kyōiku shinchō-sha, 1965. A useful popular reference to those interested in examining the Shingon theory of *sokushin-jōbutsu*.

10 Nakano Gishō. *Mikkyō no shinkō to rinri* (*Mikkyō:* Its Religious and Ethical Aspects). Tōkyō: Kyōiku shinchō-sha, 1970. An interesting work on the religious and ethical aspects of Shingon written by one of the leading contemporary Shingon scholars and practitioners.

11 Ōyama Kōjun. *Mikkyō-shi gaisetsu to kyōri*. (*Mikkyō*: Its History and Doctrine). Kyōto: Taian-dō, 1961. A comprehensive and well researched work on the history and the development of Shingon *Mikkyō* by one of recent Shingon scholars. Highly recommended.

12 ——. *Shingon Mikkyō e no tebiki*. (A Guide to Shingon *Mikkyō*), (in the *Showa bukkyō zenshū* Series, No. 6. 2.) Tōkyō: Kyōiku shinchō-sha, 196*b*. A good introductory text on Shingon dealing with Kūkai, Shingon thooght and its problematics, history of Kōya-san Monastery, Shingon practice and *maṇḍalas*.

13 Takagami Kakushō. *Mikkyō Gairon* (Introduction to *Mikkyō*). Tōkyō: Daiichi shobō, 1938 (first print). Excellent introductory work to Shingon with doctrinal themes presented in a well structured manner.

14 Takubo Shūyō. *Shingon darani-zō no kaisetsu* (An Interpretive Account of Shingon *Dhāraṇi* Literature). Tōkyō: Sanyō bijitsu insatsu, 1960. A careful study on Shingon *dhāraṇi* literature. It deals with the history of the development of *dhāraṇi* practice and literature in India, the impact of its practice and literature on the development of Mahāyāna literature, and on the development of Shingon. For the specialist.

15 Toganoo Shōun. *Himitsu bukkyō-shi* (History of *Mikkyō* Buddhism). Kyōto: Naigai Press, 1933 (first print). A new print of this book is contained in the *Gendai bukkyō meicho zenshū* (Collection of Modern Buddhological Works, Vol. 9) comp. by Nakamura Hajime, Masutani Fumio, and Joseph Kitagawa. Tōkyō: Ryūbunkan, 1964). The best among works dealing with the history of Shingon written before World War II. It deals with the Indian foundation of Tantric Buddhism, the history of Chen-yen (Shingon) and Lamaism in China, a brief historical sketch of the same in Korea, and a fuller treatment of Japanese Shingon history. Despite the date of its composition, this work cannot yet be completely ignored, because of the excellent source materials the author cites and also because the author shows considerable sophistication in handling historical data, particularly with reference to the Indian foundation. But this work also needs to be examined critically because of the vast amount of new information uncovered by both historians and Buddhologists in the last four decades, information which was not available in Toganoo's

time.

VI. Shingon Textual Studies

1 Hakeda, Yoshito S. *Kūkai: Major Works. Translated with an Account of his Life and a Study of his Thought*. New York: Columbia University Press, 1972. This work contains the translation of the following works of Kūkai:
1) "Indications of the Goals of the Three Teachings," pp. 101–139.
2) "A Memorial Presenting a List of Newly Imported *Sūtras* and Other Items," pp. 140–150.
3) "The Difference between Exoteric and Esoteric Buddhism," pp. 151–157.
4) "The Precious Key to the Secret Treasury," pp. 157–224.
5) "Attaining Enlightenment in this very Existence," pp. 225–234.
6) "The Meanings of Sound, Word, and Reality," pp. 234–246.
7) "The Meanings of the Word *Huṃ*," pp. 246–262.
8) "The Secret Key to the *Heart Sūtra*," pp. 262–275.
These are excellent translations of texts heretofore unavailable in any Western languages. However, a preface describing the central theme of a given text and a more elaborate annotation of the translation would have contributed to a better understanding of these very difficult texts.

2 Kambayashi Ryūjō. *Dainichi-kyō, Rishū-kyō Kōgi* (Lectures on the *Mahāvairocana Sūtra* and on the *Prajñāpāramitā-naya-parivarta* [a chapter on the *Mahāsankhya Vajramogha-satya-samaya-sūtra*]), (*Daizō-kyō kōgi* series, Vol. 6). Tōkyō: Tōhō shoin, 1933. An excellent translation and commentary on the *Mahāvairocana Sūtra* and on the *Prajñāpāramitā-naya-parivarta*, analyzing the contents passage by passage. Technical terms are adequately defined. An excellent source for those interested in serious studies of these two important Shingon texts. Highly recommended.

3 Kanayama Bokushō and Yanagida Kenjūrō. *Nihon Shingon no tetsugaku*. (The Philosophy of Shingon). Tōkyō: Kōbundō shōbō, 1943 (first print). This work, despite its title, is essentially an interpretive account of the *Hizō-hōyaku*. It is a useful work for a beginner to gain some understanding of the doctrinal contents of the *Hizō-hōyaku*. Kanayama Bokushō was one of the eminent Shingon scholars and practitioners of pre-war (and the period immediately following post-war) Japan. Yanagida Kenjūrō's field is Western philosophy. (He later became a left-wing writer of some sort.) But one hardly notices a Western philosophical interpretation of the *Hizō-hōyaku* in this work.

4 Katsumata Shunkyō. *Himitsu mandara jūjūshin-ron* (The Ten Stages of Mental Development). Tōkyō: Meiji shoin, 1954. This is essentially a translation of the *Jūjū shin-ron* into modern Japanese. The translation is carefully accom-

plished. But the greatest value of this work lies in citing primary sources Kūkai employed in the composition of the *Jūjū shin-ron*. It is not an interpretive work. As such, it is not designed for the popular reader but rather for advanced students in Shingon studies, particularly for those interested in philological and textual research.

5 Miyasaka Ninshō. *Dainichikyō ni kiku* (An Interpretive Account of the *Mahāvairocana Sūtra*). Tōkyō: Kyōiku shinchō-sha, 1970. A useful reference for those interested in familiarizing themselves with the general contents of the *Mahāvairocana Sūtra*. Not necessarily a source to be employed for serious research.

6 Miyasaka Yūshō. *Ningen no shujusō*. (The Destinies of Man). Tōkyō: Chikuma-shobō, 1967. An excellent interpretive account of the *Hizō-hōyaku* for the popular reader. A good classical bibliography on the *Hizō-hōyaku*, with some entries on modern works, is provided in the appendix. Even those seriously committed to investigate the *Hizō-hōyaku* might do well to examine this work written by a respectful Shingon scholar.

7 Morita Ryūsen. *Shaku makaen-ron no kenkyū*. (A Study on the Commentary on the *Awakening of Mahāyāna Faith*). Kyōto: Yamashiroya bunseidō, 1935. A writer of many works on Shingon, such as *Kōbō Daishi no nyūjō-kan* (Kōbō Daishi's concept of *Nirvāṇa*), *Shingon Mikkyō no honshitsu* (The Essence of Shingon *Mikkō*), *Himitsu bukkyō-shi* (History of Shingon Buddhism), etc., Morita is an accomplished Shingon scholar representative of the pre-war generation. The *Shaku makaen-ron* is one of the most important texts from which many of Kūkai's ideas are derived. Morita's *Shaku makaen-ron no kenkyū* is the standard work on studies of *Shakū makaen-ron*, despite the fact that it was published four decades ago. This work deals with the history of the transmission of the *Shaku makaen-ron* from China to Japan, the role that this text played in the history of the development of Buddhism in Japan, and a careful analysis and interpretation of the text itself. No comprehensive work of this kind has yet been published in recent years. Highly recommended.

8 Tajima Ryūjun. *Etude sur le Mahāvairocana-sūtra (Dainichikyō); avec la traduction commentee du premier chapitre*. Paris: Adrien Maisonneuve, 1936. This is the only available translation of the *Mahāvairocana Sūtra* (first chapter) in a Western language. The translation was made from the Chinese.

9 Takai Kankai. *Hizō-hōyaku, Ben kenmitsu nikyō-ron, Sokushin jōbutsu-gi kōgi* (Lectures on the *Hizō-hōyaku*, *Ben kenmitsu nikyō-ron* and *Sokushin jōbutsu-gi*) (Daizōkyō kōgi Series, Vol. 15). Tōkyō: Tōhō shoin, 1935. An excellent reference for those interested in a serious study of these important Shingon texts. It contains a carefully annotated translation, followed by a detailed

interpretation and analysis of the texts. Highly recommended.

10 Toganoo Shōun. *Hizō-hōyaku to kaisetsu* (An Interpretive Study of the *Hizō-hōyaku*). Kōya-san: Kōya-san University Press, 1949. The *Hizō-hōyaku* is translated into modern Japanese, with some footnotes and content analysis. A good classical bibliography on *Hizō-hōyaku* studies is provided in the appendix. Not for the popular reader.

11 Sakai Shinten. *Dainichi-kyō no seiritsu ni kansuru kenkyū*. (A Study on the *Mahāvairocana Sūtra*). Kōya-san: Kōya-san University Press, 1962 (first print), 1974 (second print). An elaborate study on the *Mahāvairocana Sūtra*, comparing the Chinese and Tibetan translations, and written by a contemporary Shingon Tibetologist and Sanskritist. An indispensable source for those interested in philological and textual study of the *Mahāvairocana Sūtra*. The Japanese syntax needs more careful editing. For the specialists.

12 *Sangō shiiki Shōryō-shū*. (A Guidline to the Three Systems of Thought and Collection of Poems), tr. into modern Japanese by Watanabe Shōkō and Miyasaka Yūshō (in the *Nihon koten bungaku taikei* Series). Tōkyō: Iwanami shoten, 1965 (first print), 1967 (second print). An important source to understand the thought of Kūkai. Carefully edited and translated into good modern literary Japanese. The *Sangō-shiiki* is a composition of Kūkai. It discusses the three systems of thought—Buddhism, Taoism and Confucianism. The *Shōryō-shū* is a collection of poems allegedly composed by Kūkai.

VII. Shingon Art

1 *ARS Buddhica—Daigo-ji*. Comp. by the Academic Council of Buddhist Art (Bukkyō geijitsu gakkai), Vol. 42. Tōkyō: Mainichi Press, 1960. A collection of studies on Daigo-ji's *Mikkyō* art with illustration and explanation.

2 *Buttō* (Buddhist *Stūpa*). Comp. by Tsujimura Taien. Nara: Gangō-ji (undated). Pictorial illustrations and identification of ancient collection of stūpas found in the monasteries of Nara.

3 *Gorintō no kigen* (The Origin of the five-story *stūpa*). Comp. by Yabuta Kaichirō. Kyōto: Bunkō-sha, 1967. Interesting essays concerning the origin and development of the five-story stūpas by art historians.

4 *Kōbō Daishi no risō to geijitsu* (Kōbō Daishi's Ideals and Art). Comp. by Mikkyō kenkyū-kai of Kōya-san. Kōya-san: Kōya-san University, 1948. An interesting work to be read by a beginner interested in Shingon doctrine and its art.

5 *Mikkyō to ōjō* (*Mikkyō* and the Imperial City). Comp. by Takeuchi Rizō and Sawa Takaaki (in the Bunka no rekishi Series, No. 5). Tōkyō: Toppan insatsu, 1969. *Mikkyō* thought and practice are described through Mikkyō art. Excellent pictures. Indispensable material for those interested in the socio-

cultural aspect of *Mikkyō*. Highly recommended.

6 Sawa Takaaki. *Kūkai no kiseki* (The Miracles of Kūkai). Tōkyō: Mainichi Press, 1973. Interesting book describing Kūkai from the perspective of art history.

7 ——. *Mikkyō no bijitsu* (*Mikkyō* Art) (Nihon no bijitsu Series, No. 8). Tōkyō: Heibon-sha, 1964. A valuable book on *Mikkyō* art. Excellent pictures with comments are presented in historical sequence. Of particular interest are the *maṇḍalas* presented in outline form. Highly recommended.

8 *Taishi no midera* (Kōbō Daishi's Monastery). Comp. and published by Kyōto: Tōji bunkazai hozon-kai, 1965. The standard work on pictorial illustrations related to the Tōji monastery. Excellent pictures.

9 Watanabe Shōkō, Shimizu Zensō. *Butsuzō hyakutai* (Hundred Buddha Statues). Tokyo: Tankō-sha, 1964. Excellent pictorial illustration and explanation of Shingon deities by a Shingon scholar and an art historian.

10 *Hokyōintō no kigen* (The Origin of the Seven-story Stūpa). Comp. by Yabuta Kaichiro. Kyōto: Sōgei-sho, 1967. This is a continuation on the previously cited stūpa study (no. 3 above), both of which are excellent sources for specialists in the field of *stūpa* studies.

VIII. Shingon *Maṇḍala*

1 Gonda Daisōjō. *Mandara tsūge* (Introduction to *Maṇḍala*). Kyōto: Heigosha, 1919. A very carefully researched work and a classic in mandala studies. But this work might be difficult to be found in many libraries. Toganoo's work (see no. 4 below) therefore is recommended instead.

2 Hamada Ryūchō. *Mandara no sekai* (The World of the *Maṇḍala*). Tōkyō: Bijitsu shuppan-sha, 1971. Useful and interesting reference on Shingon *Maṇḍalas* with illustrations.

3 Tajima Ryūjun. *Les Deux Grand Maṇḍalas et la Doctrine de l'Esoterisme Shingon*. Tōkyō: Maison Franco-Japanaise, 1959. An excellent introductory work on the *Garbhakosadhātu* and *Vajradhātu Maṇḍalas*, with illustrations.

4 Toganoo Shōun. *Mandara no kenkyū* (A Study on the *Maṇḍalas*). Kyōto: Naigai Press, 1927. The best among all possible *maṇḍala* studies in any language, this work deals with the history of the development of *maṇḍalas* in general, as well as with the two major Shingon *maṇḍalas—Garbhakośadhātu* and *Vajradhātu*—making reference to both Sanskrit and Chinese sources. Index in both Sanskrit and Chinese. Excellent bibliography. Highly recommended.

IX. Shingon Ritual and Practice

1 Akiyama Masami. *Butsuzō no insō o tazunete* (*Mudrās* in Buddhist Statues).

Tōkyō: Bunshindō, 1973. Excellent source for those interested in Shingon mudrās. Good illustrations.

2 Saunders, E. Dale. *Mudrā: A Study of Symbolic Gestures in Japanese Buddhist Sculpture*. New York: Bollingen Foundation, 1960. A good study on the Shingon *mudrā*, based upon actual research at the Kōya-san monastery, with illustrations. Though it lacks adequate doctrinal interpretation, this is the only English source on Shingon *mudrā* presented in a comprehensive manner.

3 Tamura Buemon. *Zuin-shū* (Mudrā). Kyōto: Kokusho kankō-kai, 1972 (new print). (First print in 1883). Interesting reference for those interested in *mudrās*.

4 Toganoo Shōun. *Himitsu jisō no kenkyū*. (A Study on *Mikkyō* Practice). Kyōto: Naigai Press, 1959. One of the most comprehensive works on Shingon *jisō* (ritual-practice) treated historically and analytically, making reference to a vast range of primary source materials. Excellent bibliography. Index in both Japanese and Sanskrit. Highly recommended.

5 Yamasaki Yasuhiro. *Mikkyō no meisō-hō* (Method of *Mikkyō* Meditation). Kyōto: Nagata bunshō-dō, 1974. Interesting work on Shingon meditation for those interested in the practical aspect of Shingon.

6 *Zoku Shingon-shū zensho*. (See "Collected Works on Shingon and Kōbō Daishi (Kūkai)," (no. III-8, above) for full citation and comments. This is the standard reference work on Shingon practice.

GLOSSARY OF TECHNICAL TERMS

This glossary provides definitions of technical terms employed in this work. It is limited to doctrinal terms, not terms designating places, personalities, deities and texts. Entries consist of terms in Sanskrit and in Japanese. (Romanized terms in parenthesis, whenever indicated, is the Chinese reading of a Japanese term.) Each entry is followed by Chinese (sometimes Japanese) characters. A Chinese character in parentheis refers to an alternate rendition of a Buddhist Sanskrit term in Chinese. The alternate rendition of character is not provided for all characters. It is provided only for the most commonly ones the reader may find in Buddhist Chinese texts, dictionaries and encyclopedias. No distinction is made between the 'old' and 'new' Chinese translation of Buddhist Sanskrit terms. I have selected the characters most frequently employed in Buddhist Chinese today.

Abhidharma 阿毘達磨 1. One of the three great divisions of the Buddhist Canon or *Tripiṭaka*. That section which consists of the systematic exposition and interpretation of Buddhist doctrine by early disciples and scholastics. 2. The title given to the Sarvāstivādin branch of Hīnayāna, after the time of King Aśoka, and based upon the voluminous analytical texts termed 'Abhidharma literature'. The basic doctrine is the theory of the absence of a self-essence (*anātman*, *asvabhāva*) and the theory that only momentary elements (*dharmas*) do exist within the impermanence of the cognitive process.

ācārya 阿闍梨 A Buddhist descriptive term and epithet, describing a master or teacher of doctrine and practice. Also a senior monk.

ādarśa-jñāna 大圓鏡智 In the Yogācāra Vijñapti-mātratā doctrine (consciousness-only) this term describes the transformed or purified *ālaya-vijñāna*—the post-*parāvṛtti* pure consciousness of the *bodhicitta* or Buddha-nature.

adhimukti 信解 A general Buddhist term for 'faith', signifying the security and peace of a practitioner's mind undisturbed by any doubts which normally accompany initial faith. It also means faith-understanding.

adhiṣṭhāna 加持 The Tantric Buddhist theory of doctrine and practice, which is an idealization of the mystical power of the *Dharmakāya* Mahāvairocana as the universal source of Tantric enlightenment. *Adhiṣṭnāna* is the union between the *tri-guhya* characterization of Mahāvairocana (*kāya-guhya*, *vāg-guhya*, *mano-*

guhya) and the tri-karma actions of sentient beings (*kāya-karma*, *vāk-karma*, *manaḥ-karma*).

A-ji meditation 阿字觀 The idealization of the principles of Tantric Buddhist doctrine, in a visual and oral form of the letter *A*. As the first letter of the Sanskrit alphabet, it is the source of all things (of all other letters), and the symbol both of emptiness and co-arising.

alakṣaṇa 無相 'Markless or aspectless'. A Buddhist technical term in contrast to laksana (having perceivable 'marks' or aspects), *alakṣaṇa* denotes the complete absence of any kind of perceivable mark or aspect in a phenomena or entity.

ālaya-vijñāna 阿賴耶識 The eighth level of consciousness in the Yogācāra doctrine of *vijñapti-mātratā* (consciousness-only). This is the store consciousness which contains and collects defiled seeds from discriminative cognition as well as the dormant pure seeds of *bodhicitta*. The *ālaya* is the repository of seeds and potentials; it is the basis of the first seven levels of consciousness; and that level of the mind where the karmic process thrives. The *ālaya's* close relationship to the deluded and discriminative manas produces the false impressions of an ego in the minds of sentient beings. And it is also in the *ālaya* that through *parāvṛtti* (transformation), the *bodhicitta* or Buddha-nature is awakened.

anutpāda (*akāra-anutpāda*) 本不生 Non-arising, non-creation or birth. In Hīnayāna it signifies nirvāna, no further arising or extinction; Mahāyāna Mādhyamika enlarges the concept to a universal, the Middle Path of no birth and death, and non-arising and non-destruction of phenomena and activities.

anuttarayoga 無上瑜伽 A Tantric Buddhist doctrinal and textual criterion, meaning 'the supreme yoga'.

asaṃskṛta dharma 無為法 'Unconditioned dharma'. That which is not created or does not arise, and is not produced by causation. The unconditioned is alluded to by the conceptual expressions of Buddhist truth like *bodhi*, *tathatā*, *nirvāṇa*, etc.

asvabhāva 無自性 A Buddhist technical term in contrast to *svabhāva* (own-being, essence or self-nature), *asvabhāva* denotes the complete absence of any kind of basis, own-being, essence or self-nature in any phenomenon or entity. *Asvabhāva* implies that phenomena and events originate due to the nature of co-arising (*pratitya-samutpāda*). There is also the second implication in Mahāyāna Buddhism, that the true basis, essence and nature of phenomena and events is emptiness (*śūnyatā*).

āśvāsa 蘇息 or 無畏 To 'revive the mind', to rediscover the *bodhicitta* wisdom inherent within the minds of sentient beings.

avidyā 無明 A traditional Buddhist technical term denoting 'ignorance' as the inhibition of sentient beings bound to karma and *saṃsāra*, and as the absence of an understanding of Buddhist truth and the inherent realization of one's *bod-*

hicitta.

avijñapti (karma) 無表業 An Abhidharma (e.g. Sarvāstivāda) technical term denoting non-bodily (unmanifest or unseen—mental) activity and the retributive effect which must accompany it.

bala 力 One of the ten *pāramitās* or perfections of *bodhisattva* practice. Specifically *bala* is 'power' or the constant energy necessary to enlighten all sentient beings.

bhadrakalpa 賢劫 A Buddhist measurement of time, *bhadrakalpa* is distinguished as the present era, in which a thousand buddhas of wisdom are said to exist. The previous era was a thousand buddhas of glory and the future era will be a thousand buddhas of celestial (constellar) quality.

Bhagavān 世尊 A common literary epithet of a Buddha, meaning 'the world-honored one'.

bhikṣu 比丘 An ordained male or monk, as one of the four categories of early Buddhist practitioners established by Śākyamuni.

bhikṣuṇi 比丘尼 An ordained female or nun, as one of the four categories of early Buddhist practitioners established by Śākyamuni.

bhūmi 地 A Sanskrit noun meaning 'earth, ground, site, position' with the Buddhist connotation of 'foundation' (for practice). Frequently translated as a stage.

bodhi 菩提 A traditional Buddhist term for the concept of 'enlightenment'. *Bodhi* also represents *nirvāṇa* (expiration) and *prajñā* (wisdom). *Bodhi* technically differs from nirvāna in that the latter has a negative connotation of the expiration of all delusion and liberation from all suffering, while the former connotes the positive aspect of success in achieving the wisdom of Buddhist truth.

bodhicitta 菩提心 'The mind of enlightenment'. A traditional Buddhist doctrinal concept expressing the aspiration to enlightenment, the Buddha-nature inherent in all sentient beings.

bodhisattva 菩薩 1. In early Indian Buddhism, the term was used to describe Śākyamuni (e.g. in the *Jātaka* tales) of his previous births. 2. With the rise of Indian Mahāyāna Buddhism, this term was used in contrast to *Śrāvaka* and *Pratyekabuddha*, and came to mean the compassionate Mahāyāna practitioner—who by virtue of the *bodhisattva* vows and practice of the *pāramitās*, strives to aid in the enlightenment of all sentient beings. 3. Later, the term was used, particularly in Chinese and Japanese Buddhism, as a title of respect bestowed upon an eminent monk or layman, who exemplifies Mahāyāna practice.

Brahmanism 婆羅門教 The title of an ancient Indian religious tradition which centered upon the ritual texts and sacrifices of the Vedas.

buddha 佛 An Enlightened One, an Awakener, the Knower. 1. In Hīnayāna: A successful practitioner who has realized the truth of Buddhist teachings through a meditative process, and experienced the *pariṇirvāṇa* or the total extinction of action and retribution and body and mind (referring specifically to Śākyamuni). 2. In Mahāyāna: The embodiment of enlightenment defined by the *tri-kāya* doctrine of *Dharmakāya*, *saṃbhogakāya* and *nirmāṇakāya*, and the ultimate goal of the *bodhisattva* wisdom qualified by the compassion to enlighten all sentient beings.

Buddhayāna 佛乘 The vehicle of practice resulting in Buddhahood. This term denotes the all-encompassing characteristic of *Ekayāna*, and in Shingon specifically refers to the universal realm or sphere of the *Dharmakāya* Mahāvairocana.

caitta 心所 Mentals, that which the mind possesses. In relation to the function of the mind, a *caitta* is the existence of objects or mentals which the mind utilizes in the cognitive process.

cakrakāya 法輪身 Literally 'wheel body', the 'body' which spreads the Dharma. Shingon conceives of three wheel-bodies: *svabhāvacakrakāya* (truth *per se* which is represented by *Dharmakāya* Mahāvairocana), *saddharmacakrakāya* (compassion *per se*) and *ādeśanācakrakāya* (compassion through anger). (The second and third represent attributes of Mahāvairocana.)

caryā 行 (儀軌) A Tantric Buddhist doctrinal and textual criterion, specifically referring to mental activity or meditational purpose in the practice of ritual.

caryāgiti チャリヤーギーティ A vernacular Tantric literature developed by the Sahajayāna branch of Vajrayāna.

chi (*chih*) 智 A Chinese philosophical concept, developed from the *I-ching*, and adapted by Chinese Buddhism to mean 'awareness, understanding, knowledge'. In Shingon *chi* came to denote the 'knower'. In contrast to *ri*, 'that which should be known'.

cintāmaṇi 如意宝珠 A fabulous wish-fulfilling jewel, legendarily claimed to be obtainable from the *nāga* or dragon king.

citta 心 Simple traditional Buddhist descriptive term denoting the mind.

citta-mātra 唯識 The Yogācāra doctrinal concept of consciousness-only, that all phenomena and events are of the mind and from the mind. Therefore this mind, which is the only entity of perception, cognition and discrimination, is not a fixed state but a constant flowing stream, wherein the effects of action are deposited to mature. And in contrast to the pre-realization *vijñapti-mātra* concept of consciousness-only, *citta-mātra* signifies the purified mind of true cognition, which is Buddha-nature.

citta-utpanna 發菩提心 To 'awaken the mind', to develop the realization of enlightenment, the *bodhicitta*.

Confucianism The title of the indigenous Chinese system of moral and social philosophy, based upon the writings of Confucius and Mencius, which formed the social and ethical basis for traditional Chinese civilization.

dāna 布施 One of the six *pāramitās* or perfections of *bodhisattva* practice. Specifically *dāna* is 'charity' or 'offering', the ability to present Buddhist truth or any other possession for the purpose of enlightening all sentient beings.

daśabhūmi 十地 The Buddhist technical term signifying the forty-first through fiftieth stages of the fifty-two stages of Mahāyāna *bodhisattva* practice. As the most important group of stages within this practice, the (ten) *daśabhūmi* stages are designed to realize the union of self-enlightenment and the enlightenment of others. Shingon, however, claims that the first *daśabhūmi* stage is the ultimate, incorporating within itself all other *daśabhūmi* stages.

dhāraṇi 陀羅尼 The idealization of a Tantric Buddhist principle within the context of a simple verse, which contains spiritual potential when utilized in Tantric Buddhist practice. *Dhāraṇi* is not to be confused with *mantra*, for *mantra* is a simplification of a *dhāraṇi*.

dharma 法 1. An element of existence, a perceivable element subject to asvabhāva and co-arising. 2. The truth, teachings or doctrinal laws of Buddhism which correctly describe the universal condition of sentient beings and enlightenment. 3. Codified morality.

Dharmadhātu 法界 The embodiment of Buddhist truth in the form of the realm of sentient beings or the universe. This term characterizes, for example, the world-view of the Chinese Hua-yen school of Buddhism, which by application of its Four *Dharmadhātu* theory, finds the phenomenal realm to be the only true existence, as the co-dependent relationship between delusion-suffering and enlightenment (*saṃsāra—nirvāṇa*) is established.

Dharmadhātu-svabhāva-jñāna 法界体性智 One of the five *jñānas* of Shingon doctrine. This *jṇāna* represents the universality of the truth of Shingon doctrine (the wisdom of Mahāvairocana) and encompasses the other four of these five *jñānas*, which are the *ādarsa-*, *pratyavekṣaṇā-*, *krtyānuṣthāna-*, and *samatā-jñānas* of the purified mind within Yogācāra Vijñapti-mātratā doctrine.

Dharmagupta 法蔵部 A faction which developed from the Mahīsāsaka group of the Sarvāstivādin branch of Hīnayāna Buddhism, claiming lineage from the disciple Maudgalyāyana. The Dharmagupta developed the mantra from its minor position in the Pāli Canon.

Dharmakāya 法身 One of the *tri-kāyas*, the three aspects or bodies which characterize the concept of Buddha within Mahāyāna Buddhist doctrine. The *Dharmakāya* is the Dharma-body, the embodiment of the highest Buddhist truth, which is the absolute and unconditioned Buddha-nature, otherwise termed tathatā.

Dharma-maṇḍala 法曼荼羅 One *maṇḍala* of the Shingon Four *Maṇḍala* theory which together function as doctrinal representations to portray the Six Elements theory in terms of four different aspects. The *Dharma-maṇḍala* is a characterization of the Tantric Buddhist relationship between words, letters and sounds and their potential for expressing doctrinal truth.

dharma-śūnyatā 法空 An application of the *śūnyatā* concept to the concept of *dharmas*, signifying that all elements and activities of existence have no *svabhāva* or self-essence, and implying that dharmas arise due to the nature of co-arising.

dhātu 界 A Buddhist technical term meaning 'sphere, realm, region or sense-field'. A sense-field or realm is the context which defines the limits of a particular perception or activity.

dhyāna 定 1. A general term for meditation, a practice of mental concentration which attempts to eliminate or transcend the reasoning process of the intellect and to increase awareness by the exclusion of extraneous thoughts. The general goal of an intense and well-developed *dhyāna* practice is the realization of *bodhicitta*. 2. One of the six pāramitās of *bodhisattva* practice. Specifically *dhyāna* is 'meditation', the mental concentrative practice to intuitionally experience understanding Buddhist truth which is essential for enlightening all sentient beings.

dohā ドーハ A vernacular Tantric literature developed by the Sahajayāna branch of Vajrayāna.

duḥkha 苦 Suffering or pain, and the central tenet of the first of the early Buddhist four noble truth theory—*duḥkha-satya*, that all existence is suffering. Also one of the elements in the early cyclic causational theory of *kleśa*, *karma*, *duḥkha* (delusion, action-retribution, suffering).

Ekayāna 一乗 In contrast to the doctrinal distinctions of Hīnayāna, Mahāyāna and *tri-yāna*, the Ekayāna or the One, universal and all-encompassing vehicle, is the cumulative doctrinal theme of later Mahāyāna Buddhism popularized in China and Japan. As doctrine, this concept totally asserts the Buddha-nature inherent in all sentient beings, and as practice this concept implies the encompassing or inclusion of all previous methods and disciplines of both Hīnayāna and Mahāyāna schools of Buddhism.

garbha 胎 A Sanskrit noun, meaning "womb, interior, embryo" with the Buddhist connotation of a 'fertile interior (which something develops from), the true potential'.

Garbhakośadhātu Maṇḍala 胎蔵界曼荼羅 One of the two great forms (kinds) of Shingon *maṇḍala*. This *maṇḍala* of the 'repository of truth' symbolizes the concept of the five elements as *ri*, the known. The *maṇḍala* also expresses the doctrinal relationship between *bodhicitta*, compassion and skillful means.

gati 趣 The traditional Buddhist hierarchy of sentient beings within the three realms of desire, form and non-form. This hierarchy consists of six stages of existence or destinies: hell, hungry-beings, beasts, fighting-beings, men, and gods.

genzu mandara 現圖曼荼羅 A Shingon descriptive term meaning 'iconographic *maṇḍala*'.

gorin jōshin 五輪成身 A symbolic characterization of the Shingon theory of the five elements of the universe (the jewel as space, the half-globe as wind, the trapezoid as fire, the globe as water and the square as earth). *Gorin jōshin* is the ideal combination of components to comprise the 'perfect body'. This 'five element developing-body' is a doctrinal idealization of the *Dharmakāya* Mahāvairocana which the practitioner attempts to identify with and realize as his own body.

hetu-pratyaya 因縁 A Buddhist technical term describing the process of causation, as the combination of a primary or direct cause (*hetu*) and secondary or indirect causes (*pratyaya*).

Hīnayāna 小乗 The 'Lesser Vehicle', the pejorative term used to describe early Indian Buddhist schools and practices based upon the Pāli or early Canon, specifically referring to the disciplines of the *Śrāvaka* and *Pratyekabuddha*. These disciplines and goals are taken by Mahāyāna to be individually-oriented and therefore inferior to the compassion to enlighten sentient beings of the *bodhisattva* practice.

hompushō 本不生 The Shingon term for *anutpāda*.

honji 本地 The 'fundamental essence or nature'. In Shingon, *honji* denotes *Dharmakāya* (the Buddha Mahāvairocana) and particularly the six elements as the essential nature of the *Dharmakāya* Buddha.

Hossō (Fa-hsiang) 法相 The Chinese and Japanese Yogācāra schools based upon the *Vijñaptimātratā-siddhi*. One of the thirteen major Chinese schools and eight major Japanese schools. Hossō means the 'marks or aspects of dharmas' and refers to the Yogācāra analysis of constituents and the question of the reality which underlies them.

hṛdaya 心 A Sanskrit noun, meaning 'heart, interior, core' with the Buddhist connotation of 'the essence or center, heart'.

hyōtoku-mon 表徳門 A Japanese Buddhist technical term which denotes the positive reality of all dharmas as an expression of the origins of virtue. In contrast to *shajō-mon*.

Ichinen sanzen (*I-hsin san-ch'ien*) 一念三千 'Three thousand realms in one mind'. The Tendai doctrinal and meditational concept which integrates all possible realms of sentient beings into a relationship of synthesis within the mind of an individual.

Indra's Net 帝網 Indra's Net expresses one view of the relationship between all phenomena and events in the Universe. It is a metaphor of the net in the heaven of the Brahmanic god Indra, and in this net there is a jewel affixed at the intersection of each point where one strand of rope crosses another. One jewel reflects the light of all other jewels while each of the others in turn reflects the first jewel reflecting them, and these multiple reflections continue. The jewels represent the co-dependency of individual phenomena and activity while the light represents the relationship of truth and *tathatā* to phenomenal activity.

Isshin Sangan (*I-hsin San-kuan*) 一心三観 'Three meditations in one mind'. The Tendai doctrinal and meditational concept which synthesizes three Mādhyamika concepts into a simultaneous phenomenal view: emptiness, co-dependency and the middle (which transcends the dichotomy created by positing the first two). This integration is characterized by Tendai as the three aspects of phenomena.

jisō 事相 Ritual practice in contrast to doctrine, within Shingon Buddhism.

jñāna 知 (識) 1. A Buddhist technical term denoting knowledge or intellectual judgement of phenomena and activities and their fundamental laws. Sometimes used in contrast to *prajñā* (wisdom or intuitive realization of Buddhist truth). 2. One of the ten *pāramitās* or perfections of *bodhisattva* practice. Specifically *jñāna* is 'knowledge', the intellectual understanding of Buddhist doctrine as the rational communication of Buddhist truth necessary to enlighten all sentient beings.

kaji 加持 In contrast to *honji*, the *Dharmakāya* Mahāvairocana as the fundamental nature, *kaji* refers to any manifested body or form of this nature. The interpretation of *kaji* in relation to Mahāvairocana (*honji*) became the major element in doctrinal schism within the Shingon sect. *Kaji* is the Japansee version of *adhiṣṭhāna*.

kaji-jōbutsu 加持成佛 One of the three categorie of Shingon 'instant buddhahood' theory in the *Ihon sokushin jōbutsu-gi* (The Later *Sokushin jōbutsu-gi*). It denotes that the successful realization of man as Buddha requires the *adhiṣṭhāna* integration of *tri-guhya* and *tri-karma*.

kalpa 劫 A unit of measuring time within traditional Buddhism, to denote periods of progression toward doctrinal goals. Loosely defined as an eon, Shingon interprets the concept to mean stages of progression or levels of spiritual proficiency instead of the mere temporal measurement of such.

karma 業 The basic Buddhist doctrinal concept of mental or bodily action and necessarily-resultant retribution, which establishes the context for the suffering and delusion of sentient beings.

Karma-maṇḍala 羯磨曼荼羅 One *maṇḍala* of the Shingon Four *Maṇḍala* theory, which together function as doctrinal representations to portray the Six Elements theory in terms of four different aspects. The *Karma-maṇḍala* is a characterization of the effort and activity of buddhas and *bodhisattvas* in their advocation of Buddhist enlightenment.

karuṇā 慈悲 The general Buddhist term which describes compassion as the motivation of *bodhisattva* practice, and the necessary co-relative of *prajñā* in the *bodhisattva* effort to enlighten all sentient beings.

kāya-guhya 身密 One of the *tri-guhya* Tantric Buddhist theory of doctrine and practice, *kāya-guhya* is the 'body' characteristic of the *Dharmakāya* Mahāvairocana, which parallels the *kāya-karma* (body) action of sentient beings. It is through the *adhiṣṭhāna* practice of the *mudrā* that the union between practitioner and Buddha is effected.

kāya-karma 身業 One of the *tri-karma* Tantric Buddhist theory of doctrine and practice, *kāya-karma* is the 'body' action of sentient beings. It is through the *adhiṣṭhāna* practice of *mudrā* that the union between practitioner and Buddha is effected.

Kegon (Hua-yen) 華厳 One of the thirteen major schools of Chinese Buddhism, founded by Tu-shun (557–640) and systematized by Fa-tsang (643–712), and based upon the *Avataṃsaka Sūtra*. This indigenous Chinese *Ekayāna* school is characterized by its theories of co-arising, the Four *Dharmadhātu*, the Six Aspects, and the Ten Theories of causation. Its world-view is then expressed by the term '*dharmadhātu*'. One of the six scholastic sects of Japanese Nara Buddhism.

kendoku-jōbutsu 顕徳成佛 One of the three categories of Shingon 'instant buddhahood' theory in the *Ihon sokushin jōbutsu-gi* (The Later *Sokushin jōbutsu-gi*). It denotes that successful *adhiṣṭhāna* practice of the body, speech and mind (*tri-guhya* realized in *tri-karma*) is the complete revelation of Buddha-nature as inherent in sentient beings.

kengyō 顕教 A descriptive term used by Shingon Buddhism to contrast its textual interpretation, texts, doctrine and practice, from those of all other Buddhist schools. The textual interpretations, texts, doctrines and practices of all other schools are termed the 'revealed teaching' or exoteric Buddhism. The title connotes not only the difference but also the inferiority of non-Tantric teaching in relation to Tantric teaching, in terms of the potential for enlightenment.

kleśa 煩悩 The general Buddhist technical term which describes delusion, as the natural and ordinary condition of the ignorance, suffering and discrimination of sentient beings. Delusion must be understood, purified and removed, to achieve enlightenment and recognize inherent Buddha-nature.

kriyā 所作 A Tantric Buddhist doctrinal and textual criterion, specifically referring to the physical practice of ritual, or its 'external form'.

kṛtyānuṣṭhāna-jñāna 成所作智 In the Yogācāra *vijñapti-mātratā* doctrine (consciousness-only) this term describes the transformed or purified first five levels of consciousness—which is the post-*paravṛtti* non-discriminatory perfect practice (the perception of truth) of the *bodhicitta* or Buddha-nature.

kṣānti 忍辱 One of the six *pāramitās* or perfections of *bodhisattva* practice. Specifically *kṣānti* is 'patience', the constant endurance and understanding of difficulties encountered in enlightening all sentient beings.

kyō-han (*chiao-pan*) 教判 The system of doctrinal evaluation and classification developed by Chinese Buddhist philosophers to organize and synthesize the irregular body of imported Indian Buddhist textual materials and doctrines. This ahistorical critical doctrinal apparatus was utilized by Chinese schools to develop and justify their teachings, and this model was adopted by Kūkai in soldifying Tantric Buddhist teaching and material as the basis for his Shingon doctrine and practice.

Lotus *Ekyāna* 法華一乘 The particular universal and all-encompassing vehicle or practice (ekayāna) as defined by the doctrines of the *Lotus Sūtra*.

Mādhyamika 中觀 One of the two major philosophical schools of Indian Mahāyāna Buddhism, founded by Nāgārjuna and based upon his writings. Its basic doctrinal position is the 'Middle Path'—the negation of all forms of extreme views.

Mahā-maṇḍala 大曼荼羅 One *maṇḍala* of the Shingon Four *Maṇḍala* theory, which together function as doctrinal representations to portray the Six Element theory in terms of four different aspects. The *Mahā-maṇḍala* characterizes the universality of the existence of the *Dharmakāya* Mahāvairocana. The *Samaya-*, *Dharma-*, and *Karma-maṇḍalas* act as three atrributes of Mahāvairocana.

mahāsukha 大楽 (歓喜) 'The great bliss', the union of male and female energy in Tantric doctrine.

Mahāvairocana 大日 The idealization of the principles of Tantric Buddhist doctrine in the context of *Dharmakāya*. The idealization of Mahāvairocana as the Tantric source of all truth and enlightenment, parallels the image of the light as the universal source of all life.

Mahāyāna 大乘 The 'Greater Vehicle', the self-complimentary term used to describe the later schools of Indian, Chinese and Japanese Buddhism, centering upon the bodhisattva practice.

manaḥ-karma 意業 One of the *tri-karma* Tantric Buddhist theory of doctrine and practice, *manaḥ-karma* is the 'mind' (consciousness) action of sentient beings. It is through the *adhiṣṭhāna* practice of yoga that the union between practitioner and Buddha is effected.

manas 意 The seventh level of consciousness in the Yogācāra doctrine of *vijñapti-mātratā* (consciousness-only). This is the value-judging level of consciousness, which measures, calculates and discriminates the conceptualized sensory-material it has received from the sixth level, the *mano-vijñāna*.

maṇḍala 曼荼羅 The idealization of a Tantric Buddhist principle as the symbolic embodiment of a circular diagram and its individual components. The artistic expression of doctrinal elements and their unification in the complete diagram contains spiritual potential when utilized within Tantric Buddhist practice.

mano-guhya 意密 One of the *tri-guhya* Tantric Buddhist theory of doctrine and practice, *mano-guhya* is the mind (consciousness) characteristic of *Dharmakāya* Mahāvairocana, which parallels the *manaḥ-karma* (mind) action of sentient beings. It is through the *adhiṣṭhāna* practice of yoga that the union between practitioner and Buddha is effected.

mano-vijñāna 末那識 The sixth level of consciousness in the Yogācāra doctrine of *vijñapti-mātratā* (consciousness-only). This is the sense-center of mind-consciousness which receives and collects the perceptions cognized by the first five levels of consciousness. It is said to organize or conceptualize this sensory-data.

mantra 呪 (眞言) The idealization of a Tantric Buddhist principle as an embodiment of sound. Therefore a sacred syllable or incantation which contains spiritual potential when utilized within Tantric Buddhist practice.

Mantrayāna 眞言乘 The *mantra*-vehicle or Tantric Buddhist discipline and practice which utilizes the sound expression of the *mantra*.

māra 悪魔 The traditional Buddhist theory of the three evils or poisons of greed, hate and delusion.

mārga 道 A 'path', system of precepts or structure of religious practice which leads to liberation from delusion and suffering.

mikkyō 密教 The 'secret teaching' or esoteric Buddhism, which refers to the interpretation of Buddhist texts by Tantric Buddhist doctrine, and to Tantric Buddhist texts, doctrines and practices.

mudrā 印 The idealization of a Buddhist principle in the form of a hand gesture, either in practice or in the artistic representation of a Buddhist deity.

mūla 根 A term denoting 'basic', with the Tantric Buddhist connotation of 'condition', as one of the three aspects of the Triple Formula of the *Mahāvairocana Sūtra*.

Nikāya schools ニカーヤ (部派佛教) Early Indian Buddhist doctrinal factions which began to divide a century after the Buddha's death, until they formed the twenty schools of Hīnayāna by the time of King Aśoka (ca. 256–232 B.C.).

nirbhaya 無畏 A stage of mental peace within the process of awakening, in the Shingon Six *Nirbhaya* theory. *Nirbhaya* is a state of awakening by freeing oneself from the bonds of delusion, and awakening the realization of one's inherent Buddha-nature.

nirmāṇā-Dharmakāya 変化法身 A Shingon doctrinal concept referring to the nirmānakāya aspect specifically of the Tantric Buddhist *Dharmakāya* Mahāvairocana. However this particular *nirmāṇakāya* is qualified by the audience which it discourses to—only practitioners such as *Śrāvaka*, *Pratyekabuddhas* and *pre-daśabhūmi bodhisattvas*.

nirmāṇakāya 変化身 One of the *tri-kāyas* the three aspects or bodies which characterize the concept of Buddha within Mahāyāna Buddhist doctrine. The *nirmāṇakāya* is a historical personality (e.g. Śākyamuni) who explains Buddhist teachings to sentient beings and is the embodiment of the wisdom and compassion of enlightenment subject to the limitations of the discrimination of *saṃsāra*.

nirvāṇa 涅槃 'Blowing out, extinction', the state of enlightenment attained by Śākyamuni and the Hīnayāna goal of liberation from the suffering and delusion of sentient beings. The goal of the *Śrāvaka* and *Pratyekabuddha*.

nirvikalpa 無分別心 In contrast to *vikalpa*, this is the non-discrimination resultant from the process of *paravṛtti*. *Nirvikalpa* is true cognition of experience based upon the pure seeds of Buddha-nature (which had laid dormant in the *ālaya-vijñāna* prior to *parāvṛtti*).

niṣyanda-Dharmakāya 等流法身 A Shingon doctrinal concept referring to the *nirmāṇākāya* aspect specifically of the Tantric Buddhist *Dharmakāya* Mahāvairocana. However this particular *nirmāṇakāya* is qualified by the audience which it discourses to—only deluded sentient beings within the six destinies.

pāramitā 波羅密多 In early Buddhism, the term denoted 'crossing to the other shore' (Arhatship), but in Mahāyāna the term evolved into an abstract quality which characterized a *bodhisattva*. Here it meant 'perfection', and technically there are six *pāramitās* which must simultaneously be perfected for success in enlightening all sentient beings: charity (*dāna*), morality (*śila*), patience (*kṣānti*), effort (*virya*), meditation (*dhyāna*) and wisdom (*prajñā*). There later developed ten *pāramitās*, for four supplementary perfections (practices) were included to aid in bodhisattva practice: vow (*praṇidhāna*), skillful means (*upāya*), power (*bala*) and cognition (*jñāna*).

parasaṃbhoga-Dharmakāya 他受用法身 A Shingon doctrinal concept referring to one aspect of *saṃbhoga-Dharmakāya*. Shingon divides the *saṃbhogakāya* connotation of the enjoyment body as the embodiment of the glory and perfection of enlightenment, into self-enjoyment and others-enjoyment. This is the others-enjoyment aspect.

paratantra-svabhāva 依他起性 One aspect of the Yogācāra three *svahbāva* theory dealing with the nature of cognition. *Paratantra-svabhāva* is the nature of co-dependent and conditional causation in the universe. It is traditionally likened to correctly realizing a rope to be a rope (see '*parikalpita-svabhāva*') but also understanding the elements of the rope and their relationships.

parāvṛtti See *prāvṛtti*.

parikalpita-svabhāva 遍計所執 One aspect of the Yogācāra three-*svabhāva theory*. *Parikalpita-svabhāva* is the nature of false discrimination, a belief in the *svabhāva* of elements, events, and self. It is traditionally likened to falsely conceiving a rope to be a snake, and the real fear which arises in spite of the untrue perception.

parinișpanna-svabhāva 圓成実性 One aspect of the Yogācāra three-*svabhāva* theory. *Parinișpanna-svabhāva* is the ultimate-reality (*tathatā*), the Buddhist truth which underlies all phenomena in the three realms and six destinies. It is traditionally likened to the wisdom accomplished by having realized the mistake of taking a rope to be a snake (*parikalpita-svabhāva*), and then understanding the relationship of all elements (*paratantra-svabhāva*).

paryavasāna 究竟 A technical term denoting '*kleśa*' (that which entraps sentient beings in action-retribution and transmigration), with the Tantric Buddhist connotation of 'result', as one of the three aspects of the Triple Formula of the *Mahāvairocana Sūtra*.

pātayantikā 波夜提 A monastic moral or ethical offense related to speech, as defined by precept within the early Buddhist code of discipline, the *Vinaya*.

prajñā 智慧 (般若) 1. The general term which describes wisdom as the ability to correctly understand essential Buddhist doctrine (i.e. co-arising, *asvabhāva*, emptiness, *tathatā*) to be the true circumstance of all life and activity in the universe. 2. One of the six *pāramitās* or perfections of *bodhisattva* practice. Specifically *prajñā* here means wisdom, the quality of distinguishing between delusion and truth in enlightening all sentient beings. 3. In a general Mahāyāna sense, wisdom is the necessary co-relative of compassion, in the *bodhisattva* effort to enlighten all sentient beings.

praṇidhāna 願 One of the ten *pāramitās* or perfections of *bodhisattva* practice. Specifically *praṇidhāna is* 'vow' or 'resolution', a formal spiritual declaration of the *bodhisattva's* total devotion to enlightening all sentient beings.

pratītya-samutpāda 縁起 'Co-arising or dependent co-production'. A central conception in Buddhist doctrine, which describes the relationship of all phenomena and activities within the universe, to consist of total co-dependency. Co-arising is the theory of conditioned causality which combines with the theory of the absence of any own-being, essence or self-nature (*asvabhāva*) as well as with the impermanence of all phenomena, processes and goals, to produce the Buddhist conception of reality based upon emptiness.

pratyavekșaṇā-jñāna 妙観察智 In the Yogācāra *vijñapti-mātratā* doctrine (consciousness-only) this term describes the transformed or purified *mano-vijñāna*—which is the post-*parāvṛtti* insight into particulars (individual phenomenon) of the *bodhicitta* or Buddha-nature.

Pratyekabuddha 縁覚 (独覚) A Buddhist practitioner who achieved enlightenment independent of receiving doctrinal instruction or monastic discipline and practice, based upon a thorough realization of the twelve-fold cycle of causation.

pravṛtti (or *parāvṛtti*) 轉識 The Yogācāra doctrinal process which explains the revolution or transformation of the first seven consciousness levels from being subject to delusory cognition and discrimination (and thereby depositing defiled seeds in the *ālaya-vijñāna*), to becoming purified to truthfully cognize experience based upon the pure eeds sof Buddha-nature (which had previously laid dormant in the *ālaya*).

pudgala-śūnyatā 我空 An application of the *śūnyatā* concept to the concept of *pudgala*. *Pudgala* is the early Indian Buddhist concept of the existence of a permanent self which lies beneath and unifies the experience of impersonal dharmas. *Pudgala-śūnyatā* signifies that the *pudgala* or permanent self has no *svabhāva* or self-essence, and implies that the self is due to the nature of co-arising (*pratitya-samutpāda*).

pūjā 供養 A traditional Buddhist descriptive term meaning 'to offer, to honor, veneration, worship'.

ri (li) 理 A Chinese philosophical concept, developed from the *I-ching* and adapted by Chinese Buddhism (particularly the Hua-yen school) to mean the 'essence underlying phenomena, principle, an absolute'. In Shingon *ri* as 'essence' came to denote 'the truth that should be known'. In contrast to *chi*, the 'knower'.

rigu-jōbutsu 理具成佛 One of the three categories of Shingon 'instant-buddhahood' theory in the *Ihon sokushin jōbutsu-gi* (The Later *Sokushin jōbutsu-gi*). It denotes that because of *ri* (*bodhicitta*) man is really a Buddha.

rūpa 色 A traditional Buddhist descriptive term for matter, which has mass, is capable of obstruction and disintegration.

Sahajakāya 我身 Literally 'self-body'. A *Sahajayāna* concept which realizes ultimate truth within the context of the self.

Sahajayāna サハジャ乗 A branch of Vajrayāna. Sahaja means 'self'. This school attempts to realize ultimate truth within the context of the self.

samādhi 三昧 'Trance of concentration'. A specific level of meditation which is the concentration of the mind upon a single subject or theme.

samatā-jñāna 平等性智 In the Yogācāra *vijñapti-mātratā* doctrine (consciousness-only) this term describes the transformed or purified manas—which is the post-*parāvṛtti* non-discriminatory knowledge (perception of *tathatā*) of the *bodhicitta* or Buddha-nature.

Samaya-maṇḍala 三摩耶曼荼羅 One *maṇḍala* of the Shingon Four *Maṇḍala* theory, which together function as doctrinal representations to portray the Six Element theory in terms of four different aspects. The *Samaya-maṇḍala* is a characterization through symbolic representation, of *upāya* or skillful means, to show the varieties of attitudes and methods which must be the true talent of the *bodhisattva* in attempting to enlighten all sentient beings.

saṃbhoga-Dharmakāya 受用法身 A Shingon doctrinal concept referring to the *saṃbhogakāya* aspect, specifically of the Tantric Buddhist *Dharmakāya* Mahāvairocana. This *saṃbhoga-Dharmakāya* has two aspects, *svasaṃbhoga-Dharmakāya* and *parasaṃbhoga-Dharmakāya*.

saṃbhogakāya 受用身 One of the *tri-kāyas*, the three aspects or bodies which characterize the concept of Buddha within Mahāyāna Buddhist doctrine. The *saṃbhogakāya* is the enjoyment body, the embodiment of the glory and perfection of enlightenment in its role as celestial teacher and savior. This body is the successful result of *bodhisattva* practice and serves as the vehicle of expression among buddhas and *bodhisattvas*.

saṃsāra 輪廻 Transmigration, the traditional Buddhist term which denotes the perpetual repetition of birth and death in the three realms and the six destinies (*gati*). Transmigration is due to action-retribution (*karma*) which is caused by the ignorance and delusion of sentient beings.

saṃskṛta-dharma 有為法 'Conditioned *dharma*' or all phenomena, entities and activities which arise or are produced through causation. Common phenomena in contrast to *saṃskṛta-dharma*.

Sanron (San-lun) 三論 The Chinese and Japanese Mādhyamika schools. One of the thirteen major Chinese schools and eight major Japanese schools. Sanron means the 'three *sāstras*'—the *Mūla-madhyamaka Sāstra* and the *Dvādaśa-dvara Śāstra* by Nāgārjuna, and the *Śata Śāstra* by Āryadeva.

sattva-citta 衆生心 (凡夫心) The general Mahāyāna Buddhist term denoting the deluded mind of sentient beings.

shajō-mon 遮情門 A Japanese Buddhist technical term which denotes the elimination of ordinary delusions or false conceptions. In contrast to *hyōtoku-mon*.

Shingon 眞言 One of the eight major schools of Japanese Buddhism, founded by Kūkai (774–835) and based upon the *Mahāvairocana* and *Tattvasaṃgraha Sūtra* and the *Bodhicitta Śāstra*. It is defined by Kūkai's interpretations of Tantric Buddhist doctrine and practice. The school's doctrinal importance is its esoteric utilization of *adhiṣṭhāna*, the *Dharmakāya* Mahāvairocana and the *sokushin-jōbutsu* theory ('Buddhahood realized in the present body').

Shintō 神道 'The Way of the Gods', or the indigenous Japanese worship of natural phenomena, embodied as spirits and supported by textual mythology, ritual and architecture.

shoji soku goku 初地即極 A Shingon phrase which denotes that all the fifty-two stages of *bodhisattva* practice are implicit or totally included in the first stage. By implication the phrase signifies that although the fifty-two stages are logically explained as a progression, in practice they cannot be attained in a gradual sequence.

Six Elements 六大 The traditional Buddhist and basic Shingon theory of the six elements of earth, water, fire, wind, space and mind, which comprise the universe and all entities within it. These are not physical but symbolic elements representing the Shingon Dharma.

sokushin jōbutsu 即身成佛 A Shingon phrase which describes the identity of sentient beings and the Buddha. Because all sentient beings have inherent Buddha-nature (*bodhicitta*) there exists the definite potential for realization of enlightenment by all sentient beings. Shingon characterizes this potential as realization of the *Dharmakāya* Mahāvairocana within the body (present existence) of a successful practitioner.

śraddha 信 (信心, 浄心) A general Buddhist term for 'faith' or belief (in the inherency of the Buddha-nature, the possibility of enlightenment, or the innate purity of the mind).

Śrāvaka 声聞 An early Buddhist practitioner who attempted attainment of Arhatship, based upon a thorough realization of the four noble truths. The *arhat* practice consists of four stages of stream-winner, once-returner, no-returner and arhatship. Specifically, the term refers to the direct disciples of Śākyamuni.

stūpa 佛塔 1. Originally a dome-shaped monument in Indian Buddhism, generally erected over sacred relics of Śākyamuni or upon a site consecrated as the scene of an activity of Śākyamuni. 2. Also popularly known as pagoda, a towerlike storied structure, in India, Southeast Asia, China, Korea and Japan, with symbolic connotations, which had architecturally evolved from the dome-shaped Indian Buddhist monument.

suijaku 垂迹 'Trace or manifestation of fundamental nature'. A term descriptive of a theoretical development in Japanese Shintō and folk religion, which was the result of application of the *honji-kaji* theory. In Shingon, *honji* (as the fundamental essence or nature of the Tantric *Dharmakāya* Mahāvairocana) provided the theoretical basis for the Shingon identification of Shintō deities as manifestations of Mahāvairocana's fundamental nature. Historically, the successful application of this theory hastened the acceptance and assimilation of Shingon Buddhism within Japanese culture.

śūnyatā 空 Emptiness. The basic doctrinal concept of the Indian Mādhyamika Buddhist school and a fundamental concept of Mahāyāna Buddhism. The intuitive realization that all dharmas, processes and goals are empty or absent of any own-being, essence or self-nature. As such, all things and activities exist in a co-dependent causal relationship, with emptiness as the source or basis for this relationship.

sūtra 経 One of the three great divisions of the Buddhist canon or *Tripiṭaka*. The *sūtra* is the basic scripture, in the form of a discourse or group of discourses by a buddha, upon a definite theme.

svabhāva 自性 An early Indian Buddhist technical term, related in meaning to *ātman*, and describing the own-being or self-nature of a *dharma*—the unchanging essence of any phenomena or event, which Buddhist theory denies.

svabhāva-Dharmakāya 自性法身 A Shingon doctrinal concept referring to the essence, nature or source of the *Dharmakāya* Mahāvairocana. This essence is emptiness, which possesses the spiritual potential within Tantric Buddhist doctrine and practice, to enable the Shingon practitioner to accomplish 'Buddhahood in the present body'.

svasaṃbhoga-Dharmakāya 自受用法身 A Shingon doctrinal concept referring to one aspect of *saṃbhoga-Dharmakāya*. Shingon divides the *saṃbhogakāya* connotation of the enjoyment body as the embodiment of the glory and perfection of enlightenment, into self-enjoyment and others-enjoyment. This is the self-enjoyment aspect.

tantra タントラ *Tantra per se* is pre-Buddhist and refers to religious ritual, but in post-eighth century A.D., Indian Mahāyāna Buddhism incorporated *tantras* which supplanted the *sūtra* as the chief doctrinal source and systematized Tantric Buddhism.

Tantric Buddhism 密教 A later school of Indian Buddhism, characterized by the incorporation of tantric elements (rules and rituals) in doctrine and practice.

Taoism 道教 The loose descriptive title of the indigenous Chinese philosophy based upon the writings of Lao-tzu and Chuang-tzu and folk religion based upon mythology and alchemy.

Tathāgata 如来 (如去) An epithet of a buddha, denoting 'thus gone' or complete success in the understanding and practice of enlightenment, and the wisdom and compassion implied thereof. The term, however, is translated as 'thus come' in the Sino-Japanese Buddhist context.

tathatā 眞如 The Mahāyāna Buddhist conception of the true reality which underlies all phenomenal discrimination. It is an attempt to express the inexpressible of Buddhist truth, and is translated into English as 'suchness' or 'thusness'.

tattva 眞実 A general Buddhist term which means truth, reality, and implies the truth of Buddhist doctrine and practice.

ten *tathatās* 十如是 The Tendai doctrine of ten aspects of existence or ten tathatās. The ten aspects are marks, nature, substance, potentiality, function, primary cause, secondary cause, effect, retribution, and the first nine combined as one.

Tendai (T'ien-t'ai) 天台 One of the thirteen major schools of Chinese Buddhism, founded by Chih-i (538–597), and based upon the *Lotus Sūtra*. This indigenous Chinese *Ekayāna* school is characterized by its theories on the relationship between *nirvāṇa* and *saṃsāra*, such as 'three thousand realms in one thought' (*ichinen sanzen*) and its meditative practices. A major Japanese Buddhist school.

Tri-guhya 三密 The three Tantric Buddhist 'teaching-practices of the Buddha' theory, revealed through the functions of body, voice and mind of the Shingon Buddha, Mahāvairocana. The three '*guhya*' (*kāya-guhya*, *vāg-guhya* and *mano-guhya*) are characterizations of Mahāvairocana which theoretically parallel the *tri-karma* practices of sentient beings. These parallel triads of characteristics are to be united through *adhiṣṭhāna*, the instrument of integration, which is a Tantric idealization of the mystical power of Mahāvairocana as the universal source of Tantric enlightenment.

tri-karma 三業 The three Tantric Buddhist practices of man theory, *kāya-karma*, *vāk-karma* and *manaḥ-karma*, which parallel the *tri-guhya* theory of the characteristics of the Dharmakāya Mahāvairocana. These parallel triads of characteristics are to be united through the concept (and practice) of *adhiṣṭhāna*, which is a Tantric idealization of the mystical power of Mahāvairocana as the universal source of Tantric enlightenment.

triyāna 三乘 1. The Mahāyāna categorization of Buddhist practice in terms of three vehicles or methods, the *Śrāvaka*, *Pratyekabuddha* and *bodhisattvas*. 2. A Hīnayāna categorization of three different practices toward the goal of Arhatship.

upāsaka 優婆塞 A male layman, as one of the four categories of early Buddhist practitioners established by Śākyamuni.

upāsika 優婆夷 A female 'layman', as one of the four categories of early Buddhist practitioners established by Śākyamuni.

upāya 方便 1. 'Skillful means', the infinite variety of possible methods to aid sentient beings to realize Buddhist truth and achieve enlightenment. 2. Within the *kyō-han* system of doctrinal evaluation and classification, *upāya* specifically refers to characterizing a teaching or doctrine as a temporary or provisional teaching limited by the attitudes, intelligence or experience of the audience. Positing that this *upāya* attitude formed the true motive for the (alleged temporary) doctrine's exposition, the doctrine is then reinterpreted, replaced or transcended by the utilizer of the *kyō-han* system. 3. One of the ten *pāramitās* or perfections of *bodhisattva* practice. Specifically *upāya* is the existence of spontaneous originality in methods and approaches to enlighten all sentient beings.

vāg-guhya 口密 One of the *tri-guhya* Tantric Buddhist theory of doctrine and practice, *vāg-guhya* is the voice (sound) characteristic of the *Dharmakāya* Mahāvairocana, which parallels the *vāk-karma* (voice) action of sentient beings. It is through the adhisthāna practice of *dhāraṇi* and *mantra* that the union between practitioner and Buddha is effected.

vajra 金剛 A diamond. In Tantric Buddhism, the *vajra* is the symbol of the total indestructability of Buddhist truth.

vajra-citta 金剛心 A Tantric Buddhist descriptive term signifying the 'diamond or indestructible mind', which doctrinally is the successful union of the mind of a sentient being (Tantric practitioner) with the idealized mind of the *Dharmakāya* Buddha Mahāvairocana through *adhiṣṭhāna* practice.

Vajradhātu Maṇḍala 金剛界曼荼羅 One of the two great forms (kinds) of Shingon *maṇḍala*. This *maṇḍala* symbolizes the 'knower' upon which the 'known' (*Garbhakośadhātu Maṇḍala*) is reflected.

Vajrakāya 金剛心 The diamond-body. Charaterizing the form of the Tantric practitioner as an indestructible embodiment of idealized Tantric Buddhist principles.

Vajrayāna 金剛乘 The diamond vehicle. The indestructible practice and discipline of Tantric Buddhism which guides the practitioner, through the utilization of the doctrine of emptiness, to the successful realization of truth and enlightenment.

vāk-karma 口業 One of the *tri-karma* Tantric Buddhist theory of doctrine and practice, *vāk-karma* is the voice (sound) action of sentient beings. It is through the *adhiṣṭhāna* practice of *dhārani* and *mantra* that the union between practitioner and Buddha is effected.

vāsanā-bija 熏習種 In the Yogācāra *vijñapti-mātratā* doctrine (consciousness-only), this is a 'perfuming seed' or potential. This is an attempt to describe the transference of sensory impressions by the first six levels of consciousness through the *manas* to the *ālaya-vijñāna*, where this seed will ripen to produce the retributive effects of actions.

Vātsīputrīya 犢子部 A faction which developed from the Sarvāstivādin branch of Hīnayāna Indian Buddhism, claiming lineage from the disciple Sāriputra, and advocating the controversial *pudgala* concept of the existence of a permanent self which lies beneath and unifies the experience of impersonal *dharmas*.

Vibhajyavāda 分別說部 (識婆闍婆提) A faction which developed from the Sarvāstivādin branch of Hīnayāna Indian Buddhism, of which little is known, other than the title, 'those who make distinctions'.

vijñāna 識 Cognition by discrimination. In the Yogācāra *vijñapti-mātratā* doctrine (consciousness-only) this is the general descriptive term for the discriminative quality of ordinary consciousness. The discriminative *vijñāna* becomes the non-discriminative *jñāna* through the *parāvṛtti* transformation.

vijñapti 表識 An Abhidharma Buddhist technical term denoting bodily actions and retributive effect which must accompany them.

vijñapti-mātratā 唯識 The Yogācāra doctrine that all phenomena and events are of the mind and from the mind. Therefore this mind which is the only entity of perception, cognition and discrimination, is not a fixed state but a constant flowing stream wherein the effects of action are deposited to mature. Included in this doctrine is the analysis of the mind into eight levels of consciousness (the sight-, hearing-, smell-, taste-, and touch-*vijñāna*, the *mano-vijñāna*, the manas, and the *ālaya-vijñāna*). In contrast to the *citta-mātra* concept of consciousness-only, *vijñapti-matratā* signifies the deluded mind which can only produce false discrimination because of ignorance of the buddha-nature.

vikalpa 分別 'Discrimination'. A technical term used extensively in Yogācāra, describing the ordinary delusion-based cognitive-discriminative process of the eight levels of consciousness in the minds of sentient beings.

vimokṣa 解脱 'Liberation', enlightenment, freedom or release from delusion and suffering, which is the context of the existence of sentient beings in the universe.

virya 精進 One of the six *pāramitā* or perfections of *bodhisattva* practice. Specifically *virya* is 'effort', the continual energy and enthusiasm necessary to enlighten all sentient beings.

vyavadāna 清浄 A Buddhist technical term in contrast to *saṃkleśa* (impurity), *vyavadāna* means 'to purify or cleanse what is defiled by delusion'.

yoga 瑜伽 A Tantric Buddhist doctrinal and textual criterion, specifically referring to the doctrinal and physiological methods and principles regulating meditation within the practice of ritual.

Yogācāra 瑜伽 (唯識) 派 One of the two major philosophical schools of Indian Mahāyāna Buddhism, systematized by Maitreyanātha, Asaṅga and Vasubandhu. Its basic doctrinal concept is the *vijñapti-mātratā* (consciousness-only) theory—that discrimination and false perception is based upon an analysis of the mind as eight levels of consciousness or *vijñāna*. The effect of action, characterized as 'seeds', is deposited through the first six levels, to be interpreted in the defiled manas and to mature as consequence in the *ālaya*. The school's basic position is the three svabhāva theory of existence: *parikalpita-svabhāva* or falsely-discriminated existence, *paratantra-svabhāva* or complete co-dependence and conditional causation-based existence, and *parinispanna-svabhāva* or *tathatā*, the ultimate reality-based existence.